Martin Giersich

**Real-time Intention Analysis in Teams**

Martin Giersich

# Real-time Intention Analysis in Teams

Concept of a Robust and Training-free Probabilistic System for Real-time Intention Analysis in Teams

Südwestdeutscher Verlag für Hochschulschriften

**Impressum / Imprint**

Bibliografische Information der Deutschen Nationalbibliothek: Die Deutsche Nationalbibliothek verzeichnet diese Publikation in der Deutschen Nationalbibliografie; detaillierte bibliografische Daten sind im Internet über http://dnb.d-nb.de abrufbar.

Alle in diesem Buch genannten Marken und Produktnamen unterliegen warenzeichen-, marken- oder patentrechtlichem Schutz bzw. sind Warenzeichen oder eingetragene Warenzeichen der jeweiligen Inhaber. Die Wiedergabe von Marken, Produktnamen, Gebrauchsnamen, Handelsnamen, Warenbezeichnungen u.s.w. in diesem Werk berechtigt auch ohne besondere Kennzeichnung nicht zu der Annahme, dass solche Namen im Sinne der Warenzeichen- und Markenschutzgesetzgebung als frei zu betrachten wären und daher von jedermann benutzt werden dürften.

Bibliographic information published by the Deutsche Nationalbibliothek: The Deutsche Nationalbibliothek lists this publication in the Deutsche Nationalbibliografie; detailed bibliographic data are available in the Internet at http://dnb.d-nb.de.

Any brand names and product names mentioned in this book are subject to trademark, brand or patent protection and are trademarks or registered trademarks of their respective holders. The use of brand names, product names, common names, trade names, product descriptions etc. even without a particular marking in this work is in no way to be construed to mean that such names may be regarded as unrestricted in respect of trademark and brand protection legislation and could thus be used by anyone.

Verlag / Publisher:
Südwestdeutscher Verlag für Hochschulschriften
ist ein Imprint der / is a trademark of
OmniScriptum GmbH & Co. KG
Heinrich-Böcking-Str. 6-8, 66121 Saarbrücken, Deutschland / Germany
Email: info@svh-verlag.de

Herstellung: siehe letzte Seite /
Printed at: see last page
**ISBN: 978-3-8381-1603-7**

Zugl. / Approved by: Rostock, Universität Rostock, Dissertation, 2009

Copyright © 2010 OmniScriptum GmbH & Co. KG
Alle Rechte vorbehalten. / All rights reserved. Saarbrücken 2010

# Abstract

Present-day mobility and ubiquity of computing devices make information technology accessible for user activities that are temporally and, especially, spatially distributed. Besides mobile systems this enables ubiquitous computing that – as Weiser phrased it – *"enhances computer use by making many computers available throughout the physical environment, while making them effectively invisible to the user"* (Weiser, 1993, pg. 75). Mobile and ubiquitous systems aim for autonomous and proactive assistance and therefore their infrastructure needs to be able to identify the users' needs. This has two important consequences:

1. The set of devices available for interaction may change over time. This raises the *challenge of adaptivity*: on different devices the same abstract human-computer interaction such as entering a phone number has to be rendered differently in order to make optimal use of the specific device's interaction mechanisms.

2. The structure of a user task becomes accessible to the computing system. This creates the *opportunity of proactive assistance*: if the devices in the user's environment are able to infer her current activity, they are able to trigger actions such as providing information without explicit user interaction.

In order to enable adaptivity and to use proactive assistance a concept investigated in current research on mobile and ubiquitous systems is to provide computing systems with *explicit models* of the user's behavior or tasks. Even though for both fields (adaptivity and proactive assistance) any aspects of the user's behavior or activities can be derived from psychological research on human cognition and social groups, both are seen as separate issues in system development and are addressed by different modeling concepts. This work reviews research areas of social psychology, cognitive psychology, and signal processing to collect sensible descriptions of human behavior in both group situations and problem solving situations that might be helpful to map cooperative task accomplishment in a group to a model. It examines how recent smart environments projects model the user's activities, and provides a catalogue of criteria for a *team intention model*. Then this work presents the concept of a robust and training-free probabilistic system for intention analysis and prediction in teams, and yields the experimental evaluation of the concept by applying simulation and in situ experiments. The experiments prove the validity of the presented concept and the viability of a model-based approach for the indented scenario.

The fundamental statement this work makes is that developing and incorporating explicit models of user tasks is an important aspect of mobile and ubiquitous software development methodology. Furthermore, this work contributes to recent technology and research by *1.)* providing an *in-depth interdisciplinary recherche* of the several different aspects in team behavior recognition, *2.)* providing a *concept* for modeling intention analysis and prediction for teams of users in environments of mobile and ubiquitous computing devices, by *3.)* providing an *experimental infrastructure* for simulation and in situ experiment on the proposed and other concepts, and by *4.)* providing *ideas* for the automated creation of agenda-driven team intention models that allow to recognize team objectives from observable actions of the individual team members.

Strictly speaking, the proposed approach addresses inferring the intention of a team of users within a smart meeting environment that is equipped with sensors and has access to meeting information. The key challenge is to derive and select intended team activities from the observation of multiple users by noisy heterogeneous sensors. Therefore a *team intention model* based on a hierarchical dynamic Bayesian network (DBN) is introduced for inferring the current task and activity of a *team* of users real-time. Sparse, intermittent sensor readings of the team members' positions within a meeting room are used to analyze and predict the team's current objective.

The inference tool implementation is utilizing particle filters for inference. Evaluation experiments demonstrate how knowledge about the meeting agenda can improve prediction accuracy and speed, and how reliability of agenda knowledge can influence the prediction of team behavior. Learning approaches are determined to tune prediction quality, and finally an approach is outlined that uses annotated hierarchical task trees for synthesizing models from a common basic description.

# German Abstract

Die heutige Mobilität und Omnipräsenz von Computern macht Informationstechnologie für Nutzeraktivitäten zugänglich, die zeitlich und besonders räumlich verteilt sind. Neben mobilen Systemen ermöglichen sie "Ubiquitous Computing", das – wie Weiser (1993) es sinngemäß formulierte – die Nutzbarkeit von Computern durch die Verfügbarkeit vieler gleichzeitig für den Nutzer unsichtbarer Computer in der physikalischen Umgebung verbessert. Mobile und allgegenwärtige Systeme zielen auf autonome und proaktive Assistenz hin, und deshalb muss deren Infrastruktur in der Lage sein, die Bedürfnisse der Nutzer zu identifizieren. Das hat zwei wichtige Konsequenzen:

1. Die Menge der Geräte, die für die Interaktion zur Verfügung stehen, kann sich im Laufe der Zeit ändern. Daraus ergibt sich die *Herausforderung der Adaptivität*: auf zwei unterschiedlichen Geräten muss die gleiche abstrakte Mensch-Maschine Interaktion, wie die Eingabe einer Telefonnummer, unterschiedlich realisiert werden, um eine optimale Nutzung der spezifischen Geräteinteraktionsmechanismen zu schaffen.

2. Die Struktur einer Nutzeraufgabe wird für das Computersystem greifbar. Das schafft die *Gelegenheit zur proaktiven Assistenz*: wenn die Geräte in der Umgebung eines Nutzers in der Lage sind, dessen derzeitige Aktivität zu inferieren, können sie Aktionen wie das Anbieten von Informationen ohne explizite Nutzerinteraktion triggern.

Ein Konzept, das die derzeitige Forschung zu mobilen und ubiquitären Systemen untersucht, um Adaptivität zu ermöglichen und proaktive Assistenz zu nutzen, ist, Computersysteme mit *expliziten Modellen* des Verhaltens oder der Aufgaben eines Nutzers zu versorgen. Auch wenn für beide Gebiete (Adaptivität und proaktive Assistenz) beliebige Aspekte des Verhaltens oder der Aktivitäten eines Nutzers aus der psychologischen Forschung zu menschlicher Kognition und sozialen Gruppen abgeleitet werden können, werden beide bei der Systementwicklung als separate Probleme wahrgenommen und mit unterschiedlichen Modellierungskonzepten angegangen. Diese Arbeit rezensiert die Forschungsgebiete Sozialpsychologie, Kognitionspsychologie und Signalverarbeitung, um Beschreibungen von menschlichem Verhalten sowohl in Gruppensituationen als auch Problemlösungssituationen zu sammeln, die hilfreich für die modelhafte Abbildung der kooperativen Aufgabenbewältigung innerhalb einer Gruppe sein könnten. Sie untersucht, wie jüngste "Smart Environment"-Projekte die Aktivitäten eines Nutzers modellieren, und liefert einen Kriterienkatalog für ein *Teamintentionsmodell*. Dann legt diese Arbeit die Konzeption eines robusten und trainingsfreien, probabilistischen Systems für die Intentionsanalyse und -prädiktion in Teams vor und liefert mit der Durchführung von Simulations- und "In Situ"-Experimenten die experimentelle Evaluation des Konzepts. Die Experimente zeigen die Tauglichkeiten des präsentieren Konzept und die Realisierbarkeit des modellbasierten Ansatzes bezüglich des vorgesehenen Szenarios.

Die fundamentale Aussage der Arbeit ist, dass die Entwicklung und Integration expliziter Modelle von Nutzeraufgaben ein wichtiger Aspekt für die Methodik der Entwicklung mobiler und ubiquitärer Softwaresysteme ist. Darüberhinaus leistet diese Arbeit Beiträge zu jüngsten Technologien und jüngster Forschung durch *1.*) die Lieferung einer *gründlichen interdiziplinären Recherche* der zahlreichen verschiedenen Aspekte bei der Erkennung von Teamverhalten, *2.*) die Lieferung eines *Konzepts* zur Modellierung von Intentionsanalyse und -prädiktion für ein Team von Nutzern in Umgebungen mit mobilen und ubiquitären Computern, durch *3.*) die Lieferung einer *Experimentalinfrastruktur* für Simulations- und "In Situ"-Experimente mit dem vorgeschlagenen oder anderen Konzepten und durch *4.*) die Lieferung von *Ideen* für die automatisierte Erstellung Agenda-gesteuerter Teamintentionsmodelle, die die Erkennung von Teamzielen aus beobachtbaren Aktionen einzelner Teammitglieder zulassen.

Genaugenommen befasst sich der vorgeschlagene Ansatz mit der Inferenz von Intentionen eines Teams von Nutzern in einem "Smart Meeting Environment", das mit einigen Sensoren ausgestattet ist und Zugriff auf Meetinginformationen hat. Die zentrale Herausforderung ist die Ableitung und Auswahl der geplanten Teamaktivitäten mittels der Beobachtung mehrerer Nutzer durch verrauschte und heterogene Sensoren. Dazu wird ein *Teamintentionsmodell* basierend auf hierarchischen dynamischen Bayes'schen Netzen vorgestellt, das das Inferieren der aktuellen Aufgaben und Aktivitäten eines *Teams* von Nutzern in Echtzeit ermöglicht. Spärliche, intermittierende Sensormessungen von Teammitgliederpositionen in einem Besprechungsraum werden genutzt, um das derzeitige Ziel des Teams vorherzusagen.

Die Implementierung des Inferenztools nutzt Partikelfilter für das Schließen. Evaluationsexperimente demonstrieren, wie Wissen über die Meeting-Agenda die Vorhersagegenauigkeit und -geschwindigkeit verbessern kann und wie Verlässlichkeit des Agenda-Wissens die Vorhersage des Teamverhaltens beeinflussen kann. Lernansätze werden untersucht, um die Vorhersagequalität zu tunen, und schließlich wird ein Ansatz umrissen, der annotierte hierarchische Task-Trees für die Erzeugung des *Teamintentionsmodells* aus einer gemeinsamen Grundbeschreibung nutzt.

# Theses

1. Situations are distinguished decisively by the behavior of the user that acts in it. Computing device states can indicate the dedicated circumstances a user has to handle.

2. The user's behavior is led by process-driven or task-driven intentions. In cooperative multi-user situations the social *"nature of groups"* causes the evolution of a group goal that can be interpreted as team intention.

3. The number of high-level team intentions is denumerable in a closed application domain like a *"smart meeting room"* as long as a group of users shows a cooperative behavior.

4. Roles that team members adopt with respect to a team intention can be modeled independently from the interdependencies and structures in groups.

5. The team member's behavior is goal oriented at least in the productive performing stage of the group life cycle, which is assumed for the application domain of this work.

6. Many teams act in meetings on a-priori context information like agendas and schedules, but these are just prior compiled evidences and not reliable sources for the course of a meeting, because several teams deviate from such a-priori plans during the meetings.

7. Preliminary context information like a-priori agendas that are unreliable with respect to the schedules and courses of meetings are preferable over no context information about meetings, because the unreliable but additional information improves the recognition accuracy significantly.

8. Probabilistic task models like Markov models are suitable for the purpose of modeling the situation in a *"smart meeting room"* with its inherent uncertainty factors.

9. Approximative Bayesian inference methods especially particle filters are an appropriate approach for robust reasoning on unreliable context information and sparse sensor data.

# Contents

**Abstract**     iii

**German Abstract**     v

**Theses**     ix

**1 Overview**     1
    1.1 Introduction . . . . . . . . . . . . . . . . . . . . . . . . . . . . . . 1
    1.2 Thesis Layout . . . . . . . . . . . . . . . . . . . . . . . . . . . . . . 3
        1.2.1 Agenda-driven Team DBN . . . . . . . . . . . . . . . . . . . . 4
        1.2.2 Team Intention Inference . . . . . . . . . . . . . . . . . . . . . 4
    1.3 Thesis Contributions . . . . . . . . . . . . . . . . . . . . . . . . . . 5
    1.4 Related Projects . . . . . . . . . . . . . . . . . . . . . . . . . . . . . 6
        1.4.1 Mobile Assistance Applications . . . . . . . . . . . . . . . . . 6
        1.4.2 Smart Environment Applications . . . . . . . . . . . . . . . . 11
        1.4.3 Observation, Annotation Applications . . . . . . . . . . . . . 19
    1.5 Method Matrix . . . . . . . . . . . . . . . . . . . . . . . . . . . . . 22
    1.6 Scenario . . . . . . . . . . . . . . . . . . . . . . . . . . . . . . . . . 25
    1.7 Criteria for a Team Intention Model . . . . . . . . . . . . . . . . . . 28
    1.8 Summary . . . . . . . . . . . . . . . . . . . . . . . . . . . . . . . . 30

**2 Modeling Team Intention Recognition**     31
    2.1 Introduction . . . . . . . . . . . . . . . . . . . . . . . . . . . . . . . 31
    2.2 Social Psychology Perspective on Teams . . . . . . . . . . . . . . . 32
        2.2.1 Interaction . . . . . . . . . . . . . . . . . . . . . . . . . . . . . 33
        2.2.2 Interdependence . . . . . . . . . . . . . . . . . . . . . . . . . 33
        2.2.3 Structure . . . . . . . . . . . . . . . . . . . . . . . . . . . . . . 35

|  |  |  |  |
|---|---|---|---|
|  | 2.2.4 | Goals | 37 |
|  | 2.2.5 | Cohesiveness | 39 |
|  | 2.2.6 | Stage | 39 |
|  | 2.2.7 | Relevant Essence | 41 |
| 2.3 | Cognitive Psychology View on Tasks | | 44 |
|  | 2.3.1 | Reasoning | 45 |
|  | 2.3.2 | Problem Solving | 47 |
|  | 2.3.3 | Means-ends Analysis Models | 48 |
|  | 2.3.4 | User Models | 51 |
|  | 2.3.5 | Task Models | 61 |
|  | 2.3.6 | Relevant Essence | 64 |
| 2.4 | Modeling in Signal Processing | | 65 |
|  | 2.4.1 | Neural Networks | 66 |
|  | 2.4.2 | Temporal Probabilistic Models | 76 |
|  | 2.4.3 | Relevant Essence | 85 |
| 2.5 | Summary | | 87 |

# 3 The Team Intention Model Approach — 89

|  |  |  |  |
|---|---|---|---|
| 3.1 | Introduction | | 89 |
| 3.2 | Instrumenting the Lab | | 89 |
|  | 3.2.1 | Concrete Scenario | 90 |
|  | 3.2.2 | Concrete Lab Situation | 91 |
| 3.3 | Criteria Revisited | | 95 |
| 3.4 | Agenda-driven Team DBN | | 97 |
|  | 3.4.1 | Structuring Team Tasks | 99 |
|  | 3.4.2 | Team DBN Proposal | 100 |
|  | 3.4.3 | Note on Synthesizing Team DBN | 109 |
| 3.5 | Team Intention Inference | | 112 |
|  | 3.5.1 | Inference Tasks | 113 |
|  | 3.5.2 | Bayesian Filter Approach | 115 |
|  | 3.5.3 | Particle Filter Approach | 118 |
|  | 3.5.4 | Core Tools and Team Intention Tracker | 122 |
| 3.6 | Summary | | 130 |

| | | |
|---|---|---|
| **4** | **Experiments and Conclusions** | **131** |
| | 4.1 Introduction . . . . . . . . . . . . . . . . . . . . . . . . . . . . . . . . . . 131 | |
| | 4.2 Experiment #1: Simulation Study . . . . . . . . . . . . . . . . . . . . . . . 131 | |
| |     4.2.1 Study Methodology . . . . . . . . . . . . . . . . . . . . . . . . . . 132 | |
| |     4.2.2 Results . . . . . . . . . . . . . . . . . . . . . . . . . . . . . . . . . 135 | |
| | 4.3 Experiment #2: Instrumented Field Study . . . . . . . . . . . . . . . . . . 139 | |
| |     4.3.1 Study Methodology . . . . . . . . . . . . . . . . . . . . . . . . . . 140 | |
| |     4.3.2 Results . . . . . . . . . . . . . . . . . . . . . . . . . . . . . . . . . 144 | |
| | 4.4 Summary and Outlook . . . . . . . . . . . . . . . . . . . . . . . . . . . . . 154 | |
| | 4.5 Acknowledgement . . . . . . . . . . . . . . . . . . . . . . . . . . . . . . . 159 | |
| **A** | **Core Tool Features** | **181** |
| **B** | **Results Experiment #2** | **183** |

# Chapter 1

# Overview

## 1.1 Introduction

In order to identify a suitable structure for the aspects that are addressed within the following chapters, this work starts with a brief overview on classification approaches given by representatives of the ubiquitous computing community to subdivide their research area. Reviewing the related literature many attempts to structure the methods and components that are utilized in the field of ubiquitous computing can be found.

For instance Cook and Das (2007) have described recently that components of applications from this field can be assigned roughly to four different areas:

- *Physical* – This area includes all physical devices of an intelligent environment, mainly sensors and actuators.

- *Communication* – This area contains middleware questions like device discovery, network standards and protocols as well as system ontologies.

- *Information* – This part addresses the aspects of data storage and intelligent data analysis and determines inference and prediction methods based on user models.

- *Decision* – This part searches appropriate decision making processes based on the analyzed information and chooses suitable actions to assist the users.

A slightly older classification by DeVaul et al. (2003) distinguished between *Sensing, Feature Extraction, Modeling, Inference* and *Action*. And Hightower et al. (2002) subdivided in their

Location Stack a little more technically into *Sensors, Sensor Fusion, Contextual Fusion, Activities* and *Intentions*.

Obviously *Information, Modeling, Inference* or *Intentions* are subject headings that characterize this work roughly. But the application domain that is addressed here might be divided further to respect the number of users that an application was designed for (i.e. differentiate between *Single-user* and *Multi-user* (*Team*) applications), or to reflect how the application infrastructure was set up (i.e. in decentralized, dynamic *ad-hoc* manner, or centralized and static). Also a distinction between *Mobile Assistance Applications*, *Smart Environment Applications*, and *Observation/Annotation Applications* might seem sensible.

However, a proper delimitation of application areas entails constraints for method selection in the addressed area. This work researches *Multi-user Ad-hoc Smart Environments* and addresses the central question of my research group that the department chair phrased as:

> *How can an ad-hoc ensemble find out as early as possible what a team would like to do if it would know what it could do within that ensemble?*[1]

The goal of this work on *Team Intention Recognition* for *Smart Environments* is to infer the needs of teams to enable proactive assistance in a meeting environment scenario, which includes *1.*) providing information, data, and action respectively without explicit interaction between computing system and user group, and *2.*) enabling the environment to pre-fetch media content or pre-configure system features based on predicted team intentions. Hence, the research question can be altered to:

> *How can an ad-hoc smart environment optimally support a* **team** *of users in a meeting* **without** *explicit interaction?*

This work presents an approach for modeling team behavior for ad-hoc smart environments, which allows to infer intentions of teams to prepare goals for interaction with smart environments. It also addresses learning statistics parameters for the team intention model. From the mentioned focus the following relevant areas of research can be derived:

*1.) Modeling,* and *2.) Inference*

---

[1] My department's chair coined that phrase during a research seminar session in summer term 2008.

Before starting the review of outstanding projects from the ubiquitous computing field and the identification of relevant methods from those projects' applications, the next two sections outline the overall structure of this thesis, provide a quick look at the chapters, and lay claim to the contributions made.

## 1.2 Thesis Layout

This work is organized as follows: Subsequent to the next two sections the work starts in Section 1.4 with a review of related projects from the application domain to identify relevant methods for the with this work aspired conception. A method matrix in Section 1.5 clearly summarizes the identified methods. Then, in Section 1.6, the scenario is formulated which describes the situation this work is designed for and indicates the constraints for method selection that can be derived from this delimitation. In Section 1.7 a catalogue of criteria outlines which requirements the aimed concept of a team intention model has to meet.

The overview chapter is followed by three separate chapters (i.e., Chapters 2, 3 & 4). Originating from implications that can be derived from the criteria for a team intention model identified in Section 1.7, Chapter 2 digs into research areas, which are closely related to single person and group behavior. The review includes social psychology approaches (see Section 2.2) for categorizing the *"nature of groups"* and modeling group processes (e.g. group interaction, group structure, group goals), and cognitive psychology approaches (see Section 2.3) for structuring and modeling (single person) human behavior. Here, especially aspects related to *thinking* like *reasoning* and *problem solving* are determined. Furthermore the signal processing area (see Section 2.4) is reviewed regarding its approaches for the recognition of behavior patterns – whether model-free or model-based.

In Chapter 3 first the scenario from Section 1.6 is adapted to delimitate it from related work in Section 3.2. Then, after an overview of the features of the prototype laboratory – called *"SmartApplianceLab"* – that is built into a room of my department shown in Figure 1.1, the criteria from Section 1.7 are revisited under a more concrete perspective in Section 3.3. Here the findings from Chapter 2 are considered, and the constraints just as much as the capabilities stemming from architectural and infrastructural decisions made on behalf of my department's research objectives as well as from the construction and structure of the physical smart environment are incorporated.

Figure 1.1: SmartApplianceLab at University of Rostock

Then, by means of the two focus areas *modeling* & *inference* mentioned in Section 1.1 this work's concept is described. The next two subsections describe briefly the content of the related Sections 3.4 & 3.5. By the end of Chapter 3 the concept is proven with the introduction of an experimental infrastructure in Section 3.5.4.

Afterwards, in Chapter 4, two experiments (simulation in Section 4.2 and in situ in Section 4.3) are described, which were realized with the developed experimental infrastructure. These experiments were selected to evaluate the concept. Thus, results of the agenda driven team activity recognition are discussed. Finally, Chapter 4 summarizes findings from this work in a comprehensive conclusion in Section 4.4.

### 1.2.1 Agenda-driven Team DBN

Merging findings from the reviews in social psychology, cognition science, and signal processing with the criteria of this work, Section 3.4 presents a *team intention model* based on dynamic Bayesian networks (DBN), which represents a robust way to technically model cooperative group behavior at least for the described scenario and enables filtering and prediction of intended group activities with the support of a-priori knowledge about the group situation.

### 1.2.2 Team Intention Inference

In Section 3.5 inference tasks for the proposed model are identified. Then follows a detailed description of the Bayesian inference approach and inference mechanisms based on particle filters. Requirements for an implementation are collected and an architecture is introduced that specifies components and modules of the experimental infrastructure. Finally, usage of the implemented tools is outlined.

## 1.3 Thesis Contributions

The previous section indicated where contributions to the area of Smart Environment generally and Smart Meeting Rooms specifically can be expected. This work examines how recent smart environments projects recognize and eventually model the user's activities, and provides a matrix of relevant methods and a catalogue of criteria for a *Team Intention Model*. Furthermore, it reviews the research areas of social psychology, cognitive psychology, and signal processing to collect descriptions of human behavior in both group situations and problem solving situations.

Focusing on – in terms of Cowell et al. (2007) speaking – rather *technological* than *scientific* modeling and a proper inference of team behavior this work then presents the concept of a robust and training-free prior knowledge probabilistic system for real-time intention analysis in teams, and yields the experimental evaluation of the concept applying simulation and in situ experiments.

The fundamental statement this work makes is that developing and incorporating explicit models of user tasks is an important aspect of mobile and ubiquitous software development methodology. It proposes to extract findings from psychological fields to enhance explicit models for better or at least more flexible recognition of team cooperation. Furthermore, this work contributes to recent technology and research by providing

- an *in-depth interdisciplinary recherche* of the several different aspects that are related to team behavior recognition,
- a *concept* for modeling intention analysis and prediction for teams of users in environments of mobile and ubiquitous computing devices,
- an *experimental infrastructure* for simulation and in situ experiment on the proposed and other concepts, and
- *ideas* for the automated creation of agenda-driven team intention models that allow to recognize team objectives from observable actions of the individual team members.

## 1.4 Related Projects

Mobile assistance applications and smart environments are tools that help users with their real world problems and tasks either out in the field or in office, school, and home environments. They can acquire knowledge about users and their environments. To do so, sensors observe states of both users and environment. These states are interpreted by a model to infer or predict a user's needs resulting in a strategy that enhances the user's experience of the environment. Activity observation and annotation tools have a special role. Here, the acquired knowledge about users and their environment does not directly result in assisting strategies and action. Rather, the information is utilized to record *Persona*[2] and *Role*-corpora, which then are evaluated in studies on medical, psychological, or usability aspects.

For this section on related projects the earlier mentioned distinction between mobile assistance applications, smart environment applications, and activity observation and annotation applications is picked up to make a rough categorization of projects. Smart environments of course is the most related category to this work but nevertheless both other categories also provide interesting insights in how modeling, inference, and learning can be addressed.

### 1.4.1 Mobile Assistance Applications

Under this category all tour-guides or personal navigation systems ever produced could be mentioned. But, since this would obviously be beyond the scope here, and the primary goal of this work is to prepare a concept of a system for intention analysis and prediction of team behavior in smart environments on behalf of agenda knowledge and location data, in this section only three outstanding projects – the *Location Stack*, the *Place Lab* and *Opportunity Knocks* – are described in more detail because those are interesting from the perspective how location could be modeled and higher level activities could be inferred.

**Location Stack** The *Location Stack* model proposed by Hightower et al. (2002) was driven by the conclusions drawn from a survey on location systems for ubiquitous computing (Hightower and Borriello, 2001a,b). With this survey a seven-dimensional taxonomy was put in by Hightower and Borriello to characterize localization systems. Variables of the property vector

---

[2]Persona designates *"an individual's social facade or front that especially in the analytic psychology [...] reflects the role in life the individual is playing [like] the personality that a person (as an actor or politician) projects in public"* (Merriam–Webster Online Dictionary, 2008a)

*Overview*

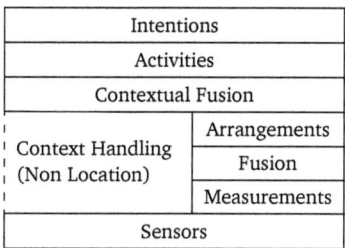

Figure 1.2: The seven layers of the Location Stack design abstraction. (*Source*: Adapted from Hightower et al. 2002, pg. 23)

reached from *1.) physical vs. symbolic* and *2.) absolute vs. relative* locations over *3.) localized local computation*, *4.) recognition*, *5.) accuracy and precision* to *6.) cost*, and *7.) limitations*. Since existing location systems were rather tuned for some few application specific aspects than for enabling the full range of the feature vector[3], the survey was motivation for designing the Location Stack. The aim was to propose a robust standardized software abstraction that connected multiple sensing technologies to benefit from aggregate properties, which would have been unavailable when using location systems individually.

In Hightower et al. (2002) some design principles were specified that location systems for mobile or location-enhanced application – and so the Location Stack – should rely on. Fundamental measurement types (e.g., distance, angle, proximity, or asserted position), which always exist in such applications, were combined in standard ways and enabled standard object relationship queries. Additionally, at sensor level, measurements were always concerned with uncertainty about the location. This uncertainty should be preserved for higher abstraction levels, such that those are able to propagate correct uncertainty information. In addition, location and context data in such applications were typically not used directly but to enable recognition about users' activities and inference of their needs.

The Location Stack design abstraction consisted of the seven layers shown Figure 1.2. The *sensors* layer collected sensor observations in various forms of raw data. In the *measurements* layer raw inputs were transformed to normalized representations that also implied uncertainty values based on the particular sensor models. The *fusion* step continually merged measurements to a sort of probabilistic statement about positions and orientations of objects. Due to different capabilities of different sensors redundancies or contradictions were able to influ-

---

[3]Note, that the same realization applies to nowadays location systems.

ence the combined uncertainties of object locations. Reasoning about the relationships (e.g., proximity, or containment) between objects was done within the *arrangements* layer. The *contextual fusion* layer allowed merging of location knowledge with other non-location contextual information of a situation. The *activities* and *intentions* layers added the specific semantics of the individual ubiquitous computing application, where the activities were the application's interpretations of environment states given the combined information from contextual fusion, and intentions were the users' needs in relation to those recognized activities.

In Hightower et al. (2003) an implementation of some layers of the Location Stack was presented. Besides some sensor technology device drivers, a database service, and a simulation service the framework primarily contributed at the fusion layer. They applied Bayesian filter techniques including *multi-hypothesis tracking*, namely *particle filters* to address both basic sensor fusion and simultaneous identity estimation for multiple tracking targets. The decision for particle filters was made on basis of a survey on Bayesian filter implementations performed by Fox et al. (2003). Here, different approaches were assessed regarding their abilities to manage measurement uncertainty and to perform multi-sensor fusion and identity estimation. Hightower et al. described their decision for particle filters as due to the "*typically very uncertain and multi-modal [...] belief over the person's location*" (Hightower et al., 2003, pg. 6) when using multiple more or less inaccurate ID sensors. Furthermore, they recommended to constrain possible location hypotheses (i.e., particles) of a person and utilize Voronoi graphs of free space – as described by Liao et al. (2003) – to restrict the spreading of particles around the motion of users in an environment.

A second aspect that was addressed with the Location Stack fusion algorithms was the data association problem in multi-target tracking with anonymous sensors. Track confusions during tracking were able to induce wrong associations of identities. A solution proposed by Schulz et al. (2003) used a multi-hypothesis tracking approach in which particle filters and Kalman filters were combined. Due to the accuracy of the anonymous sensors used for that scenario users could be tracked using Kalman filters and multiple hypotheses regarding the identities of people were maintained using particle filters. Here, each particle reflected one hypothesis about the identity of a tracked user, which was a set of identity annotated Kalman filters.

For the arrangements layer just a few operators were provided. Current probabilistic location estimates were used to produce a probabilistic output that denoted the confidence of a certain arrangement, for example, that a user was in front of a certain object or an object was within a certain region. Finally the upper layers, activities and intentions, were not addressed by the implementation. But Hightower et al. (2003) indicated that the design for these layers could be based on the same approaches as used for the fusion and arrangements layers to support the higher level recognition and learning tasks that characterize these layers. Some progress made on methods for these layers can be found in Place Lab and Opportunity Knocks described next.

**Place Lab**  *Place Lab*[4] was a localization project at Intel Research in collaboration with the University of Washington in Seattle. It was engaging in the provision of location-enhanced or mobile applications. Planetary-scale low-cost indoor and outdoor positioning was envisioned, which was listening for radio signals from already existing infrastructure such as 802.11 access points, GSM cell phone towers, and fixed Bluetooth appliances. A multi-platform software base and a community-driven beacon database[5] offered a low barrier of participation, either for privately determining a location or for sharing hotspot information.

Technically interesting for this work was the Place Lab client. This was the mobile assistance application that in this case had to deliver adequate position estimates from heterogeneous, noisy sensor sources. LaMarca et al. (2005) described that the client consisted of roughly three components – the spotter, the mapper, and the tracker. The first two were rather straightforward, since they just read accessible cell-identifiers and looked them up in the beacon-database to obtain latitude and longitude or other information of the requested base-stations. Then the collected data was streamed to the tracker to produce estimates of the user's position. The tracker component contained knowledge about some related system properties like signal propagation in various physical environments and was also able to incorporate additional information like map data for a position estimation. Besides a simple tracker with Venn diagram-style range triangulation, a Bayesian particle filter tracker was included to utilize the rich model knowledge (Hightower and Borriello, 2004). This tracker was an implementation of the previously described Location Stack abstraction.

Another aspect of Place Lab was to enable a match between the latitude and longitude a location estimation provided and colloquial place names, like "Home", "Work" or this special

---

[4]It should not be confused with the PlaceLab at MIT, which was an initiative of *House_n* project and TIAX to build *"an apartment-scale research facility where new technologies and design concepts can be tested and evaluated in the context of everyday living"* (PlaceLab, 2008, pg. 1). This lab is open to various research groups and primarily used to collect sensor data as well as Persona and Role-corpora for evaluation.

[5]Place Lab's beacon database was transfered to the community *wigle.net* as major research ceased in 2006.

italian restaurant's name the inner circle is familiar with. To address this issue, Hightower et al. (2005) introduced a learning mechanism based on the collection of radio signal fingerprints that they called BeaconPrint algorithm. Roughly summarized the algorithm segmented a signal log at stable signal situations by adding a waypoint. Waypoints issued from a repeated visit of the same location were merged with the already known one. Note that this algorithm rather addressed the notification of someone's favorite places than the assignment of a certain semantics to a recognized place. A related approach was chosen for the Opportunity Knocks prototype of the ACCESS project described next.

**Opportunity Knocks**  The objective of the Assisted Cognition in Community, Employment and Support Settings (ACCESS) project at University of Washington was to enhance the quality of life for persons with cognitive disabilities through computer-based memory and problem solving aids. A major part of the efforts made in this project, that evolved from the Assisted Cognition project introduced by Kautz et al. (2002), was focused on *Opportunity Knocks*[6] – a prototype described by Patterson et al. (2004) that logged location sensor data to recognize a user's mode of transportation and learn typical locations of activities. The system was built to support the memory of users from the target group by monitoring deviation from the usual daily routine, detecting a likely aberration, and providing guidance back on track.

Patterson et al. (2003) described a Dynamic Bayesian Network (DBN) to infer and learn modes of transportation. The model used GPS sensor data as observable input for the DBN. Then multi-hypothesis tracking, namely particle filter, was applied to reason about the most probable mode of transportation. They distinguished between three different transportation mode values: *BUS*, *FOOT*, and *CAR*, which obviously provided different motion patterns. The model also incorporated learning of conceptual locations (e.g., bus stop or parking lot) where transitions in the transportation mode may occur to improve tracking and prediction.

In Liao et al. (2004) and Patterson et al. (2004) an expanded version of this model was explained. This hierarchical DBN additionally modeled a *trip segment* layer and a *goal* layer. The new trip segment level predicted in addition to the transportation mode also the route of transportation and at the goal level the goal location was inferred. Of course, a new goal location only could be applied when the user reached the end of a trip segment.

---

[6]This prototype was also know as *Activity Compass* in the Assisted Cognition project context (Patterson et al., 2003).

In latter publications Liao et al. (2005b,a, 2007) switched to Conditional Random Fields, namely Relational Markov Networks, to handle the increasing amount of prediction constraining information (e.g., locations of restaurants and shops or the fact that a person works at a number of different locations) that naturally occur in an unrestricted mobile environment.

### 1.4.2 Smart Environment Applications

In principle this section, too addresses upper layers of the Location Stack just mentioned. It contains a selection of Smart Environments projects from office, school, or home surrounding. The descriptions examine applications semantics and how activity recognition and intention inference were realized.

**Classical User Interfaces**

**Active Badge** One of the first Smart Environments was the *Active Badge* system from Cambridge University Computer Laboratory. Want et al. (1992) stated that the system was designed as an aid for telephone receptionists. It incorporated a location system that consisted of personalized unique infrared signal sending badges and a set of receivers in the various rooms of the laboratory. Badges sent out their identity signal every 15 seconds and the receivers made their signal detection available for the application throughout the network.

Then, with every detected signal the application updated the recognized – or better associated – state of the corresponding person. States were provided to the receptionists in form of a lookup table of names against dynamically updating fields containing a description of the location and the nearest telephone extension.

Additionally, a kind of likelihood was displayed that indicated how probable it was that someone could be found at the associated location. 100% meant stable sighting, below 100% indicated the person was moving around. Periods of non-sighting graded from 5 minutes to more than a week with displaying first the last time, then the last day, and finally the indication ´AWAY´. The receptionists then had to formulate their intentions explicitly using command-line queries that the system provided (e.g., ´FIND (name)´, ´LOOK (location)´, or ´FIND (name)´).

## Adaptive User Interfaces

**EasyLiving** Brumitt et al. (2000) put the goal of Microsoft's *EasyLiving* system as to aggregate diverse devices into a coherent user experience. At the heart of the system the *EasyLiving Geometric Model* (EZLGM) abstracted the perceptional part of the system from the application semantics. According to Brumitt and Shafer (2001), EZGLM stored *entities* for all interesting objects (including persons) within the environment. Then *measurements* connected the entities forming an undirected graph where a measurement edge described position and orientation of one entity in relation to another entity. Additional entities stored information about their physical expansion, the uncertainty of their position, and other contextual knowledge. Krumm et al. (2000) explained in detail how the localization of multiple inhabitants using stereo computer vision was realized. Additionally EasyLiving utilized pressure mats, thumbprint reader, and keyboard login to localize and identify persons. For detecting the moveable devices (e.g., wireless keyboard or RF mouse) in the environment a combination of color and shape cues from camera images was processed (Brumitt et al., 2000).

EZLGM kept track of the latest perceptions and provided the information to the application layers where all input and output devices as well as several small software pieces (e.g., web browser or a person's whole desktop) were encapsulated in unique services. Various UI adapting demo applications enabled the inhabitants, for instance, to control different output devices with one moveable input device[7] or to move their desktop session to the nearest screen.

**Interactive Room** At Stanford University the Interactive Workspace project built the *Interactive Room* (iRoom) to research adaptive interfaces for multi-display environments. Similar as in EasyLiving, the idea of Fox et al. (2000) was to *1.*) equip a multi-user meeting space with a variety of displays (i.e. three touch-sensitive SmartBoard displays, a bottom-projected table, and a front-projected screen) and multiple wireless mice, keyboards, and PDAs, and *2.*) enable this space to allow one input device to manipulate multiple output devices, or respectively vice versa.

But in the iRoom no location system was used. Instead the centrally managed computational glue, which was called *iROS*, just knew iRoom's screen topology (Johanson et al., 2002b). Spatial proximity, therefore, was not used for moving data, moving control and dynamic

---

[7]Or vice versa; different input devices could control a specific personalized application like the "contact anyone anywhere" example mentioned by Shafer et al. (1998).

application coordination, respectively, but for explicit service selection by the users. The iROS merely provided with its components *Data Heap*, *Event Heap*, and *iCrafter* an architecture where the UI tools could dock (Johanson et al., 2002a). As Ponnekanti et al. (2002) further described a central contribution of the project was the seamless provision and adaption of control interfaces for iRoom devices to the different appliances (e.g., Java-enabled notebook vs. PDA without Java installed) that different users brought into the iRoom environment. Therefore an interface managing application on top of *iCrafter* encapsulated the whole process of selection and provision of the adequate UI.

**Neural Networks**

**Adaptive House**  Goal of the *Adaptive House* project was to build a home, which adjusted itself to schedules and lifestyle of its inhabitants and at the same time minimized energy costs. Therefore a realty of the University of Colorado at Boulder was equipped with various sensors and actuators. According to Mozer et al. (1995) roughly seventy-five sensors monitored various aspects of the environment (e.g., temperature, ambient light, sound level, motion, door status, etc.), and actuators influenced parameters including air and water, lighting, or ventilation. In Mozer and Miller (1998) and Mozer (1998) a control system for this home automation setting called ACHE was introduced to adapt the actuators optimally.

ACHE, an acronym for Adaptive Control of Home Environments, consisted of several components. First sensor information were collected by an *occupancy model* and an *anticipator*. The occupancy model determined the currently occupied zones within the house using motion detectors and a finite-state model, but naturally could just react to sensor readings. And for this reason an additional anticipator was built to predict an impending zone occupancy and to issue actions before this zone became occupied. Conceptionally, a standard single-hidden-layer neural network[8] was chosen, which utilized occupancy model data as a training signal.

Then a *state estimator* formed a high-level state representation that encoded information relevant for decision making. Central information were, of course, user activities, which were derived from the patterns that the occupancy model and the anticipator net provided (e.g., if Bob is vacuuming, expect many zone changes in a short time; if he is reading quietly in a corner, expect few zone changes). An *orienting mechanism* applied event-based segmentation

---

[8]*"with 107 inputs, 50 hidden units, 8 output units, direct input-output connections, and a symmetric sigmoidal activation function"* (Mozer and Miller, 1998, pg. 382).

to gate the decision making process. That required the determination of salient events, which were defined to be: *1.)* anticipation of zone or region entry or exit, *2.)* significant change in the outdoor light level, and *3.)* change in inhabitant activities.

Finally, the decision making component, called *Q-learning controller*, implemented reinforcement learning, particularly Q-learning[9], to sample trajectories in state space. But according to Mozer (2005) Q-learning was not guaranteed to converge optimally, because ACHE was not able to determine exact observations for both location of users and their needs at the moment.

**iDorm** The University of Essex equipped a dormitory room (*iDorm*) with various non-intrusive sensors including light, temperature, and humidity sensors as well as pressure mats or motion sensors to monitor users within a natural environment. Additionally an adaptive interface allowed inhabitants to configure the available actuators (e.g., heater, fan, lights, blinds, or PC based application). Centralized *control points* in the room then used the monitored sensor data and user interventions to adopt the behavior that the inhabitants desired.

For this purpose different approaches were introduced. Besides a proposal for an intelligent fuzzy agent system by Doctor et al. (2005), Rivera-Illingworth et al. (2005) suggested an agent-based approach, which was premised on an Adaptive Neural Network. This network was derived from the Evolving Connectionist Systems (ECoS) paradigm proposed by Kasabov (2002) and, hence, could adapt itself to the monitored environmental data by adding neurons to the hidden layer whenever the observation could not be explained with the already existing structure of the network.

After a training phase the net covered normal conditions and – applied to monitor the iDorm – detected new conditions. Depending on the scenario these new states could be regarded as new preferred behavior or as abnormal behavior (e.g., in a medical case of emergency). Besides usual *input*, *hidden*, and *output layer* the network also incorporated a temporal recurrent component – the so-called *memory layer* –, which allowed to capture temporal dependencies in the data.

---

[9]*"Given a fully observable state and an infinite amount of time to explore the state space, Q-learning is guaranteed to converge on an optimal policy"* (Mozer, 2005, pg. 277).

## Plan Recognition

**Intelligent Room** MIT's Agent-based Intelligent Reactive Environment (AIRE) project[10] researched how localization and recognition techniques could enable natural multimodal human-computer interfaces in intelligent spaces. Their *Intelligent Room* was built upon an agent software system called Metaglue. Coen et al. (1999) explained how the Metaglue middleware organized communication issues between perceptual agents, central services, and appliance agents or actuators respectively.

At perceptual level, computer vision was used to localize the inhabitants. Brooks (1997) described that for this purpose two cameras observed the whole room from the rear and tracked users relying on adaptive background differencing. Identification of persons was realized by comparing a single person's rectangular bounding box with predetermined sets of rectangles.

To determine the activities of users finite state machines (FSM) were applied to the system. Inoue (1996) described how they were modeled to recognize what happened in the room. These grammars provided temporal coherence that constrained the interpretation. At person level the room could distinguish between *walking, standing, sitting,* or *pointing*[11]. Picking up a user *walking* through the entrance only a few transitions to new activities were possible. Two higher level grammars were provided on top of the person level. One grammar recognized multi-person activities like *hand shaking*, or *talking*, and the other distinguished some group contexts (i.e., *meeting, presentation*). The intended system actions were again initiated by the user group explicitly, even though a natural multimodal interface with gesture and speech recognition was available.

**SmartOffice** Another very similar project on natural multimodal interfaces for Smart Environment was the Monica project at the French National Institute for Research in Computer Science and Control (INRIA). Their *SmartOffice* used a centralized agent framework, where a so-called supervisor kept track of the current states of all agents.

Le Gal et al. (2001) mentioned that multiple cameras estimated separately inhabitant positions using color based face trackers and estimated locations were fused using a Kalman filter. Activity recognition was at the same granularity as in AIRE project. It divided motion patterns

---

[10] AIRE itself was part of the MIT project Oxygen and contributed to the so-called E21 – environmental devices.
[11] Pointing was recognized by two additional cameras mounted next to the presenter screens. Coen (1998) described the usage of background differencing and color processing to register pointing gestures (i.e., pointing by hand and laser pointing).

into *coming in, going out, sitting down, rising,* and *walking* in the four main directions. A training phase was applied to compute a multidimensional histogram for each activity, which exhibited probabilities of possible outputs for a given activity. The actual activity recognition process, then, was not used to guess user intentions, but just to assist for the location tracking process. Some recognitions were used to start or stop tracking (e.g., *coming in, going out*) and others helped to determine specific locations (e.g., *sitting down, rising*). Therefore this system too was driven by explicit multimodal user interaction through voice and gesture solely.

**Intelligent Classroom**  The *Intelligent Classroom* from Northwestern University Illinois was designed for a different purpose. The aim of Franklin (1998) was to support user activities in classrooms; i.e., assist lecturers while holding their speeches. Therefore the classroom attempted to understand everything that speakers did in terms of a high-level explanation of actual activity. The perceptional part of the system consisted of video cameras that observed the environment to notice gestures by tracking speaker's head, hands, and feet and microphones that recorded speech to extract phrases from a small vocabulary.

Franklin et al. (2002) explained that a lecturer's possible activities were described by a kind of hierarchical finite state machines. Triggered by the sensor observations, a plan recognition mechanism was used to identify which activity out of a predefined library the user was actually performing. Based on this, the lecture room automatically showed assistive behavior like in the example mentioned by Franklin and Hammond (2001, pg. 166) where the lecturer wanted to play a video and the classroom cued the tape, set the video source, and started the VCR.

**Probabilistic Parsing**

**MavHome**  Heierman III et al. (2001) gave five recommendations for the construction of Smart Environments: *1.*) adapt for dynamic device collection, *2.*) automate usage of simple devices, *3.*) learn occupants' behavior, *4.*) allow user intervention, and *5.*) learn temporal patterns. The Managing an Adaptive Versatile Home (*MavHome*) project from University of Texas at Arlington addressed those issues. In Das et al. (2002) an agent framework was introduced, which consisted of a hierarchy of rational agents that act to meet the overall goals of home automation and energy optimization. The architecture distinguished between house-level, room-level, and appliance-level agents and incorporated several algorithms for the recognition and prediction of an inhabitant's activities.

Besides sliding window mechanisms like the Smart Home Inhabitant Prediction (SHIP) algorithm or the Episode Discovery (ED) mechanism described in Cook et al. (2003b), the probabilistic parsing approach was considered. In Cook et al. (2003a) the Active-LeZI (ALZ) algorithm for localization or activity prediction respectively was explained. This algorithm based on Lempel-Ziv parsing for data compression and was closely related to the LeZi-update algorithm that Bhattacharya and Das (1999) proposed for tracking mobile users in personal communication service networks. Therefore alphabets of locations or activities were defined. With every observation a history (i.e., a string that was composed out of entities of the alphabet) was updated and parsed by ALZ into a trie-style[12] dictionary. The nodes of this dictionary preserved the statistics to compute the conditional probability for the next location or activity.

**Aware Home** The *Aware Home* was intended, as Kidd et al. claimed, as an *"environment that is capable of knowing information about itself and the whereabouts and activities of its inhabitants"* (Kidd et al., 1999, pg. 191). To do so, the Aware Home Research Initiative at Georgia Tech built a two-floor home with identical and independent living spaces. Additionally, a control and observation room was established in the basement of this house. Several different sensing components, including cameras and pressure mats, were installed into both flats to observe and identify the inhabitants. The substantial equipping of Aware Home allows for various research directions. Behavioral observations were, of course, possible as well as research on passive biometric identification. Orr and Abowd (2000), for example, described an approach based on *ground reaction force*. This concept from biomechanics provided unique signatures of the inhabitants' footsteps, which could be compared with prerecorded footstep signatures to identify persons. But besides that various approaches for activity recognition were investigated.

One approach was described by Moore and Essa (2002). Here, a model of a stochastic context-free grammar (SCFG) was defined that described the rules of activity and assigned them probabilities. This model was closely akin with the proposals for probabilistic parsing of Bobick and Ivanov (1998) and Ivanov and Bobick (2000). Within all systems the Earley-Stolcke parsing algorithm was utilized for parsing the sequence string of atomic activities provided by a lower level recognition mechanism.

---

[12]*"[A] trie, or prefix tree is an ordered tree data structure that is used to store an associative array where the keys are usually strings. Unlike a binary search tree, no node in the tree stores the key associated with that node; instead, its position in the tree shows what key it is associated with. All the descendants of any one node have a common prefix of the string associated with that node, and the root is associated with the empty string."* Wikipedia (2008)

**Probabilistic Plan Recognition**

**Aware Home – continued**  Another recognition approach was described by Hamid et al. (2003). They proposed a simple Dynamic Bayesian Network (DBN) for activity recognition from video observation. The hidden states in this system reflected the atomic actions such as *holding*, *moving*, or *inserting* and the observable states contained vectors of tracking data, including features such as the relative distances between objects as well as their velocities, direction, etc.

Particle filters were used to track object movement and the probability of a certain particle state, then, was measured in terms of how well an observation fitted to statistical features, which were color and orientation histograms of the tracked objects. This approach was, among others, tested in the Aware Home *living* scenario as well as in a *classroom* scenario, which rather resembled the Classroom 2000/eClass project; a project that was also implemented at Georgia Tech and is described in the following Section 1.4.3.

**Surveillance System**  A research group from Computer Science Department of the Australian Curtin University of Technology investigated methods for activity recognition. Nguyen et al. (2003) described a *Surveillance System* that aimed to detect a user's activities as he moved around in an office building or – as in Duong et al. (2005) – in a home environment.

At the sensor level user paths were observed by a set of ceiling-mounted cameras. A floor plan of the environment was subdivided into a set of square-meter sized cells and a multiple-camera tracking module assigned the detected movement of the user to a list of visited cells (i.e., cell ID and the duration of each cell visit were stored).

Then, to deduce activities from the observed footprints real-time this group proposed several approaches based on *probabilistic* plan recognition. In Bui et al. (2000) an Abstract Hidden Markov Model (AHMM) was introduced to represent the execution of hierarchical plans from the application domain stochastically. Later the AHMM was extended with the capability to remember certain states in plan execution. The enhanced Abstract Hidden Markov mEmory Model (AHM$E$M) was presented to overcome earlier limitations (Bui, 2002, 2003).

A slightly different approach was pursued by Duong et al. (2005). A two-layered Switching Hidden Semi-Markov Model (S-HSMM) was suggested, which modeled activities of daily living (ADL) such that at the bottom layer atomic activities and their duration (e.g, staying in cell *'at stove'* for 10s) were represented using HSMMs, while the top layer abstracted the different high-level activities where each high-level activity (e.g., *'making coffee'*) was made of sequences of atomic activities.

### 1.4.3 Observation, Annotation Applications

Applications or projects listed in this section have, respectively, the same demand for activity recognition and intention inference as the examples in the previous Section 1.4.2. But the work that is presented here does not need to come up with strategies for the configuration of environments. Coming primarily from surroundings such as medical monitoring and behavioral or usability study, these projects utilized the user observation only for the purpose of automatic activity annotation. Hence, some of the projects are even realized in an offline post-processing manner.

**eClass aka Classroom 2000**  In Abowd et al. (1996) the *Classroom 2000* project at Georgia Tech was introduced. This project from the college classroom domain served exclusively as a note taking facility, which collected various kinds of information during lessons. Later named *eClass* (Brotherton and Abowd, 2004) it recorded the lecturer's slide history, the notes of the lecturer from a marker board, audio and video footage as well as student notes or questions.

Then, immediately after a lesson the multimedia material was compiled into a time-lined webpage, which was accessible for students' review. Key events derived from slide content (e.g., URLs) or interactions such as a slide change were used to index the media content along the timeline. But unlike the earlier mentioned Intelligent Classroom, the eClass did not try to recognize special gestures or activities[13] to enable focusing on particular details.

Instead it continuously recorded all data from all resources, letting student reviewers weight the content for themselves later. Brotherton and Abowd (2004) found that eClass, which was fully deployed in actual classrooms, was apparently very popular with students. Many claimed that they were better able to participate in the class since they were freed from distracting continuous note-taking.

---

[13]Nevertheless other researcher at Georgia Tech determined activity recognition and intention inference for classroom scenarios, such as in the earlier mentioned approach of Hamid et al. (2003) (cp., Section 1.4.2).

**Smart Kindergarten**  A related project called *Smart Kindergarten* (SmartKG) was established at UCLA. According to Srivastava et al. (2001) it was intended to not only collect information from sensors but also to fuse and interpret them. Additionally SmartKG should react appropriately upon those interpretations. Therefore video and audio observation was installed into a kids classroom and a sensing appliance named *iBadge* was developed. The iBadges were worn by the small inhabitants as well as integrated into toys. All badges together formed a sensor network, which provided the data from these appliance, including position and orientation.

Latter publications from this project indicated that the focus was apparently shifted to an observation-only approach. In Chen et al. (2002) the focus was described as on *"[s]patially dense but unobtrusive sensors [that] continually capture interactions among students, teachers, and common classroom objects"* (Chen et al., 2002, pg. 49) and the main research issues then were *1.*) if a behavioral model for the behavior of kids in a classroom context could be developed, and *2.*) if so, if this model could be implemented using sensor-based measures. In SmartKG (2003) the project proposed a 60-node Bayesian network to capture the collaborative processes in its observational environment. With 48 observable nodes they inferred four hidden variables: first, *overall collaboration* (whether collaborative processes were observed in the group), which was a function of two others: *interaction* and *engagement*, and finally *group existence*, which based on proximity measures. Later Savvides and Srivastava (2005) clarified in-depth the self-configuring location-discovery process.

**Smart Meeting Room Task**  The goal of *Smart Meeting Room Task* (SMaRT) – a joined project of the Interactive Systems Laboratories (ISL) at Carnegie Mellon University and Karlsruhe University – Waibel et al. (2003, pg. 752) phrased as *"to provide meeting support services that do not require explicit human-computer interaction"*. Efforts on monitoring user activities using both video and audio analysis should provide the basis for appropriate reaction of a meeting room to users' needs. Even though Waibel et al. claimed comprehensive smart environment behavior in their scenario, the main result of this project was a meeting corpus (Burger and Yu, 2002), which provided information about the speaking style depending on the meeting type, and a meeting browser, which had the ability to efficiently capture, manipulate and review all aspects of a meeting.

The meeting browser incorporated the tracking and identification approach described by Yang et al. (2000) that used multimodal input based color appearance of the video signal, audio signals and face detection to identify attendees of a recorded meeting automatically. Waibel et al. (1998) and Schultz et al. (2001) described the other components of the meeting browser application. Raw audio and video sources were recorded and a speech recognizer provided user-by-user transcription, which again could have been summarized. Additionally, neural network-based visual cues from face and gaze tracking and discrete HMM-based auditory cues including ringing telephones, knocks on doors, or even sound texture differences between different speaking situations helped to index the meetings.

Recent publications from ISL, for example Wojek et al. (2006), came up with activity recognition approaches akin to those mentioned earlier (cp., Survailience System in Section 1.4.2) and the following approach of the M4 project.

**Multimodal Meeting Manager**   The EU IST-Programme sponsored *Multimodal Meeting Manager* (M4) project was focused on the realization of a system to enable structuring, browsing and querying of an archive of automatically analyzed meetings. Therefore a series of meetings took place in a meeting room at IDIAP equipped with multiple sensors (i.e., cameras and microphone arrays). Those sessions were recorded and made available as M4-corpus. Utilizing corpus data researchers from several involved institutions determined different approaches to structure and annotate the pre-recorded meetings.

In McCowan et al. (2003, 2005) a first method was presented that assumed a discrete set of group activities and viewed a meeting as a sequence of such activities. The goal then was to recognize the turn-taking pattern from sensor data, which would allow a segmentation of the meeting into those group activities. McCowan et al. proposed Hidden Markov Models (HMM) to derive auditory and visual features automatically. Zhang et al. (2004) came up with an extension that addressed the issue known from social psychology, that individual actions and interactions were on different semantic levels. In their two-layer HMM framework they considered this point by providing separate layers for the recognition of individual actions performed by each person, such as writing and speaking, and group activities.

The person-layer models were asynchronous HMMs respecting that some asynchrony might exist for the group activities but recognition was akin to the model by McCowan et al.. The upper group layer, then, used results from the person-layer recognizers as input as well as features from the raw sensor stream that could not be associated with individual persons. Dielmann and Renals (2004) transformed the two-level HMM into a graphical representation, namely a Dynamic Bayesian Network (DBN). Interpreting group activities as a sequence of several actions, they added *counter* and *enabler nodes* to their model. As a second variation a multi-stream DBN was proposed, which processed features from different sources independently at the person level, and integrated them at the upper group level. Al-Hames and Rigoll (2005) used a similar model.

Finally, Zhang et al. (2006) recently proposed another DBN with a two-level structure, namely player (i.e., a single person or individual) level and team level. A single person's activities were modeled as a conventional HMM. The activity states of all persons at a certain moment were parent nodes to the team state node and thus potentially influenced the team state. In addition to those conditional parents a switching node decided which particular activity was to affect the team activity. The team node itself in turn just had an impact on an individual person's activities in the next time step. This also implied that there is no direct affection between a current team state and its previous state, but only the described two-level bi-directional influence.

Zhang et al. (2006) esteemed the team level as an aggregation of the individual's behaviors, where the contribution of a certain person's behavior was described by the distribution over the switching node variable. The probability distribution was automatically learned from data in an unsupervised fashion and in the end this model outperformed with its influence values a method that took the proportions of time during a meeting which each participant spoke to quantify influence.

## 1.5 Method Matrix

The previous sections described several projects from the ubiquitous computing community. The described projects showed several aspects that could matter within this work for the choice of a modeling approach and the selection of appropriate inference methods and learning algorithms. This section should reflect and summarize methods seen with other projects to emphasize methods which are worth to be analyzed in more detail. Tables 1.1 & 1.2 provide matrices of the reviewed projects and identified relevant aspects.

This overview allows some interesting observations. First, the most frequently used classification technique of the presented related projects are Hidden Markov Models (HMM). In Table 1.1 can be found that six projects from this extensive view into the state of the art clas-

*Overview*

sified at least atomic activities using a form of HMMs. This is followed by five occurrences of both Neural Networks (NN) and Dynamic Bayesian Networks (DBN). Since DBNs generalize HMMs (Murphy and Paskin, 2001), the state of the art shows a strong tendency for an application of a probabilistic model-based approach to the problem definition of this work. This tendency can also be found in Table 1.2, where a count of eight probabilistic approaches faces six and five entries in the other categories respectively. Furthermore, the review shows that only a few ubiquitous computing projects so far addressed cooperative team behavior

Table 1.1: Matrix summarizing *Modeling* aspects of the described related projects.

|  | Mobile Assistance | | | Smart Environment | | | | | | | | | | Observation, Annotation | | | |
|---|---|---|---|---|---|---|---|---|---|---|---|---|---|---|---|---|---|
|  | Location Stack | Place Lab | Opportunity Knocks | Active Badge | Easy Living | Interactive Room | Adaptive House | iDorm | Intelligent Room | SmartOffice | Intelligent Classroom | MavHome | Aware Home | Surveillance System | eClass | Smart Kindergarten | SMaRT | M4 |
| **Modeling** | | | | | | | | | | | | | | | | | | |
| Team Approach | | | | | ■ | | | | | | | | | | | ■ | | ■ |
| **Sensors** | | | | | | | | | | | | | | | | | | |
| Vision | | | | ■ | | ■ | | ■ | ■ | ■ | ■ | | ■ | ■ | | ■ | ■ | ■ |
| Discrete (IR) | ■ | ■ | | | ■ | | ■ | ■ | | ■ | | ■ | ■ | | ■ | ■ | | |
| Continuous (RF) | ■ | | ■ | ■ | ■ | | | | | | | | | | | ■ | | |
| **Classification** | | | | | | | | | | | | | | | | | | |
| NN | | | | | | ■ | ■ | | ■ | | ■ | ■ | | | | ■ | | |
| FSM | | | | | | | | | | | ■ | | | | | | | |
| SCFG | | | | | | | | | ■ | | | | | | | | ■ | |
| BN | | | | | | | | | | | ■ | | | | | | | |
| HMM | | | | | | | | | ■ | ■ | | | ■ | ■ | | | ■ | ■ |
| DBN | ■ | | ■ | | | | | | | | | | | | | | | |
| CRF | | | | | | | | | | | | | | | | | | |
| others | | | ■ | | ■ | | | | | | | | | ■ | | | | |

NN – Neural Network    HMM – Hidden Markov Model
FSM – Finite State Machine    DBN – Dynamic Bayesian Network
SCFG – Stochastic Context Free Grammar    CRF – Conditional Random Fields
BN – Bayesian Network    others – Look-up Lists & Tables, Geometry Models,
        Linear Classifiers, *k*-Nearest Neighbor

(cp. with Table 1.1). Some of them (e.g., Interactive Room, eClass[14]) addressed this issue through explicit interaction without incorporating any inference and prediction approaches. Others (e.g., Smart Kindergarten, M4) addressed team intention recognition by annotating

---

[14]eClass was used actually for hindsight selection of recorded observation content and, thus, is an example for offline explicit interaction.

Table 1.2: Matrix summarizing aspects of the described projects related to *Inference*.

| | Mobile Assistance | | | Smart Environment | | | | | | | | | | | Observation, Annotation | | | |
|---|---|---|---|---|---|---|---|---|---|---|---|---|---|---|---|---|---|---|
| | Location Stack | Place Lab | Opportunity Knocks | Active Badge | Easy Living | Interactive Room | Adaptive House | iDorm | Intelligent Room | SmartOffice | Intelligent Classroom | MavHome | Aware Home | Surveillance System | eClass | Smart Kindergarten | SMaRT | M4 |
| **Inference** | | | | | | | | | | | | | | | | | | |
| **Training** | | | | | | | ■ | ■ | ■ | ■ | ■ | | ■ | ■ | | | ■ | |
| **Approach** | | | | | | | | | | | | | | | | | | |
| Connectionist | | | | | | ■ | ■ | | ■ | | | ■ | | | | | ■ | |
| Rule-based | | ■ | | ■ | | | | | ■ | ■ | | | | | ■ | | | |
| Probabilistic | ■ | | ■ | | | | | | | | ■ | ■ | | ■ | | | ■ | ■ |
| **Recognition** | | | | | | | | | | | | | | | | | | |
| Real-time | ■ | ■ | ■ | | ■ | ■ | ■ | ■ | ■ | ■ | ■ | ■ | ■ | | | ■ | ■ | ■ |
| Offline | | | | ■ | | | | | | | | | | ■ | ■ | | | |
| **Inference** | | | | | | | | | | | | | | | | | | |
| Particle Filter | ■ | | ■ | | | | | | | | | | ■ | ■ | | | | |
| LBP | | | | | | | | | | | | | | | | | ■ | ■ |

LBP – Loopy Belief Propagation (marginalization) aka. Viterbi (maximization)

| | Location Stack | Place Lab | Opportunity Knocks | Active Badge | Easy Living | Interactive Room | Adaptive House | iDorm | Intelligent Room | SmartOffice | Intelligent Classroom | MavHome | Aware Home | Surveillance System | eClass | Smart Kindergarten | SMaRT | M4 |
|---|---|---|---|---|---|---|---|---|---|---|---|---|---|---|---|---|---|---|
| **Learning** | | | | | | | | | | | | | | | | | | |
| Supervised | | | | | | ■ | | | | | | ■ | | | | | | |
| Reinforcement | | | | | | | | ■ | | | | | | | | | | |
| Clustering | | | | | | | ■ | | | | | | | | | | | |
| EM | ■ | | | | | | | | | | | | | ■ | | | ■ | |
| M(P)LM | | | | | | | | | | | | | | | | | | |
| Fingerprint | | ■ | | | | | | | | | | | | | | | | |

Supervised – Backpropagation    Reinforcement – model-free Q-Learner
Clustering – Fuzzy C Means + Hierarchical Clustering    EM – Expectation Maximization
M(P)LM – Maximum (Pseudo) Likelihood Maximization    Fingerprint – Beaconprint

Overview

observations of group behavior in an offline manner. The scenario Section 1.6 will show that in this work a realtime approach is needed to enable a proper inference of team intentions in a Smart Environment like my department's SmartApplianceLab that forms dynamically in an ad-hoc manner. To the best of my knowledge no solution exists that realizes an implicit control of an ad-hoc Smart Environment by means of an real-time inference approach for team intention recognition.

In addition, some other not that strong relations might be seen in Tables 1.1 & 1.2. The matrices show that Neural Networks need to be trained. Finite State Machines (FSM) and HMMs seem to be adequate to recognize vision patterns. DBNs are used when continuous but sparse and noisy sensor input needs to be processed.

And finally, the inference and learning techniques strongly depend on the utilized model; i.e., inference in Conditional Random Fields (CRF), for instance, is usually realized using Loopy Belief Propagation (LBP) or respectively Viterbi and Particle Filters usually enable inference in DBNs. Learning in Neural Networks mainly employs supervised or reinforcement learning methods, whereas DBN model parameters are typically tuned applying Expectation Maximization (EM).

## 1.6 Scenario

Design and assembly of the ubiquitous computing applications realized by the different projects rely on definitions of their particular application domain. Some were designed for outdoor assistance, others found their usage in indoor environments. Some were envisioned to react immediately, others just recorded the scene to be processed later on. Some focused on optimizing the environment in either way without having users involved, others relied on explicit interaction with the inhabitants.

A common approach to define the focus of an application is to put this into a scenario of the envisioned usage of this piece of software. This section provides a scenario for a Smart Meeting Room Environment that uses the concept proposed by this work. The scenario emphasizes the key objectives for the intended system in a prosaic manner to indicate directions and delimitations of research in this work. Since this is a work on team support for Smart Environments, a thought by Grudin (2002) is put at the beginning who tried to give a reason for the little success of ubiquitous computing applications in the wild. He argued with the very little change in human nature and group dynamics over the past millions of years and stated:

> *A [...] reason we are reluctant to adopt new meeting support technologies is that unlike with a personal productivity tool, experimentation occurs in public. We learn by making mistakes, but mistakes in this domain are often embarrassing. To avoid problems, the use of trained facilitators and technology experts is recommended, but they divert attention from the meeting "owner." Process and status are altered. [...]*
>
> *Support technologies that have succeeded (blackboard...) are those that minimally alter the social dynamics. The message for ubiquitous computing is that these technologies, too, must meld with human social dynamics. They should not focus exclusively on improving productivity if this requires us to change fundamental aspects of how we interact"* (Grudin, 2002, pg. 75).

Keeping this statement in mind and remembering the ubiquitous computing vision of into the background vanishing appliances phrased by Weiser (1991) my department is interested in researching group support without explicit interaction in a smart ensemble that was dynamically formed by fixed and mobile smart appliances. The following scenario respects these preliminary considerations, describes potential capabilities for such an ad-hoc Smart Environment, and thus provides the boundaries for this work.

Consider a Smart Meeting Room Environment designed to incorporate inhabitant tracking and environment monitoring as well as occupancy schedule and meeting agenda retrieval. The room is equipped with sensing devices (e.g., RF-positioning sensors, motion sensors, luminosity sensors) and acting appliances (e.g., steerable projectors, motor screens, motor window blinds) that form an ad-hoc ensemble together with brought-in devices including notebooks and mobile projectors. In such a room, situated in a company's IT department, a meeting of a software design group could be appointed.

Therefore chief architect *Penny* announces the meeting using the internal calendar management system of this company. With her announcement she provides an outline of agenda items that should be addressed during the meeting. Maybe the meeting is structured like in the agenda of Figure 1.3 where first software architect *Sheldon* should present his thought about an envisioned software design. Then software architect *Leonard* provides his presentation and after that it is the turn of chief architect *Penny* to present. Afterwards a discussion

*Overview*

**Topic**
- ☐ Software Architecture Meeting
  *Smart Appliance Lab*
- ☐ 10:00 Presentation of Proposal of Software Architect Sheldon
- ☐ 10:05 Presentation of Proposal of Software Architect Leonard
- ☐ 10:10 Presentation of Proposal of Chief Architect Penny
- ☐ 10:15 Discussion of Proposals

Figure 1.3: Preliminary agenda of a meeting

on those presentations is scheduled. Additionally invitations are sent to both software architects *Sheldon* and *Leonard*. Since the announcement is made by their boss *Penny*, they will probably confirm the announcement and prepare their presentations. In parallel the calendar management system of the company informs the Smart Meeting Room that this meeting is appointed and the persons *Sheldon*, *Leonard* and *Penny* will probably show up at the agreed meeting time to probably process the agreed agenda.

Shortly before the appointed meeting time the two software architects *Sheldon* and *Leonard* enter the Smart Meeting Room. Assuming all employees and visitors of the company are wearing identifiable RF-badges, the room immediately knows who is walking in. Luminosity sensors measure available light so that the appliance ensemble in the room can decide whether it should provide additional light (e.g., turn on lamps, lift motor blinds). The calendar management system indicates that a meeting is about to begin. Hence, the ensemble goes into a meeting stand-by configuration where screens and projectors are prepared to provide their assistance.

As chief architect *Penny* walks in a short gossip starts, occupants walk to their seat and open their brought-in notebooks. The notebooks add themselves dynamically to the ensemble and make the presentations of their owners available to the room. Then, the meeting starts and deviating from the preliminary agenda *Leonard* goes to the presentation stage to give his talk.

But the environment recognizes this deviation, infers that the team decided to bring forward the presentation of *Leonard* and puts his presentation on the screen just before he enters the presentation stage. Additionally the light situation is adjusted to enable optimal viewing conditions. After *Leonard*'s contribution, the team turns back to the agenda and *Sheldon* presents. Finally, chief architect *Penny* moves for presentation, and every speaker is proactively provided with his particular presentation. During the subsequent discussion light may adjust again and the presenting appliances change to and stay in stand-by modus, just in case an occupant wants to show something additionally. In the end of the meeting the attendees grab their mobile appliances and leave the room. Now the remaining appliance ensemble in the room can go to energy saving or re-calibration mode and can rest until the next scheduled meeting. End!

Some may say: 'That is not that fancy and visionary scenario that I expected'. But note, it is the attempt to provide a scenario that is akin with the earlier mentioned visions to minimize embarrassment in usage of Smart Environments as well as its obtrusiveness or potential for distraction from the substantial tasks. It emphasizes the research directions of my department, namely implicit interaction and ad-hoc dynamic ensembles. And finally, the scene indicates a set of criteria to which this work can provide a handsome contribution with the proposed concept of a robust and training-free prior knowledge probabilistic system for real-time intention analysis in teams. The next section highlights those criteria.

## 1.7 Criteria for a Team Intention Model

Taking the scenario from the previous section as a source of marginal conditions for this work, a set of criteria can be identified that are relevant to the design of the desired system for Smart Meeting Rooms. Other criteria derive from the physical layout of the department's laboratory *SmartApplianceLab*[15] and its built-in sensing technologies. Moreover a third source for constraints exists, which is my demand to provide a flexible experimental infrastructure. This also influences the criteria catalogue. Typical questions that must be considered for an appropriate selection of a modeling approach are:

- How complex is the model development? (How much knowledge does the system designer need for the creation of a model? What cognitive complexity does the model definition require?)

- How is the relation of complexity versus precision in the model?

- How will statistic parameters of the model be trained? (Is it usable before or without training? How much training is required before the model is usable?)

- How is the model created? (Manually, extracted from annotated task models, or learned structurally respectively?)

---

[15]The laboratory infrastructure of the department is described in Section 3.2.2.

*Overview*

The mentioned scenario indicates that the envisioned Smart Meeting Room should be a very open environment, where a dynamic ensemble of mobile and of course also built-in appliances forms the basis for the capabilities and features of the environment. The dynamism of this infrastructure implies that it could not be foreseen at design or training stage respectively and valuable training data would hardly be available. Considering those questions, one issue is that the proposed concept should pursue a *training-free prior knowledge approach*. Secondly, the meeting room is open to various groups of various sizes with various meeting practices. That is, the context, namely the inhabitant identities and the meeting agendas, changes from meeting to meeting, too. Furthermore, the dynamic character of the Smart Meeting Room leads to two other criteria for modeling proper intention recognition. An adequate model must allow *easy changes or extensions* of either *the lexica of team activities* or *the size of teams* (i.e., the number of team members) to allow a flexible handling of the various team settings just mentioned. Additionally, as team intention analysis and prediction is used in the real-world surrounding of an assistive Smart Meeting Room it is mandatory that the proposed concept provides *real-time recognition* and *prediction*.

Another aspect is that the modeling approach has to deal with physical infrastructural constraints. Acting under the observation of, for instance, an audio-vision system may be found embarrassing. Additionally, a company deployment of audio-vision-based recognition may raise security concerns by that company, because recorded confidential meeting content may be abused. Therefore, my department decided to rely recognition on simple unobtrusive sensor data. For this work a part of the sensing information provided by the Ubisense Platform indoor-positioning system is used. In the case of the described scenario these are the 2D-positions for each of the three team members, namely a six-dimensional feature vector of position data. But the concept should allow the usage of even simpler sensor hardware (e.g. proximity sensors), too. From this it follows that the proposed concept must enable *robust recognition from simple*, maybe sparse or noisy, *sensor data*.

Finally, it seems reasonable to keep track of recognized finished team activities, because most items on a meeting agenda already finished will not appear again within the same meeting. Hence the concept must allow to consider this fact with a kind of *team activity history* that enables an adaptation of recognition. In contrast, single user activities as part of team activities can obviously appear multiple times and thus an added value from a history could not be expected. This is just one reason to allow for *separate modeling of team and user activities*. In any case it provides a more flexible model, which is needed for an experimental infrastructure with flexible tools.

In summary, the relevant criteria for the team intention model are *1.)* pursuance of a **training-free prior knowledge approach**, *2.)* capability of using **various lexica of team activities** (i.e., agendas), *3.)* allowance for **easy extensions** (e.g., to larger teams), *4.)* support of **real-time recognition**, *5.)* provision of **robust recognition** from simple sensor data, *6.)* tracking of **team activity history**, and *7.)* **separate modeling** of complex team and atomic user activities.

## 1.8 Summary

The current chapter identified a number of techniques and methods from related work that could be valuable for the planned concept of a system for team intention analysis. It described the envisioned usage scenario, to which the compiled concept should contribute, and defined a set of criteria the concept should follow. Besides a detailed discussion of selected techniques from the method matrix in Section 1.5, the next chapter provides insight into research topics related to human behavior. It describes how subfields of psychology, namely social psychology and cognitive psychology, structure behavior of individuals and dynamics of groups. Findings from those well-established research areas may provide additional information relevant to the criteria catalogue defined in the previous Section 1.7. Just before the introduction of this work's modeling approach in the next chapter the criteria are revisited to incorporate knowledge on human individuals and group behavior.

# Chapter 2

# Modeling Team Intention Recognition

## 2.1 Introduction

This chapter enlightens about how knowledge about human behavior and roles in individual as well as group situations can help to model team intention recognition. In the *collaboration* community it is widely accepted to consider research on cognition and social aspects in teams for modeling approaches (Grudin, 2002; Hayne et al., 2003) and also some earlier mentioned work on activity annotation referred to psychological approaches (McCowan et al., 2005). Therefore this chapter represents the attempt to identify work and founding methods from the related fields of psychology that influenced design decisions made regarding this work's approach of modeling team intention recognition for smart environments with a *team intention model*.

After explaining the psychological background of this work, selected methods from signal processing are described in more detail. The selection of those methods relies on the findings from Section 1.5, where the most promising methods with respect to the criteria specified in Section 1.7 were extracted from the approaches used by related projects work. Interestingly enough, the course of the sections in this chapter follows in parallel the same hierarchy levels as introduced later in the proposed Team DBN. Starting at the team task level with aspects from social psychology the chapter continues with the user task level in the cognitive psychology section and finally ends at the sensor signal level with a review of the more technical field of signal processing.

## 2.2 Social Psychology Perspective on Teams

While intention recognition in Smart Environments is an ongoing research domain and the focus on teams rather than single users is not really established yet, in psychology exists the field of social psychology which is focused on group behavior. A Merriam–Webster definition describes social psychology as *"the study of the manner in which the personality, attitudes, motivations, and behavior of the individual influence and are influenced by social groups"* (Merriam–Webster Online Dictionary, 2008b), and an extensive amount of literature on group behavior is already available in the social psychology area. A review of this literature might provide helpful insight into the structure of meetings and information present in teams. Because these are aspects relevant to my approach that sustain the proposed team (execution) intention model a summary of the social psychology perspective on teams should be included.

The structure of this paragraph is mainly influenced from work done by Forsyth (2006) who gave an excellent overview on Group Dynamics. He identified properties and dynamics that all kinds of groups possess and divided the so called *"nature of groups"* into six categories – interaction, interdependence, structure, goals, cohesiveness, and stage. These categories are picked up for the further structure of this section.

Table 2.1: Categories of IPA (Interaction Process Analysis) System from 1950 and revised 1970 (*Source*: Adapted from Bales 1970)

| General Categories | | IPA 1950 | | IPA 1970 |
|---|---|---|---|---|
| A. Positive (and mixed) actions | 1. | Shows solidarity | 1. | Seems friendly |
| | 2. | Shows tension release | 2. | Dramatizes |
| | 3. | Agrees | 3. | Agrees |
| B. Attempted answers | 4. | Gives suggestion | 4. | Gives suggestion |
| | 5. | Gives opinion | 5. | Gives opinion |
| | 6. | Gives orientation | 6. | Gives orientation |
| C. Questions | 7. | Asks for orientation | 7. | Asks for orientation |
| | 8. | Asks for opinion | 8. | Asks for opinion |
| | 9. | Asks for suggestion | 9. | Asks for suggestion |
| D. Negative (and mixed) actions | 10. | Disagrees | 10. | Disagrees |
| | 11. | Shows tension | 11. | Shows tension |
| | 12. | Shows antagonism | 12. | Seems unfriendly |

### 2.2.1 Interaction

Bales (1950) identified two classes of interactions that are characteristic for group situations. One is task interaction. It usually covers behavior that focuses on goals a group wants to achieve with its work or projects. Therefore members of a group have to motivate each other and coordinate their skills and resources so that the group can dispose decision to succeed with their plans. When a group of software engineers present their suggestions of a software architecture to each other and the chief software architect and discuss those presentations to agree on a common interface definition, the interaction of the group is task focused.

The second class of interaction is focused on relationship – the interpersonal and social aspects occurring in groups. With socio-emotional interaction group members try to sustain the linkage of members to one another and to the group. This does not directly lead to task completion but helps to create and maintain group well-being. It occurs if a member needs support that others will help with a shoulder to lean on or constructive suggestions or if someone of the group does not follow the norms that he will be criticized and made to feel uncomfortable.

The Interaction Process Analysis (IPA) from Bales (1950, 1970) relies on this distinction between task and relationship interaction processes and provides a measure for the interaction process in group situations. Therefore the conversation during a group-meeting is broken down into sequences of IPA categories (see Table 2.1).

An elaboration of IPA is the also process-based SYMLOG system (System of Multiple Level Observation of Groups) from Bales et al. (1979), where it was assumed that behaviors vary in three dimensions: U*pward – dominant* vs. D*ownward – submissive*, P*ositive – friendly* vs. N*egative – unfriendly*, and F*orward – accepting authority* vs. B*ackward – non-accepting authority* (see Figure 2.1). The observation here concentrates on the attitudes of the individual group members.

### 2.2.2 Interdependence

In most kinds of groups interdependences exist. According to Wageman (2001) group members influence parts of other members actions, thoughts or feelings. For instance the success of the chief software architect from the scenario in Section 1.6 is depending on how excellent her software engineers complete their work. She can personally do best but if her engineers

| Label | & General Behavior |
|---|---|
| U | Active, dominant, talks a lot |
| UP | Extrovert, outgoing, positive |
| UPF | A Purposeful, democratic task leader |
| UF | An assertive, business like manager |
| UNF | Authoritarian, controlling, disapproving |
| UN | Domineering, Tough-minded, powerful |
| UNB | Provocative, egocentric, shows off |
| UB | Jokes around, expressive, dramatic |
| UPB | Entertaining, sociable, smiling, warm |
| P | Friendly, egalitarian |
| PF | Works cooperatively with others |
| F | Analytical, task-oriented, problem-solving |
| NF | Legalistic, has to be right |
| N | Unfriendly, negativistic |
| NB | Irritable, cynical, won't cooperate |
| B | Shows feelings and emotions |
| PB | Affectionate, likable, fun to be with |
| DP | Looks up to others, appreciative, trustful |
| DPF | Gentle, willing to accept responsibility |
| DF | Obedient, works submissively |
| DNF | Self-punishing, works too hard |
| DN | Depressed, sad, resentful, rejecting |
| DNB | Alienated, quits, withdraws |
| DB | Afraid to try, doubts own ability |
| DPB | Quietly happy just to be with others |
| D | Passive, introverted, says little |

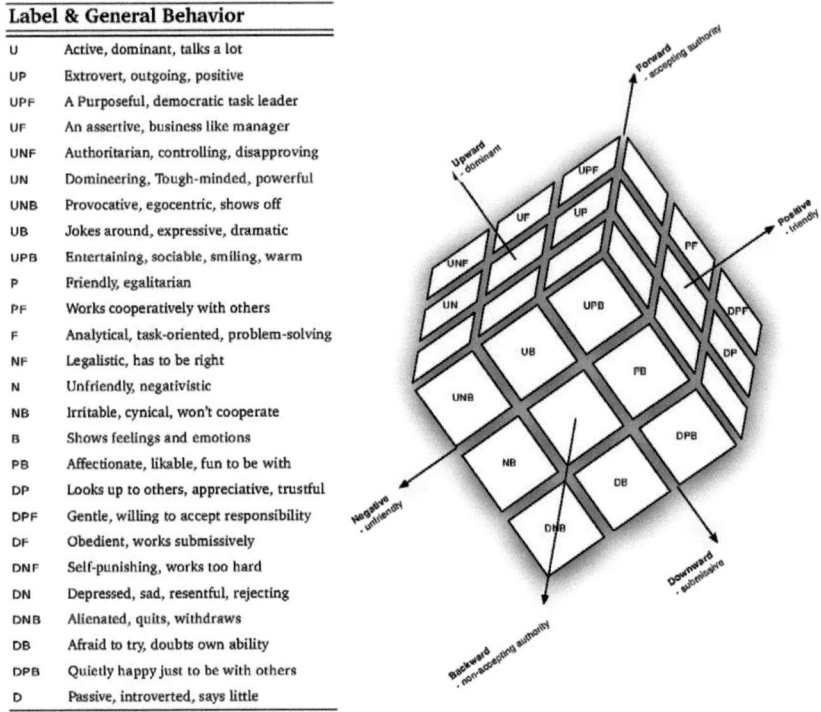

Figure 2.1: The three-dimensional SYMLOG-space shows 26 directions of behavior resulting from a combination of the six main directions. The description of the general behavior is listed left. (*Source*: Adapted from Bales et al. 1979, pp. 61, 63)

do not succeed then she fails. So this member of a group is strongly interested in a supportive and assistive climate within the group. Thus, he will probably influence the other group members in this direction.

In strong hierarchies the relation of staff members to the boss is an example for nearly unilateral interdependence, as he influences his employees much stronger then the other way round. But in other groups with less distinctive hierarchies a rather mutual influence is probable (see Figure 2.2): Either as a sequential interdependence where one member influences another member who then influences the next or as reciprocal interdependence where two or more members may influence each other. If a group is nested in a larger environment multilevel interdependence probably occurs and the group is able to influence, or can be influenced by, others outside the group.

*Modeling Team Intention Recognition*

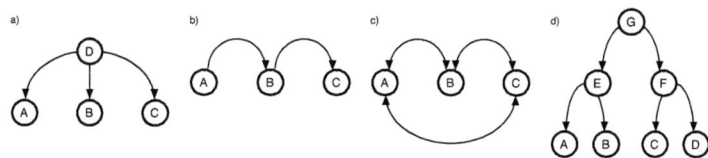

Figure 2.2: a) Unilateral interdependence, b) Sequential interdependence, c) Mutual, reciprocal interdependence, and d) Multilevel interdependence (*Source*: Adapted from Forsyth 2006, pg. 12)

### 2.2.3 Structure

A group is not a randomly composed entity, but rather shows predictable organizational patterns. Regularities exist that determine who bears responsibility, who reports to whom, or who assists whom. The group structure is formed by these regularities that Forsyth (2006) categorized as roles, norms and inter-member relations.

Roles define the expected behavior of a person that takes a certain position within a group. Fundamental roles in most group configurations are leaders and followers. Moreover Benne and Sheats (1948) identified additional roles that should exist in every well-balanced group. Besides many other important roles are the information seeker, information giver, elaborator,

Table 2.2: Types of roles in groups (*Source*: Adapted from Benne and Sheats 1948, pp. 41–49)

| Role | Function |
|---|---|
| **Task Role** | |
| Information seeker | Emphasizes getting the facts by calling for background information from others. |
| Information giver | Provides data for forming decisions, including facts that derive from expertise. |
| Elaborator | Gives additional information – examples, re-phrasings, implications – about points made by others. |
| Procedural technician | Cares for operational details, such as materials, machinery, and so on. |
| **Relationship Role** | |
| Encourager | Rewards others through agreement, warmth, and praise. |
| Harmonizer | Mediates conflicts among group members. |
| Compromiser | Shifts his or her own position on an issue in order to reduce conflict in the group. |

Table 2.3: Various types of norms (*Source*: Adapted from Forsyth 2006, pg. 171)

| Common Features | Description |
| --- | --- |
| Prescriptive norm | A consensual standard that identifies preferable, positively sanctioned behaviors. |
| Proscriptive norm | A consensual standard that identifies prohibited, negatively sanctioned behaviors. |
| Descriptive norm | A consensual standard that describes how people typically act, feel, and think in a given situation. |
| Injunctive norm | An evaluative consensual standard that describes how people should act, feel, and think in a given situation rather than how people do act, feel, and think in that situation. |

procedural technician, encourager, harmonizer, and finally the compromiser (see Table 2.2). But the behavior of group members, their action and interaction is also related to implicit or explicit norms of a group that describe what is suitable and what is an outrage in a certain situation. Norms are usually grouped to be prescriptive, proscriptive, descriptive, or injunctive (see Table 2.3) and derive from various types of social relations that exist in groups. Some are based on status and authority, and others are based on liking and affection. The most common types are status, attraction and communication.

Status in a group is often derived from the hierarchy within a group. The boss or the professor has more prestige than rank-and-file members. But status can also be earned in groups where people start from the same basis. Members with extraordinary aptitudes or hard-working members may gain higher status.

Attributes that have little relation to the focus of a group but rely on widespread but denied prejudices may have the opposite influence, as the higher status of men vs. women, Whites vs. Black, older people vs. younger people. These two types of status allocation are covered by the *"Expectation-States Theory"* introduced by Berger et al. (1992).

Attraction forms the sociometric structure of a group (Doreian, 1986). In the same way as some group members have higher status than others some people are more liked than others. Sociometry – introduced by Moreno (1934, revised 1953) – is the underlying technique to determine a group's social relationship where group members are asked who they like the most and who they dislike the most. Statistical summarization then identifies the popular individuals and the isolated members. Several studies use this method to group the attraction

# Modeling Team Intention Recognition

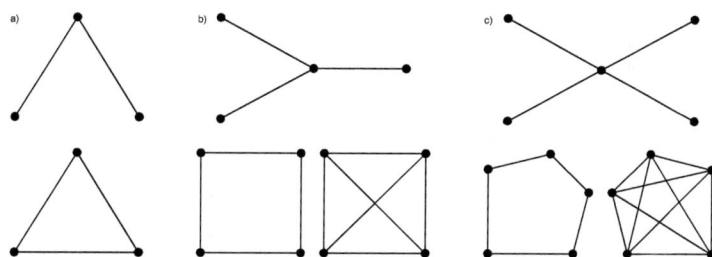

Figure 2.3: a) Three-person networks: wheel (top), comcon (bottom), b) Four-person networks: wheel (top), circle, and comcon (bottom), c) Five-person networks: wheel (top), circle, and comcon (bottom)(*Source*: Adapted from Shaw 1978)

of peers from *"popular"* to *"rejected"* as a group measure of the social competence (Coie et al., 1990; Newcomb et al., 1993).

Communication in groups is rather centralized than decentralized where leaders usually send and receive information from the others. A centralized communication network tends to be most efficient as long as the group's communication rate is low enough to route all information. If the amount of information raises too high the central node becomes a bottleneck. As argued by Shaw (1978), communication than can break down resulting in a fading group structure. Typical centralized and decentralized communication networks for small groups are shown in Figure 2.3. Note that the communication in these examples is bidirectional but networks with one-way communication links can also exist.

The structure of a group is the often underestimated core of most dynamic group processes. People spend much time to comply with requirements of a role in a group and find themselves in conflicts if they fail to match demands or violate norms that a group defined over time. If some people form a subgroup based on liking and disliking their influence within the group raises compared to isolated group members. If a member controls information exchange in a group, this also increases his influence on the others.

### 2.2.4 Goals

Groups exist for a certain reason. Members form a group to pursue common goals. Groups make it easier to achieve goals. That's why work is rather done by groups than by individuals. But groups engage in so many different things, they create ideas, research for solutions, present approaches, discuss proposals, and develop respectively deploy implementations. This opens various options to classify group goals.

A prevailed and accepted classification of group tasks is the *"Circumplex Model"* by McGrath (see Figure 2.4). It provides four basic categories: Generating, Choosing, Negotiating, and Executing. In a generating task a group can as well create approaches to their problem definition (creativity task) as develop strategies to achieve their goals (planning task). Choosing tasks exist when groups have to decide about what is the one correct solution to their problem (intellective task). If the goal can be achieved in many different ways the group must decide which way to go (decision-making task). When groups are negotiating, two kinds of tasks are relevant too, the group must either resolve differences in group members' opinions about the group goal (cognitive-conflict task), or a negotiation addresses rather social or sta-

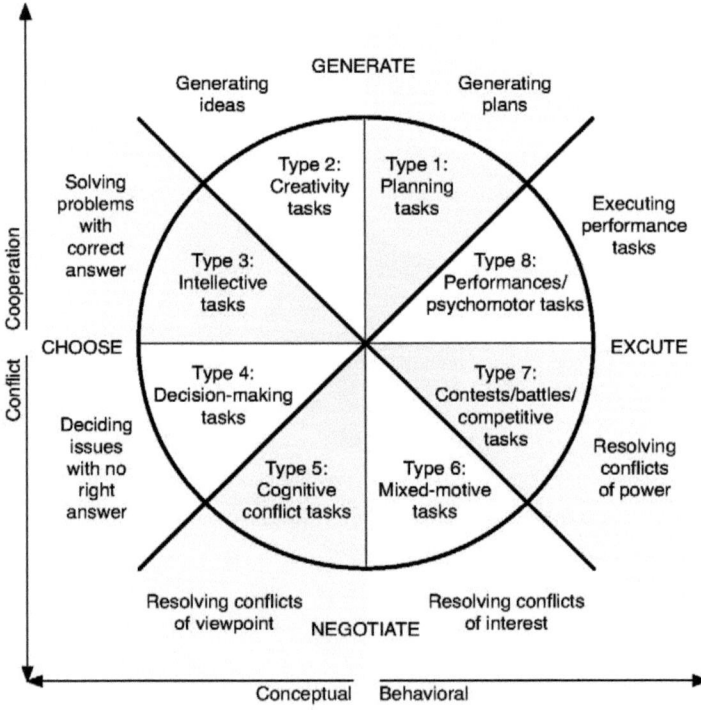

Figure 2.4: McGrath's task circumplex orders the eight basic undertakings for groups along two continua: cooperative – competitive and conceptual – behavioral (*Source*: Adapted from McGrath 1984)

tus competition (mixed-motive task). And finally, most groups actually do things, and while executing groups can just perform tasks (performances) or they act in competition to other groups (contest/battles). Note that in a group not all categories of the Circumplex Model must exist. Various groups just perform a subset of tasks (McGrath, 1984).

### 2.2.5 Cohesiveness

Groups are not just a set of independent individuals. Whenever a group is forming its members build a unified social entity over time that is more than the sum of the individual members. This observation has its root in the emergence property, a key principle of Gestalt psychology. Cohesiveness describes the solidarity and integrity of a group. The quality of cohesiveness may differ regarding the nature of a group, but according to Dion (2000) a group would fall apart if they had not a minimum of cohesiveness.

### 2.2.6 Stage

The nature of a group is also influenced by time. Starting with a bunch of unrelated individuals the group process assigns members to roles, sets up communication, or forms friendships. People join and leave, and the group sometimes shows strong unity where in other situations the cohesion is not that distinctive. Changes in a group over time follow predictable patterns. As depicted in Table 2.4, Tuckman identified five stages of group development: the *Forming* phase, *Storming* phase, *Norming* phase, *Performing* phase (Tuckman, 1965), and *Adjourning* phase (Tuckman and Jensen, 1977).

*Forming* is the phase where group members get to know each other. All act polite and first social relation are developed. In the *Storming* phase the first conflicts appear and the group seeks for a solution to improve the performance of the group. The *Norming* phase is governed by the development of standards for behavior and roles that regulate behavior. During the *Performing* phase the group works as a unit and very goal oriented. This is the stage of the highest progress regarding the group goals. In the *Adjourning* phase the progress stops because the mission was completed (or for some other reasons), and the group dissipates. Groups tend to oscillate forth and back between the task oriented issues and the socio-emotional issues of those stages. So sometimes group members work hard on goals but other times strengthening their interpersonal bonds, argued Bales (1965).

Table 2.4: The five stages of group development after Tuckman (*Source*: Adapted from Tuckman 1965)

| Stage | Major Processes | Characteristics |
| --- | --- | --- |
| Orientation: *Forming* | Members become familiar with each other and the group; dependency and inclusion issues; acceptance of leader and group consensus | Communication is tentative, polite; concern of ambiguity, group's goals; leader is active members are compliant |
| Conflict: *Storming* | Disagreement over procedures; expression of dissatisfaction; tension among members; antagonism toward leader | Criticism of ideas; poor attendance; hostility; polarization and coalition formation |
| Structure: *Norming* | Growth of cohesiveness and unity; establishment of roles, standards, and relationships; increased trust, communication | Agreement on procedures; reduction in role ambiguity; increased "we-feeling" |
| Work: *Performing* | Goal achievement; high task orientation; emphasis on performance and production | Decision making, problem solving; mutual cooperation |
| Dissolution: *Adjourning* | Termination of roles; completion of tasks; reduction of dependency | Disintegration, withdrawal; increased independence and emotionality; regret |

From an individual perspective people also experience changes in their group socialization. It is not that a person is instantly a fully integrated member of a group, rather this socialization process also runs through stages. Moreland and Levine (1982) developed a model of group socialization of individuals joining a group (see Figure 2.5), and distinguish between *Investigation* stage (The individual is still outsider but interested in joining a specific group), *Socialization* stage (The person has entered the group, and now learns norms, and takes responsibilities according to his assigned role), *Maintenance* stage (The group member has to learn new ways, and accept disliked responsibilities).

If the individual successfully acts within the group he stays on *Maintenance* stage. If he fails to meet the requirements of group structure he enters *Resocialization* stage where the group reminds the individual to abide group norms. If the group member continues failing he probably will leave the group, and with leaving enters *Remembrance* stage.

*Modeling Team Intention Recognition*

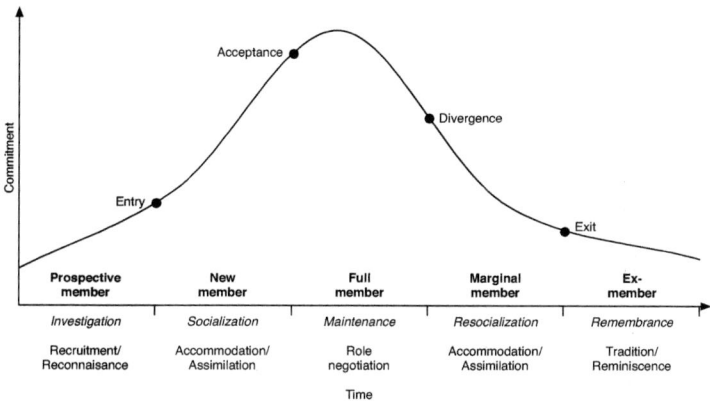

Figure 2.5: The five types of roles (e.g., new member, full member) and five role stages (e.g., socialization, maintenance) from Moreland and Levine's model of group socialization. Points on the curved line mark the four role transitions (*Source*: Adapted from Moreland and Levine 1982)

### 2.2.7 Relevant Essence

From the categories described above I identified *interaction* and *goals* as most relevant to the design of a team intention model because these aspects of group nature are focused on actual tasks and goals of an existing team. The other categories consider a team's life-cycle or well-being. Clearly, this can influence team intentions too, but on a higher level and in longer term than I required for my proposal of a *team intention model*. That is why *cohesion* is completely beyond the scope of this work.

For the *stage* category it is considered that teams which match the meeting scenario outlined in Section 1.6 operate in the most productive *performing* stage (see Table 2.4), where *interdependence* and *structure* of these teams are well-established. It is assumed that the teams are homogeneous with members having equal rights, and without a special polarizing of *roles*, *norms*, or *status*. This assumption was taken into account by choosing *mutual reciprocal interdependence* (see, Figure 2.2) for the approach. Furthermore the *structure* of the team in the scenario is a *three-person comcon network* (see Figure 2.3) where everyone communicates with each other. That is a focus that allows to center on the task respectively goal-oriented team processes.

Assessment methodologies in social psychology range from self-report measures and struc-

Table 2.5: Different Coding Systems for Group Meetings in Social Psychology

| System | IPA | | | |
|---|---|---|---|---|
| Basis | Process-based | | | |
| Lexicon | Positive actions | Answers | Questions | Negative actions |
| | show solidarity; | give suggestion | ask for orientation | disagree |
| | show tension release | give opinion | ask for opinion | show tension |
| | agree | give orientation | ask for suggestion | show antagonism |
| System | Task Circumplex | | | |
| Basis | Task-based | | | |
| Lexicon | Generate | Choose | Negotiate | Execute |
| | planning task | intellective task | cognitive conflict task | contest or battle |
| | creativity task | decision-making | mixed-motive task | performance |

tured observational measures to physiological measures, among others (Forsyth, 2006). Obviously the observational approach is particularly relevant in a smart environment setting with sensor and actor appliances. Sensor appliances in this context can act as the described observers. They objectively observe team meeting situations from an external point of view. On the other hand according to Suchman (1995) an observation turns under the influence of the context into an interpretation or analysis of the observer. Therefore intention analysis based on sensor data and prior knowledge fits well into the observational paradigm of social psychology. Observations in social psychology usually try to reach objectivity by using coding systems of group behavior. As stated by McCowan et al. (2005) the codes of these particular categorizations are non-overlapping and cover the duration of an entire meeting. Relevant to my approach is the distinction between process-based and task-based coding systems; i.e. between coding systems where the codes describe behavior to observe in group processes and others where the codes separate specific tasks.

An example for a process-based coding system is the Interaction Process Analysis (IPA) proposed by Bales (1950) mentioned in Section 2.2.1. It provides a measure for the interaction process in group situations. Observers listen to a meeting and break the verbal content into sequences of IPA categories (see Table 2.5). An elaboration of IPA is the also process-based SYMLOG system (System of Multiple Level Observation of Groups) by Bales et al. (1979). Observation here concentrates on attitudes of the individual group members.

The Circumplex Model of Group Tasks mentioned in Section 2.2.4 introduced by McGrath

(1984) is a representative of task-based coding systems. This model distinguishes between four basic goals: generating, choosing, negotiating, and executing tasks. These basic categories are subdivided further into a dictionary of eight different group tasks (see Table 2.5). Others extended the dictionary with group tasks they observed in their specific setting (Ward et al., 1995).

Observing group behavior using the categorization of coding systems has direct relevance for the design of a team intention tracking tool. Usage of a coding system enables observers to separate out stages of group situations like meetings, and enlarge them into agenda topics. According to Bales (1950), categories are made to develop the framework of major events during an observation.

Transferring this experience from social psychology to the application field of smart environments, intention analysis can be considered as a structured observational measurement with the challenge to recognize continuous, non-overlapping sequences of entries from a coding system. Since a coding system provides nothing else than a dictionary of meeting events, it is intelligible that an a-priori meeting agenda is a good candidate for such a lexicon.

Summarizing this section on social psychology, this subject area provides valuable background knowledge for a design of a team intention tracking tool. I have learned that

- the "nature of groups" includes much more than task or goal-oriented acting of a team respectively , but
- interdependences and structures in groups can be modeled in forms where team members have equal rights,
- sensor observations in a smart environment fit well to the observational technique called *structured observational measure,*
- usually coding systems are applied with this technique to recognize group events objectively and systematically, and
- an a-priori agenda can be utilized as a coding system, because categories of such a dictionary are selected to reveal an agenda of group events.

After identifying relevant social aspects for observing and inferring team behavior it is now mandatory to determine if it is possible to model behavior of individual humans. Therefore the chapter switches from team level to user level and now reviews approaches from cognitive psychology including human-computer interaction aspects. The findings are presented in the next section.

## 2.3 Cognitive Psychology View on Tasks

Cognitive psychology is another psychological field relevant to my proposal as it investigates a human's mental states. Merriam–Webster defines cognitive psychology as *"a branch of psychology concerned with mental processes (as perception, thinking, learning, and memory) especially with respect to the internal events occurring between sensory stimulation and the overt expression of behavior"* (Merriam–Webster Medical Online Dictionary, 2008).

Cognitive psychology is interested in describing the mental processes that occur between a stimulus and the related response. It is concerned with all human activities rather than some portions of it from a cognitive point of view. As claimed by Neisser (1967) the question that cognitive psychology addresses is how a sensory input is transformed, reduced, elaborated, stored, recovered, and used by a human processor. Metaphors and terminology used in cognitive psychology are rather computational and research is fairly intermeshed with artificial intelligence research as a significant aspect of the interdisciplinary subject of cognitive science.

Table 2.6: Major research areas in cognitive psychology.

| Perception | Categorization | Memory |
|---|---|---|
| General perception, | Category induction and | Sensory memory |
| Psychophysics, | acquisition, | Short-term or working memory |
| Attention and Filter theories, | Categorical judgement | Long-term memory |
| Pattern recognition, | and classification, | Declarative memory |
| Object recognition, | Category representation | Procedural memory |
| Time sensation | and structure | Autobiographic & flashbulb memory |
| | Similarity | False & constructive memory |

| Knowledge Representation | Language | Thinking |
|---|---|---|
| Mental imagery | Numerical cognition | Choice theory |
| Propositional encoding | Grammar and linguistics | Concept formation |
| Dual-coding theories | Phonetics and phonology | Decision making, Judgment |
| Mental models | Language acquisition | Logic, formal & natural reasoning |
| | | Problem solving |

Besides others the main categories in cognitive psychology are perception, memory, learning (with knowledge representation and language aspects), and thinking (see Figure 2.6). As I look at cognitive psychology with the motivation to gain insights to how to model human behavior I restrict my investigations to aspects of cognitive psychology that are related to user modeling, reasoning and problem solving strategies. In the following sections I first focus on reasoning and problem solving. Later I explain some well-known approaches that address different aspects of modeling.

### 2.3.1 Reasoning

Reasoning is a means of inferring new information from existing knowledge. Humans use three different types of reasoning in everyday situations that differ significantly: *deductive*, *inductive*, and *abductive* reasoning (Dix et al., 2004). *Deductive* reasoning utilizes given premises to deduce a logically necessary conclusion:

> Premises: If it is Friday then she will go out and dance.
> It is Friday.
> Conclusion: Therefore she will go out and dance.

As the derive is just the logical conclusion it must not reflect one's understanding of truth:

> Premises: If it is Friday then the next day will be Monday.
> It is Friday.
> Conclusion: Therefore the next day will be Monday.

Both above conclusions are totally valid but the second collides with the knowledge about the normal order of days in a week. The other way round people often infer invalid conclusions if they use their world knowledge in reasoning processes:

> Premises: Some female people are students.
> Some students learn diligently.

An obvious conclusion for the above example might be 'Some female people learn diligently'. This of course is an invalid deduction because there is no statement saying if all students are female. So it is possible that all diligent students are non-female, but people assume a certain amount of shared knowledge (e.g., the common view that males are less laborious than females) and use it to shortcut the deduction process.

With *inductive* reasoning people generalize from experiences to reason about non-experienced cases. For example, if all polar bears that a person had seen during his life had white fur he will assume that polar bears in general are white. This always includes some uncertainty because it is not possible to prove the assumption to be true. The best way to strengthen the belief is to collect evidence that sustains the induction. *Inductive* reasoning is useful while learning about the environment. Since a person can never check all polar bears on earth he will tend to trust his knowledge that has been inferred inductively.

*Abduction* is the third reasoning type, and it infers from an observed fact to its cause. With this method people try to explain events they observed. An example could be that a person knows from stereotypes if he recognizes a trailer combination with yellow license plates on a german autobahn that the driver is a camping enthusiastic Dutch man. As one would expect this is an uncertain assumption because other explanations could validate the observed situation. Maybe when his car passes the trailer he notices that actually a french license plate is mounted on that truck. With this more detailed evidence his assumption now might be that a French man is the driver. But as long as no better evidence endorses an alternative explanation people infer reasons by so-far knowledge and cleave to the inferred cause[1]. The summary in Table 2.7 reflects the relationship between these three different ways to conclude about domains of interest from experience and knowledge.

---

[1] BTW stereotypes have been utilized by some early user behavior modeling approaches (e.g., Rich, 1979).

Table 2.7: Classical terminology and relationships for the three types of reasoning.

*Deduction* takes a *Case* of the form $X \Rightarrow Y$, matches it with a *Rule* of the form $Y \Rightarrow Z$, then adverts to a *Fact* of the form $X \Rightarrow Z$.

*Induction* takes a *Case* of the form $X \Rightarrow Y$, matches it with a *Fact* of the form $X \Rightarrow Z$, then adverts to a *Rule* of the form $Y \Rightarrow Z$.

|  | Deduction | Induction | Abduction |
|---|---|---|---|
| Premiss | Rule | Case | Fact |
| Premiss | Case | Fact | Rule |
| Conclusion | Fact | Rule | Case |

*Abduction* takes a *Fact* of the form $X \Rightarrow Z$, matches it with a *Rule* of the form $Y \Rightarrow Z$, then adverts to a *Case* of the form $X \Rightarrow Y$.

## 2.3.2 Problem Solving

In contrast to *reasoning* that gathers new information from already known facts, *problem solving* is the process to find solutions to unexplored ventures from the knowledge that people have. It is characterized by the human ability to adapt available information and come up with original creative solutions for new situations.

The view how people solve problems changed over time. Behaviorism claimed that solving problems is reproductive, e.g., it uses a reproduction of known feedback or a trial and error approach. Gestalt psychologists extended this theory with a productive part. Productive problem solving also employs previous experiences but utilizes insight into the problem domain and restructuring of the problem itself to come up with a solution.

A well-kown experiment that focused on the question if insight and restructuring can lead to problem solutions was the analysis of the *pendulum problem* implemented by Maier (1931). The setup of the experiment was as follows: in a room two pieces of string were hanging from the ceiling. Additionally the room was equipped with tools like pliers, poles and extensions. The subjects had the task to tie the strings together but the problem was that those two pieces were too far apart to reach both of them at once. The subjects provided various solutions but without the insight that the plier could be used as pendulum weight only a few provided this solution. Other subjects received the pendulum insight as an experimenter moved a string and then came up with the obvious pendulum solution.

An element of problem solving that is reminiscent of the understanding of productive restructuring and insight is the use of analogies. The suggestion about analogies is that people use existing knowledge about a domain similar to the problem domain to map solutions from the known field to the new problem. This process was observed with experiments that provide subjects with analogous stories. Gick and Holyoak (1980) assigned the following task to their study subjects:

> *A doctor is treating a malignant tumor. In order to destroy it he needs to blast it with high-intensity rays. However, these will also destroy the healthy tissue surrounding the tumor. If he lessens the rays' intensity the tumor will remain. How does he destroy the tumor?*

The experimenters observed that only about 10 % found the solution to fire a set of low-intensity rays from different directions that converge at the tumor without any hints. But this number increased significantly to around 80 % if the subjects were provided with this analogical story from Gick and Holyoak (1980):

> *A general is attacking a fortress. He can't send all his men in together as the roads are mined to explode if large numbers of men cross them. He therefore splits his men into small groups and sends them in on separate roads.*

The large number of subjects spotting this analogy came from the semantically close relation of both stories. But not all analogies work that well. If an analogy is semantically not close enough to the original problem, then people often have no benefit from it for achieving the requested task.

Newell and Simon (1972) introduced the problem space. It consists of so called *problem states*. With this approach a problem always has an initial state and a goal state. Problem solving then is the process to move from former to latter state. Therefore it tries to find a sequence of state transition operators that allow a legal transformation from initial to goal state.

Solutions to problems can take the form of algorithms for manageable circumstances, or heuristics are employed if a huge problem space cannot guarantee a solution. Different problem solving models were proposed for navigating problem spaces, where the path from initial state to goal state was generated in various fashions. Depending on what is required these models tested if it is possible at all to find a path or tried to find the fastest, most efficient, and/or most likely path.

### 2.3.3 Means-ends Analysis Models

One example is *means-ends analysis*. This is a heuristic approach that first compares initial state and goal state and then tries to find an operator that reduces the difference between both. Besides Newell and Simon's General Problem Solver model various other approaches were proposed. I will review some of them during the next paragraphs.

**General Problem Solver**

A basic means-ends analysis example is the General Problem Solver – GPS by Newell and Simon (1972). The problem solving strategy of this model is based on a depth-first search.

GPS separates the task from the problem solving mechanisms. This enables the use of the same problem solving strategy for a wide range of tasks. In this model only the task information needs to be adjusted to alter the model for new goals.

Using GPS an agent can access a set of objects and knows the goal states that are expected for these objects. It identifies the objects' states and is able to refine them using operators. The agent then calculates the difference between actual states of the objects and their goal states and utilizes operators to lessen the difference. The reduction process is in many circumstances not linear but mostly realized recursively. Differences between the current states and the goal states that are difficult to eliminate are divided into sub-goals with differences that are easier to eliminate. Recursion by 'sub-goaling' is utilized as long as a progression towards the ultimate goal states is made.

**Standford Research Institute Problem Solver**

An implementation using the GPS strategies is the problem solver STRIPS (*Stanford Research Institute problem solver*) provided by Standford Research Institute by Fikes and Nilsson (1990). In STRIPS a collection well-formed formulas (*wffs*) in first-order predicate logic define the world. For the initial or current state the conjunction of those *wffs* is $True$. The goal state of a problem is also modeled as a set of *wffs* and the goals are achieved or the problem is solved if the goal state is part of the current world state. The operators have preconditions and the results phrased as *wffs*. The precondition denotes whether or not an operator can be applied. If it was applied the resulting *wffs* are added to the world model and some other *wffs* might be removed.

Technically STRIPS uses a theorem prover to realize the GPS strategies. The prover attempts to show that a goal follows from the defined world model. If the proof is successful the goal is achieved, if not the proof fragment is used to illustrate the difference between the current state and the goal.

Then STRIPS selects operators that allow the proof to proceed and validates the preconditions of these operators. If some preconditions of the selected operators are unsatisfied these are adopted as sub-goals and the problem solving process is repeated recursively.

**State, Operator and Result Architecture**

In 1990 Newell proposed the *state, operator and result* (originally shortened SOAR, but now referred as Soar) architecture as an implemented architecture for general cognition. Soar is not a specific problem solver, but the effort to provide a minimal collection of mechanisms for the complete range of intelligent behavior. The underlying structure enables a system built upon Soar to *"perform the full range of cognitive tasks, employ the full range of problem-solving methods and representations appropriate to the tasks, and learn about all aspects of the tasks and its performance on them"* (Laird et al., 1987). This is realized by incorporating several aspects of general intelligence into the architecture. According to Laird et al. (1987) these aspects include:

- *Physical symbol-system* – A general intelligence must be realized with a symbolic system.

- *Goal-structure* – Control in general intelligence is maintained by a symbolic goal system.

- *Uniform elementary representation* – There is a single elementary representation for declarative knowledge.

- *Problem space* – Problem spaces are the fundamental organizational unit of all goal-directed behavior.

- *Production system* – Production systems are the appropriate organization for encoding all long-term knowledge.

- *Universal 'sub-goaling'* – Any decision can be an object of goal-oriented attention.

- *Automatic 'sub-goaling'* – All goals arise dynamically in response to impasses and are generated automatically by the architecture.

- *Control-knowledge* – Any decision can be controlled by indefinite amounts of knowledge, both domain dependent and independent.

- *Weak method* – The weak methods form the basic methods of intelligence and the system derives its power from acombination of them.

At the problem space level Soar is a collection of interacting problem spaces and each problem space consists of states and operators that – applied to states – deliver new states. The task or goal to a problem space is introduced by a specification of an initial state and at least one coveted state. If the knowledge to apply an operator to the current state is enclosed then state transition is straight-forward. But if a precondition is not satisfied and knowledge is missing then several techniques known from human behavior observation are applied (for instance, search other problem spaces to locate the necessary knowledge or decide without additional knowledge to probable errors and apply error recovery routines).

### 2.3.4 User Models

This section briefly catalogues some of the more notable user models that have mainly been used from the human-computer interaction research community to analyze user interfaces and identify usability issues of software products.

**Task Action Grammars**

Task Action Grammars (TAG) introduced by Payne and Green (1986) follow a slightly different approach than the hierarchical representations of the user's task and goal structures mentioned so far. This linguistic approach focuses on the interaction part of the human-computer interaction triangle in terms of a task language. A well-known representative of linguistic HCI modeling is Reisner's use of the Backus-Naur-Form (BNF) (Reisner, 1981) to define an action language on a purely syntactic level.

Ignoring semantics however makes it difficult to measure the cognitive load of interaction processes that are described as a grammar. TAG aims to enable statements about cognitive load in terms of the learnability of an interface. To overcome the lack of semantics in BNF Payne and Green included elements called parametrized grammar rules.

Using these rules within a definition of an interaction process allows emphasizing consistency or congruence of an interface and encoding the user's world knowledge (e.g., up is the opposite of down). It is argued that consistency is related to the user's understanding. And as it influences the complexity of a rule set consistency also reflects the mental load of an interaction process.

Consistent interfaces that make use of already known elements can be described in TAG with more compact rule sets than others. The relative comparisons between the length of rule sets for different interface designs then enables the learnability measures. Compare the following three interfaces for moving a toy around the floor:

Common interface:
Command interface 1:
    name[Direction = left] → 'go 712'
    name[Direction = right] → 'go 956'
Command interface 2:
    name[Direction] → F('FORWARD')
*     name[Direction = forward] → 'FORWARD'
*     name[Direction = backward] → 'BACKWARD'
    name[Direction] → F('L')
*     name[Direction = left] → 'L'
*     name[Direction = right] → 'R'
Command interface 3:
    name[Direction] → known-item[Type = word, Direction]
*     name[Direction = forward] → 'FORWARD'
*     name[Direction = backward] → 'BACKWARD'
*     name[Direction = left] → 'LEFT'
*     name[Direction = right] → 'RIGHT'

(*Source*: Adapted from Dix et al. 2004, pg. 435, and Payne and Green 1986, pg. 105)

It becomes clear how TAG incorporates properties of consistency, congruence, and world knowledge into grammar rules. The first interface uses machine code addresses that are hard to remember to initiate a movement in a certain direction. In the second version commands can be associated to some feature sets where it is easy to infer the according opposite command if one is known. And the third interfaces just uses consistent commands known to english-speaking users.

Note that starred rules are generated from their parent rules utilizing world knowledge and therefore just the parent rules are counted in measures of complexity. So, in the shown example one would assume that learnability for interface three is best, and that can also be derived from the rule sets, where interface three requires three rules less than interface one.

## Goals, Operators, Methods, and Selection Rules

The well known Goals, operators, methods, and selection rules model GOMS was introduced by Card et al. (1983). It is a very good example for the class of cognitive user models that allow reasonable estimation of users' internal processes and prediction of effects on human-computer interaction that rely on those processes. GOMS comes in several flavors that make different assumptions or restrictions.

The plain GOMS version also referred to as CMN-GOMS sets the basis – i.e., defines the four elements that are common to all versions. As one may notice from the meaning of the acronym these four elements are as follows:

- *Goals* – are assignments that the user has to accomplish. They describe what the user wants to achieve and help to remind him where to return in case of occurring errors.

- *Operators* – are basic actions performed in service of a goal. They affect either the system state or the user's mental state.

- *Methods* – are sequences of operators that accomplish a goal. They are the actual hierarchical goal decompositions into sequences of subgoals and/or operators.

```
GOAL: ICONIZE-WINDOW
    .   [select GOAL: USE-CLOSE-METHOD
    .           .       MOVE-MOUSE-TO-WINDOW-HEADER
    .           .       POP-UP-MENU
    .           .       CLICK-OVER-CLOSE-OPTION
    .           GOAL: USE-L7-METHOD
    .           .       PRESS-L7-KEY]
```
( *Source*: Adapted from Dix et al. 2004, pg. 423)

- *Selection rules* – are principles to decide which method is chosen if more than one method is available to accomplish a goal. Instead of random selection of a method GOMS attempts to predict the use of a method.

  Therefore details about the particular user, the current state, and the goal state are captured in rules. These rules then enable the selection of an appropriate method.

User Sam:
>RULE 1: Use the CLOSE-METHOD unless another rule applies.
>RULE 2: If the application is 'blocks' use the L7-METHOD.
>
>(*Source*: Adapted from Dix et al. 2004, pg. 423)

A simplification to GOMS is the Keystroke Level Model (KLM) introduced by Card et al. (1983). It makes assumptions that frame a very restricted version of GOMS. In KLM only seven operations are allowed and the goals, methods, and selection rules part is blinded out. The user can solely 1.) press a key $K$, 2.) press a button on pointing device $B$, 3.) move a pointing device to a specific location on screen $P$, 4.) perform dragging with the pointing device $D$, 5.) move his own hand to a certain location $H$, 6.) prepare mentally $M$, or 7.) wait until a command execution is finished $R$. Using this model all operations are arranged as sequences where placing of *physical motor* operations is straight-forward. The *mental preparation* operation is usually put at the beginning of a command – i.e., a sequence of pointer and keystroke operations. And a command is followed by a *system response* operation if it is reasonable that the computer needs some time for the execution of the command. Times for all seven atomic tasks – $\{T_K, T_B, T_P, T_D, T_H, T_M, T_R\}$ – are determined empirically and once all operations needed for a task are scheduled the calculation of the total execution time $T_{execute}$ is trivial.

$$T_{execute} = T_K + T_B + T_P + T_D + T_H + T_M + T_R \qquad (2.1)$$

A variation to GOMS – the Natural GOMS Language (NGOMSL) was introduced by Kieras (1988) and refined in Kieras (1997). Kieras' intention was to provide an easy to use model similar to KLM with the power and flexibility of standard GOMS. As GOMS, NGOMSL assumes that goals will expand to a hierarchical structure of strictly sequential subgoals, methods, and operators, but it provides a structured natural language which enables a program-like representation of the procedures that a user must learn and execute to achieve a certain goal.

The execution time is predicted similarly to KLM but the ability to estimate the learning time makes NGOMSL a unique approach. NGOMSL derived this property from its cognitive complexity theory (CCT) roots (Kieras and Polson, 1985) that will be described in Section 2.9. Predicting the learning time also requires counting the amount of atomic NGOMSL statements. Then, *"the length of the methods, and the amount of transfer of training from the number of methods or method steps previously learned"* (Kieras, 1997, pg. 3) allow statements about the learning time. The total learning time $T_{learning}$ consists of terms of the sum pure method learning time $T_{PML}$, long term memory item learning time $T_{LTM}$, and training procedure execution time $T_{TPE}$. Thus:

$$T_{learning} = T_{PML} + T_{LTM} + T_{TPE} \qquad (2.2)$$

where $T_{PML}$ is the number of atomic NGOMSL-statements $n_{NGOMSL}$ multiplied with a certain learning time parameter *ltp* that reflects differences of learning time in different learning situations (e.g., according to Kieras (1997) 30*sec* for rigorous procedure training and 17*sec* for a typical learning situation):

$$T_{PML} = ltp \times n_{NGOMSL} \qquad (2.3)$$

LTM item learning time $T_{LTM}$ is the number of LTM chunks accessed for a procedure $n_{Chunks}$ multiplied with an empirical access time parameter *atp* (e.g., the Model Human Processor parameter from Card et al. (1983) of 10*sec* per chunk). Thus:

$$T_{LTM} = atp \times n_{Chunks} \qquad (2.4)$$

One chunk is added 1.) for each familiar pattern in the retrieval cue, 2.) for each familiar pattern in the retrieved information, and 3.) for the association between the retrieval cue and the retrieved information. And $T_{LTM}$ is only counted if the item is not known to the user before.

$T_{TPE}$ considers similarities in the methods of a procedure. It is based on the suggestion that similar parts in a procedure reduce learning time. To estimate the time that can be saved from transfer of training 1.) candidate methods for transfer must be identified, 2.) methods must be generalized, 3.) occurrences must be counted, and 4.) learning time for all but the first occurrence must be deducted from overall $T_{learning}$.

As KLM, NGOMSL breaks task down to the lowest level of atomic operators to enable reasonable time predictions. From statements at this "keystroke" level one can assume that a user knows how to execute them and that reasonable empirical time estimates for learning and execution are available. But it does not consider situations where users do things in a parallel, multitasking fashion.

Here a variation that was introduced by John (1990) and Gray et al. (1993) provides remedy.

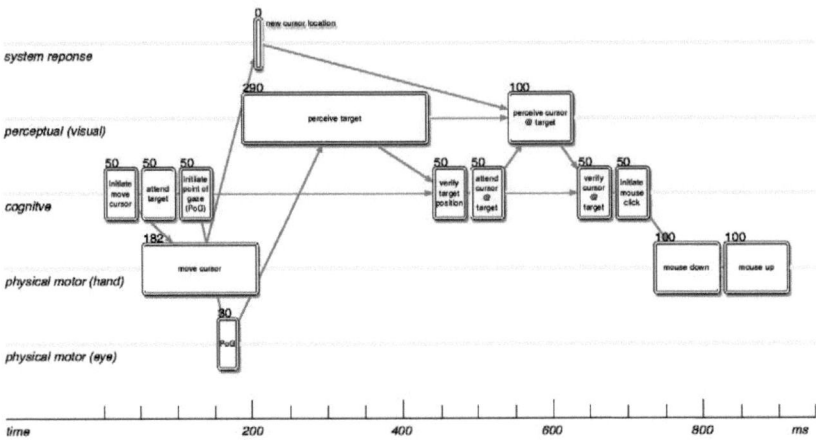

Figure 2.6: PERT-style view of a CPM-GOMS model for carefully moving the cursor to a target and clicking the mouse button. (*Source*: Adapted from John et al. 2002)

The CPM-GOMS is the most complex version of GOMS and incorporates two key features: a Cognitive Perceptual Model and the Critical Path Method (CPM) with PERT-charts[2].

CPM-GOMS is unique because of its CPM elements that allow parallel processing of several operation categories. It distinguishes between system response time and three different categories of operators: perceptual, cognitive, and physical motor operators, where perceptual operators can be e.g. visual or aural perception. Physical motor operators are things like hand movement, eye movement, or verbal responses. These categories of human activities can be executed in parallel and thus enable goal decomposition in a multitasking fashion where actions can overlap to happen in parallel (see Figure 2.6).

CPM-GOMS is the most economically successful variation of GOMS, but it is also by far the most complicated to model. It takes usually hours to model a minute-long task. Recent work proposes tool support for the modeling process – e.g., Apex in John et al. (2002) that automates the difficult task of interleaving the cognitive, perceptual, and physical motor resources underlying common task operators.

---

[2]PERT (Program Evaluation and Review Technique) is a network model that allows random activity completion and was developed in the 1950s for a large US Navy project.

## Modeling Team Intention Recognition

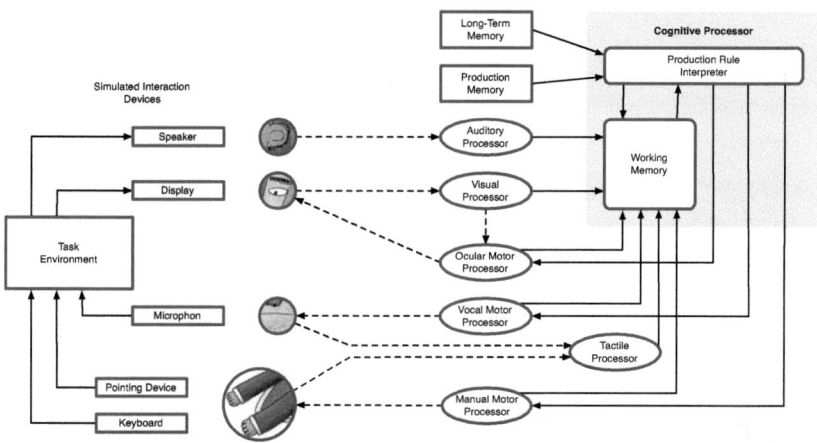

Figure 2.7: **Overview of** the EPIC architecture. Performances of task are simulated by the interaction of an EPIC modeled simulated human (on the right) with a simulated task environment (on the left). Simulated perceptual-motor organs on one side and simulated interaction devices on the other side form the interface. Solid lines indicate the information flow, whereas dashed lines mark mechanical control. (*Source*: Adapted from Kieras and Meyer 1995, pg. 4)

**Executive Process-Interactive Control**

The distinction between particular peripheral sensory-motor processors and cognitive processors also influences the design of some cognitive architectures. Executive Process-Interactive Control (EPIC) by Kieras and Meyer (1995) is a typical representative of this approach that is especially suited for the modeling of human multimodal performance on parallel tasks. With EPIC a model can be described where the process to achieve complex multimodal goals is formulated as a set of production rules.

In contrast to other architectures like Soar in Section 2.3.3 and ACT-R described next the production rule interpreter, which is basically the cognitive processor, is embedded in a strict surrounding of different perceptual and physical-motor processors (see Figure 2.7). This make EPIC mainly useful for explorations regarding the questions how the human ability to perform multiple tasks in parallel influences performance speed and accuracy, and where the performance bottlenecks in complex multimodal situations are.

Kieras and Meyer argued that *"limitations on human ability are all structural; that is, performance of tasks may be limited by constraints on peripheral perceptual and motor mechanisms,*

57

*rather than a pervasive limit on cognitive processing*" (Kieras and Meyer, 1995, pg. 3). Therefore the EPIC architecture provides detailed but fixed sets of mechanisms with mostly fixed empirical substantiated time properties for this peripheral processor. That reduces the degrees of freedom in model construction and draws the focus to the cognitive processes.

For example the visual processor models the eye including a retina. The retina contains three zones around a focal point; that is, *a)* the fovea with a 1° viewing angle, *b)* the parafovea that covers 10°, and *c)* the periphery (60°). The fovea can capture for example the content of a button label, whereas the parafovea recognizes information about what kind of objects occupy a screen region. The periphery finally just notices if an object recently appeared or disappeared. From appearance to pattern recognition of a screen object EPIC assumes different fixed standard delays. The occurrence of an object in the periphery is noticed after 50*ms*, the recognition of properties (e.g., shape) takes an additional 100*ms*, and finally the perception of certain patterns in the fovea lasts 250*ms*. Other processors of the architecture are realized in a similar fashion, because the design of EPIC aims at the explicit linkage between detailed mechanisms to handle perceptual-motor processes and a procedural cognitive task analysis represented by production-system models (Kieras and Meyer, 1995).

**Adaptive Character of Thought Theory**

The Adaptive Character of Thought (ACT-R) theory introduced by Anderson (1993) and summarized in Anderson (1996) stands in a long line of earlier cognitive models developed by Anderson. ACT theory originated as the human associative memory (HAM) theory (Anderson and Bower, 1973). HAM dealt with the question how memory could be represented and how such a representation was related to experimental observation. With the upcoming distinction between declarative and procedural knowledge in the seventies the theory was enhanced to ACTE (Anderson, 1976), which embodied these new issues. In ACT* (Anderson, 1983) production rules reflected the assumptions about neural and psychological functionality at that time. The current ACT-R system enabled the tuning of knowledge representation, acquisition, and deployment.

Knowledge representation in ACT-R is a closed interleaving of declarative and procedural knowledge. Like in Soar (see Section 2.3.3) and in EPIC (see Section 2.3.4) procedural knowledge is defined as set of production rules. A production rule represents a task goal in its conditions. Subgoals that form an abstract, hierarchical structure on human behavior

IF  the goal is to solve an equation
   and a number has been read
   and there is no second argument
THEN  store it as the second argument.

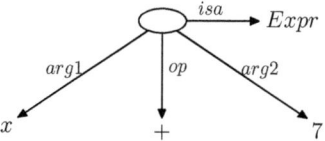

Figure 2.8: This is a step taken from an equation solving process. The figure on the right shows a declarative knowledge chunk and indicates how the second argument of the equation $x + 4 + 3 = 13$ is stored in it. On the left the corresponding production rule is shown. (*Source*: Adapted from Anderson 1996, pg. 358)

while execution might be created recursively . Production rules apply if their preconditions are satisfied by knowledge currently available in either working memory or long-term memory. Both of them hold declarative structures. So, preconditions and effects of a production are mentioned as declarative knowledge.

Declarative knowledge in ACT-R is represented as chunks – i.e. schema-like structures that hold pointers to their categories (e.g. $isa \mapsto Expr$) and additional pointers that encode the contents (e.g. $arg1 \mapsto x$, $op \mapsto +$, $arg2 \mapsto 7$). Figure 2.8 indicates how the second argument from the example is stored in a declarative knowledge chunk and reflects what granularity of analysis of human cognition is recommended by ACT-R in order to obtain "faithful models" (Anderson, 1996).

Long-term knowledge and the evolving understanding of the problem – i.e., the goal state are represented by production rules and chunks. Besides representation ACT-R also addressed knowledge acquisition – i.e., the origin of rules and chunks. As a matter of principle chunks in ACT-R originate from actions of production rules (like in Figure 2.8) and production rules can be created from the encodings in chunks.

Additionally chunk encoding from the environment was incorporated as an independent source to avoid a 'the chicken and the egg' causality dilemma. Perceptual components synthesize object features into chunk representations in ACT-R's working memory and recognize the objects. This process is identical to the process of categorizing objects given a set of properties. This is the way a stimulus is prepared for use as declarative knowledge in production rule conditions.

Production rules on their part are simply transformations of chunks. ACT-R either uses them to find some mappings from knowledge that satisfy conditions directly or restructures or subgoals the production rules respectively. Therefore ACT-R mimics examples of similar solutions either by providing the right chunks required to bridge transformations or by specifying a sequence of subgoals that can be achieved from current knowledge.

The third major issue addressed by ACT-R was knowledge deployment. It addresses the problem, how to select appropriate knowledge in certain situation. This causes a serious problem in systems where a large amount of knowledge is available for solving problems and searching the whole problem space becomes slow. ACT-R therefore provides a two-pass solution that quickly identifies relevant knowledge.

An activation process pinpoints the knowledge structures (chunks and production rules) that are most likely to be relevant for achieving the goal state in background. Then those structures determine the problem solving process (just as in other approaches – e.g., Soar, EPIC). The activation process introduced as rational analysis by Anderson (1990) calculates odds for knowledge that refer to the likelihood that this knowledge will be used in a certain situation. For ACT-R Anderson (1996) claimed that the human mind combines general usefulness and contextual appropriateness to infer what knowledge to use in a certain context and put this in the equation[3]:

$$activation\_level = base\_level + contextual\_priming \qquad (2.5)$$

In the calculation Bayesian inference is implicitly used where the posterior probability $p$ of a hypothesis **h** being correct given some evidence **e** is:

$$\frac{p(\mathbf{h}|\mathbf{e})}{p(\bar{\mathbf{h}}|\mathbf{e})} = \frac{p(\mathbf{h})}{p(\bar{\mathbf{h}})} \times \frac{p(\mathbf{e}|\mathbf{h})}{p(\mathbf{e}|\bar{\mathbf{h}})} \qquad (2.6)$$

and therefore:

$$posterior\_odds = prior\_odds \times likelihood\_ratio \qquad (2.7)$$

Transformed to log terms this is:

$$\log posterior\_odds = \log prior\_odds + \log likelihood\_ratio \qquad (2.8)$$

similar to Equation (2.5), where *activation_level* reflects log *posterior_odds*, *base_level* is implicitly log *prior_odds*, and *contextual_priming* correlates to log *likelihood_ratio*. The actual

---

[3]Equations (2.5 – 2.8) all adapted from Anderson 1996, pg. 360

activation of a chunk structure in ACT-R is realized this way[4]:

$$A_i = B_i + \sum_j W_j \times S_{ji} \qquad (2.9)$$

where the activation of a chunk $i$ ($A_i$) is the sum of the activation base-level of this chunk $B_i$ (i.e., how likely was an activation of $i$ in the past) and a term that represent the contextual-priming. Contextual priming is calculated by the sum of all products representing the weight of a contextual chunk $j$ and its associative strength to $i$.

In summary, ACT-R encodes things of the environment in declarative knowledge. Procedural knowledge contains encodings of observed transformation processes. The application of either declarative or procedural knowledge can be tuned by encoding the statistics of knowledge use, which helps to organize knowledge according to complex goal structures.

### 2.3.5 Task Models

Task models are normative approaches from the human-computer interface design field that have been developed as a means for formally describing human problem solving behavior in situations where task-driven interactions of users with computing devices take place. Human perception and interpretation of information were barely considered in human-computer interface design until task models bridged the gap. Designing task models aims at the identification of those interaction techniques that are most valuable in assisting users to perform their intended tasks.

A *task model* is a breakdown of a composite activity into individual atomic steps, between which a partial order may be defined, roughly speaking: a "plan", that mainly can be induced by the preconditions and effects of the individual atomic steps. The term "action" will denote an atomic step of a task. The concept of task models originates from *cognitive psychology* as well as from *signal processing*, which will be reviewed later in Section 2.4.

In the area of human-computer interface design, hierarchical task graphs are used where tasks can be refined by sub-tasks and their ordering constraints. With respect to hierarchical task models, one of the most popular notations is the ConcurTaskTree notation introduced by Paternò (1999).

---
[4]Equation (2.9) adapted from Anderson 1996, pg. 361

Table 2.8: Temporal operators specified in CTT. (*Source*: Adapted from Paternò 1999; Mori et al. 2002)

| | | |
|---|---|---|
| Enabling | $(\alpha \gg \beta)$ | $\beta$ cannot begin until $\alpha$ was performed. |
| Choice | $(\alpha \,[]\, \beta)$ | $\alpha \wedge \beta$ are enabled. Once one has started the other one is disabled. |
| Enabling & Info-Passing | $(\alpha \,[]\!\!\gg\, \beta)$ | $\beta$ cannot begin until $\alpha$ was performed, and information produced by $\alpha$ is used as input for $\beta$. |
| Concurrency | $(\alpha \,|||\, \beta)$ | $\alpha \wedge \beta$ can be performed in any order, simultaneous, or overlapping. |
| Concurrency & Info-Exchange | $(\alpha \,|[]|\, \beta)$ | $\alpha \wedge \beta$ can exchange information while performing concurrently. |
| Order Independence | $(\alpha \,|=|\, \beta)$ | $\alpha \wedge \beta$ can be performed in any order, but when one has started it has to be finished before the other one can start. |
| Disabling | $(\alpha^* \,[\!\!>\, \beta)$ | $\alpha^*$(usually an iterative task; indicated by an asterisk) is completely interrupted by $\beta$. |
| Suspend-Resume | $(\alpha^* \,|\!\!>\, \beta)$ | $\alpha^*$ can be interrupted by $\beta$. When $\beta$ terminates $\alpha^*$ can be reactivated from the state reached before. |

**ConcurTaskTree Environment**

The ConcurTaskTree Environment (CTTE) described by Mori et al. (2002) is a toolkit that provides support for design and analysis of complex task models for multi-user applications. Task models are described in the ConcurTaskTree notation (CTT) proposed by Paternò (1999). As abstraction levels of tasks can range from very high level decisions for problem solving strategies to very concrete actions (such as pressing a specific button), task models evolved a hierarchical tree-like structure similar to other cognitive modeling approaches (see Section 2.3.3 or Section 2.3.4).

The ConcurTaskTree notation includes a set of operators to describe temporal relationships of hierarchically structured tasks. Each task is associated with a type, a category, attributes, and objects to manipulate. CTT uses graphical syntax to enable easy interpretation of the logical structure of a task. A compound activity is represented by a task tree. Each node in the tree represents a task. Composite tasks may be broken down into subtasks. For each task node it may be specified if this activity is executed by the user, by the application, or by an interaction between user and application, or between cooperating users.

In addition, the possible execution sequences of a composite task's sibling nodes may be further constrained by temporal relations such as "$\alpha \,|=|\, \beta$" ($\alpha$ and $\beta$ may be executed in any

*Modeling Team Intention Recognition*

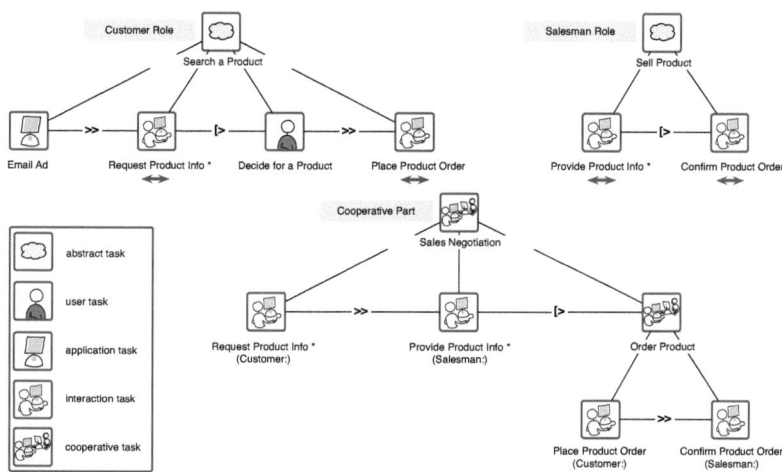

Figure 2.9: Cooperative task model specifying a simplified sales negotiation situation. (*Source*: Adapted from Paternò 1999; Dix et al. 2004)

sequence) or "$\alpha \gg \beta$" ($\alpha$ has to be executed before $\beta$). Table 2.8 shows and explains the other temporal operators specified for the ConcurTaskTree notation.

Figure 2.9 presents typical task trees, describing a rather simplistic sales negotiation between a customer and a salesman. Initiated by an email advertisement a customer requests some product information via an online application. A sales person on the other end responds to the request with the provision of information for the requested product. As indicated by the *-operator customer and salesman can iterate over a bunch of products until the customer decides for a product. Then the customer has to order a product via the application to concretize his decision. This confirmation finally enables the sales person to confirm this specific product order on his part. With both confirmations the goal of the sales negotiation task is achieved, and negotiation ends.

In spite of the fact that in this example cooperation of two individuals is incorporated, task models are more often used to specify the behavior of individual users interacting with a software system. A simulation environment such as the CTTE proposed by Mori et al. (2002) that allows generation of user interfaces from task models provides valuable insights into the dynamic behavior of the model. With simulation it is possible to compare two models that describe similar tasks, or to analyze large specifications where global and local views have to be considered. This way human-computer interface design can reflect findings from the precise analysis of what users want to do with a software system, and is able to define interfaces that are related very closely to tasks of application users.

### 2.3.6 Relevant Essence

With respect to the *team intention model* for smart environments that is introduced in this work the field of cognitive psychology has provided some valuable insight into human behavior. I was most interested in reasoning and problem solving aspects that are part of human thinking. These categories of cognitive psychology offered a large body of approaches to model human behavior. So, the first and most essential realization was that it is admissible to model human behavior.

The next aspect that I could extract from the pool of approaches was that human reasoning and problem solving is goal oriented. People turn to specific tasks in order to achieve certain goals. Originating from an initial state they try to find an efficient path of state transformations to reach the desired goal state. Most often subdividing composite tasks into individual atomic actions is employed to tackle a certain problem in a "divide & conquer" manner. Models from means-ends analysis models (see Section 2.3.3) to task models (see Section 2.3.5) pick up this approach and formulate hierarchies of subtasks with preconditions and effects as paths for solving problems or in other word achieving desired goals. Interesting with respect to the team intention model is that – like in CTTE (see Section 2.3.5) – cooperative multi-user tasks are divided into individual subtasks for the persons involved.

Let us elaborate on the task enabling preconditions. In cognitive psychology models the execution of a task is initiated by satisfied preconditions. Satisfaction then again is induced by knowledge that could be either perceived from the environment (perceptual processor), remembered from long-term memory, or reasoned by combining perception and memory in adequate way. Several of the approaches mentioned above – especially the user models CPM-GOMS (see Section 2.3.4), EPIC (see Section 2.3.4), or ACT-R (see Section 2.3.4) – addressed the knowledge acquisition question. They provided separate channels or processors for perception, effectors, or memory. ACT-R even incorporates a probabilistic weighting function to assess how essential a certain knowledge chunk is for the next state transformation (see Equations (2.5 – 2.9)).

Summarizing this section on cognitive psychology, this subject area provides valuable knowledge on how to structure a team intention model. I have learned that

- modeling human behavior is possible at all; even cooperative behavior can be modeled,
- usually hierarchical structures are applied to reflect typical problem solving strategies,
- the temporal sequence is tied to preconditions and effects of a certain action,
- the knowledge for solving problems is derived from perception, memory, or reasoning.

However, hierarchical task models are mostly used to specify the behavior of users interacting with a software system. They allow to describe the basic temporal structure of compound activities. For *inferring* the activity of a user from sensor data, additional information is needed: a specification of how input stimuli (sensor data) are related to a certain output (execution sequence). The next sections review current approaches sensor signal level – *connectionist* as well as *probabilistic* – that address this question.

## 2.4 Modeling in Signal Processing

In *signal processing*, models have been developed as a means for estimating the actual behavior of a signal source. Depending on the purpose of modeling and the quality of observation data, different modeling approaches have been found suitable for achieving intelligent behavior.

If the data is precise and covers the significant information of an operating process, then a *connectionist*[5] method, like a *neural network*, is probably the right choice for modeling. Such a method can also yield good solutions if the problem is not understood quite well but a large amount of precise data was collected (Dix et al., 2004).

On the other hand, if only incomplete and noisy observations are available, but a-priori knowledge can be brought into design, a *probabilistic* approach for modeling provides the better solution. The fundamental algorithmic method here is *Bayesian Filtering*: Given a hypothesis about a signal source's behavior repertoire, a hypothesis about which behavior will cause what

---

[5]According to the Merriam–Webster definition connectionism is "*a school of cognitive science that holds that human mental processes (as learning) can be explained by the computational modeling of neural nets which are thought to simulate the actions of interconnected neurons in the brain*" (Merriam–Webster Online Dictionary, 2008c) with a number of interconnected processors.

observation, and a set of noisy observations, a Bayesian filter will yield the most probable explanation for the observed data, that is, the most probable behavior of the signal source given those observations.

This section provides selective insight into these two large areas of signal processing. Selection was derived from the criteria catalogue in Section 1.7. Related smart environment projects from current research usually apply similar methods to address signal processing. The significant methods from the *project×method*-matrices (cp., Figures 1.1 & 1.2) receive a detailed review in this section.

### 2.4.1 Neural Networks

Neural networks arose from the connectionist community that claimed that parallel distributed processing models would be an adequate way to model cognitive processes of the microstructure of human thought. The first contributions came from Rosenblatt (1958). But after a critical analysis of this work published by Minsky and Papert (1969) interest on neural network has been waned until the mid-Eighties of last century. Then, Rumelhart et al. (1989b) and McClelland et al. (1988) coined the term *parallel distributed processing* (PDP) for cognitive information processing. In their respected eponymous companion they described the interactions of large numbers of single entities called *units*, which send to each other *excitatory* and *inhibitory signals*. Applying PDP to cognitive tasks, sets of units stand for possible hypotheses and interconnections between units reflect the constraints that exist between different hypotheses.

On a time scale of seconds and minutes human cognition – the process between sensory stimulation and the overt expression of behavior – shows a noticeably sequential character (see Section 2.3). But remember for instance the CPM-GOMS model of 'carefully moving the cursor to a target and clicking a mouse button' shown in Figure 2.6. Although the macrostructure of this task forms almost a sequence of actions, some perceptual and physical motor actions start in parallel to cognitive actions. The question that is addressed by connectionism is how the internal structure of an atomic action from symbol-manipulating approaches like CPM-GOMS can be explained and modeled incorporating knowledge about the physiology of the brain.

Sequential modeling, which is widely utilized in symbol-manipulating approaches for the macrostructure of human cognition, is rejected by connectionists for the microstructure of human thought because, as Feldman and Ballard (1982) emphasized, biological hardware is just too sluggish for sequential models. Neurons operate on a milliseconds time scale (Rumelhart et al., 1989b) whereas desktop PCs run $10^6$ times faster on a nanoseconds time scale. If the symbol-manipulating "computer metaphor" is replaced by the connectionist "brain metaphor" as representatives of connectionism wish, this means that for processing a certain action in appropriate time only around a hundred time steps can be involved. This constraint that Feldman (1985) stated as the "100-step program" constraint leads connectionists to the assumption that considerable parallelism must be involved in models for microstructure cognition.

Utilizing the "brain metaphor" connectionism argues that micro-structural processing of human thought incorporates neuron-like *units*, which can be split into *input*, *hidden*, and *output* entities, and synapsis-like *connections*, which form relationships between neurons and can be modeled through directed weighted links between units. Eight major aspects for PDP-style connectionist models were identified by Rumelhart et al. (1989b, pg. 46):

- a *set of processing units*,

- a *state of activation*,

- an *output function* for each unit,

- a *pattern of connectivity* among units,

- a *propagation rule* combining inputs and current state of a unit to a new activation level,

- a *learning rule* whereby patterns of connectivity are modified by experience, and

- an *environment* within which the system must operate.

Figure 2.10 illustrates these basic aspects. A model consists of a set of units indicated by the larger circles in the drawing. If $N$ is the number of units then units can be ordered in a way of which the $n$-th unit is designated as $u_n$. At a certain moment $t$ each unit $u_n$ holds an activation value $a_n^{(t)}$. This value is processed by an output function $f_n$ to produce an output $o_n^{(t)}$. This output is propagated through a set of unidirectional connections to the other units of the model, which is represented by the lines in the figure. The strength of a connection between two units determining the effect that one unit $u_m$ has on another unit $u_n$ is incorporated into the model by a weight $w_{nm}$. Thus the input from one unit $u_n$ is the result of weighting the output of $u_m$ accordingly. From the connected units all of the inputs of the same type $p$ are

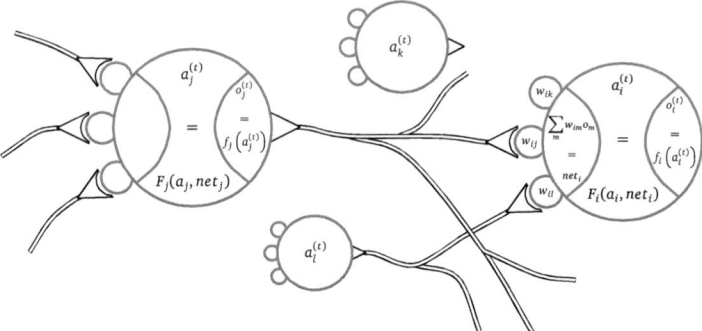

Figure 2.10: Basic components of a parallel distributed processing model. (*Source*: Adapted from Rumelhart et al. 1989b, pg. 47)

combined by some specific propagation rule[6] resulting in the net input $net_{pn}$ (If all input is of the same type the first subscript can be suppressed). Then the activation function $F_n$ takes the current activation value of the unit $a_n^{(t-1)}$ from the previous run of $F_n$ and the net input $net_n$ to compute a new activation state $a_n^{(t)}$.

Processing the state of activation of a model is primarily done by applying two functions to the activation values of each unit. These are the output function $f_n$ and the activation function $F_n$. In Figure 2.11 the transfer functions utilized usually are depicted. For the output a mapping of the current activation value of a unit to an output signal is defined. In some cases the

---

[6]Usually addition is used for this purpose.

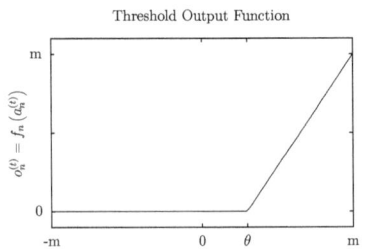
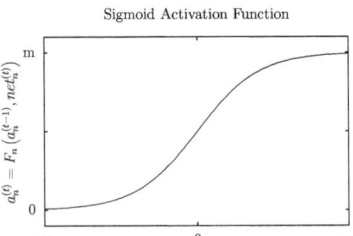

Figure 2.11: The basic processing functions of a parallel distributed processing model. (*Source*: Adapted from Rumelhart et al. 1989b, pg. 47)

output value is desired to be equal to the activation value. Then the identity function

$$o_n^{(t)} = f_n\left(a_n^{(t)}\right) = a_n^{(t)} \qquad (2.10)$$

is employed. But more often $f_n$ is some sort of threshold function as indicated by the left curve in Figure 2.11. That way a unit has no effect on other units unless its activation value surpasses a certain threshold value $\theta$.

In principle the same assumptions apply for activation functions. The simplest case, again, is the identity function where the new activity value $a_n^{(t)}$ inherits the value of net input $net_n^{(t)}$:

$$a_n^{(t)} = F_n\left(a_n^{(t-1)}, net_n^{(t)}\right) = net_n^{(t)} \qquad (2.11)$$

Another possibility is to use threshold functions, where the net input $net_n^{(t)}$ must surpass a certain threshold $\theta$ to influence the activation value. Some activation functions allow for the fact that there is maybe no net input for a unit and utilize the current activation value $a_n^{(t-1)}$ for a slow decay instead of an instant deactivation of that unit. If activation values are assumed to be continuous usually sigmoid activation functions as represented by the right curve in Figure 2.11 are chosen.

In other special cases the activation value of a unit is assumed to be, for instance, the probability that this specific unit is $ON$. Then, the likelihood is provided by a stochastic activation function $F_n$ like the following one introduced by Hinton and Sejnowski (1983) for the *Boltzmann machine*[7]:

$$a_n^{(t)} = F_n\left(a_n^{(t-1)}, net_n^{(t)}\right) = p\left(o_n^{(t)} == ON\right) = \frac{1}{1 + e^{-net_n^{(t)}}} \qquad (2.12)$$

where the activation value of a unit $a_n^{(t)}$ is the probability $p$ that the output of this unit $o_n^{(t)}$ takes the value $ON$. Note that in that case only the net input contributes to the computation of $p\left(o_n^{(t)} == ON\right)$. The output functions $f$ in such stochastic units usually apply deterministic step functions (e.g. $\{1,0\}$ or $\{1,-1\}$). Obviously, it is also conceivable to put the stochastic part of those units into the output function.

The modification of a PDP-style connectionist model is a function of utilizing experiences made

---

[7]The Boltzmann machine is a stochastic recurrent neural network in which the random variation of the network is built into stochastic activation functions of the units.

over time to learn connectivity patterns. Rumelhart et al. (1989b) have identified three kinds of modification, there are *1.*) the development of new connections, *2.*) the loss of existing connections, and *3.*) the adjustment of the strengths of existing connections. In approximation the first two kinds can be considered as special cases of the third simply by changing the weight $w_{nm}$ away from 0 or vice versa respectively. For the third kind of modification over the years many different learning rules (e.g., the perceptron learning rule (Rosenblatt, 1958), competitive learning (Grossberg, 1976), the Widrow-Hoff or delta rule (Sutton and Barto, 1981), or back-propagation (Rumelhart et al., 1989a)) were developed that are more or less variants of the basic idea described by Hebb (1949, cited by Rumelhart et al., 1989b, pg. 53): "*If a unit $u_n$ receives an input from another unit $u_m$; then, if both are highly active, the weight $w_{nm}$, from $u_m$ to $u_n$ should be strengthened.*" Furthermore, approaches from related fields like optimization (e.g., simulated annealing (Hinton and Sejnowski, 1983)) were introduced to overcome early issues in converging and finding optimal model configurations.

The dominant form of PDP-style connectionist models are *artificial neuronal networks*. Admittedly the literature distinguishes between *biological neural network* (BNN) and *artificial neural networks* (ANN) but although the "brain metaphor" was heavily influenced by BNNs this work does not address the biological form of neural networks further than mentioned to this point. Henceforth the term *neural network* is used in the meaning of *artificial neural network*. ANNs usually refer to *Multi-layer Perceptrons* introduced with the PDP Volumes (Rumelhart et al., 1989b; McClelland et al., 1988), since those replaced the *Single-layer Perceptron* of Rosenblatt after the neural network crisis. Although there are many different types of neural networks, connectionists distinguish primarily between *feedforward neural networks*, which are networks wherein no directed cycles are allowed, and *recurrent neural networks* where connections can form directed cycles and incorporate dynamic systems theory. Brief descriptions of these concepts follow.

**Single-layer Perceptrons**

The earliest and simplest kind of neural networks were *Single-layer Perceptrons* first described by Rosenblatt (1958). His so-called *Perceptron* model consisted of a *retina* (set of inputs) and *association units* (output layer). The input values were forwarded from the retina to the output layer, where the inputs were combined with weights. Units of the output layer, then, triggered the associated threshold output functions to produce the particular output values.

## Modeling Team Intention Recognition

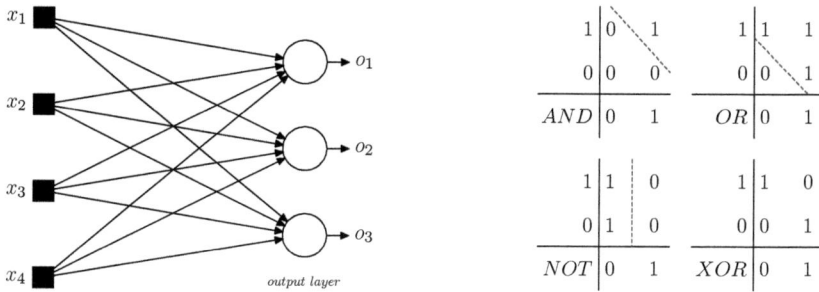

Figure 2.12: Single-layer Perceptron (left) and linear separability in common logic functions (right).

As indicated by the network on the left side of Figure 2.12 each input value is connected to each unit in the output layer[8]. Computation of output $o_n$ of the $n$th unit of a perceptron can be described by:

$$o_n = f(a_n) = f\left(\sum_m w_{nm} x_m - \theta_n\right) \quad (2.13)$$

where $x_m$ is the $m$th input, $w_{nm}$ is the weight for the connection from $m$th input to $n$th output, $\theta_n$ is the bias or offset and $f(\cdot)$ is the step output function.

But this first attempt on artificial decision making had several limitations. Those were fully realized by Minsky and Papert (1969) in their review on perceptrons. They found that only *linearly separable* problems (cp., with the examples on the right side of Figure 2.12) could be solved by single-layer perceptrons. To show this limitation they chose the *exclusive-or* (XOR) problem as a simple example for linear inseparability. A solution to this problem would require a layer of internal units. But at that time no reliable training method for such a network was available, which caused a regular crisis of research on connectionist-style systems.

**Multi-Layer Perceptrons**

Connectionist-style systems rekindled with the introduction of networks with layers of internal units and an appropriate training method for these networks. The so-called *Multi-layer Perceptrons* incorporated usually one or two hidden layers which process the input values before they are proceeded to the output layer. Input values represent some feature external to

---
[8]In the literature this kind of networks are also referred to as *two-layered* networks considering inputs as a layer, too. But since just the values from the input set are relevant as facts for the network there is no actual reason to mention this set as a separate layer.

the net. The values are provided to each hidden unit that is connected to the input. Then, each of these hidden units calculates its own activation value from the received input values. After that activation values are passed either to the units of the output layer or if another hidden layer exists they are propagated to this layer's units. Whether another hidden layer or output layer, here units compute their activation values in the same way as before. If an output layer was reached the output functions producing a network's output are applied in addition to the activation values.

**Feedforward Neural Networks**  The sort of Multi-layer Perceptron illustrated above could be a feedforward neural network (FNN). As indicated by the network in Figure 2.13, signal activation flows forward in one direction from the inputs over units on hidden layers to the output units. The signature of a network's output depends on the weights or connection strengths between units respectively. To produce an optimal solution the appropriate weight for each connection must be found. Those could be set by hand, but as a typical neural network might have a couple of hundred weights a training phase is needed to find the optimal set of weights.

In principle training algorithms follow a cycle to refine the weight values in a neural network. Starting with a random assignment of weight values this cycle includes the following: *1.)* run the network with input values from a training set and a tentative set of weights, *2.)* compare the inferred output values to the expected output from the training set and compute the difference, *3.)* average the differences from the entire set of training data to an error value, *4.)* propagate the error backward through the network and compute the gradient of change in error with respect to changes in weight values, and *5.)* adjust the weights to reduce the

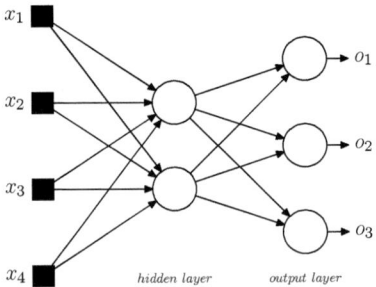

Figure 2.13: Feedforward Neural Network.

error. This type of training typical for Multi-layer Perceptrons is called *back-propagation* and was first described by Rumelhart et al. (1989a). Back then they used the gradient descent algorithm to adjust the weights towards convergence. Nowadays faster and more reliable converging algorithms are used at the core (e.g., simulated annealing (Hinton and Sejnowski, 1983), wake-sleep algorithm (Hinton et al., 1995), or a hybrid Monte Carlo method (Neal, 1996)). But a backward propagation of error information through the neural network is used by nearly all training algorithms even though the term back-propagation is often associated with the gradient descent version of Rumelhart, Hinton, and Williams.

**Recurrent Neural Networks** In neural networks like those mentioned above repeated presentations of the same input vector lead to same output every time. But this static quality is in contrast to the dynamic character of most human behavior. Humans remember repeating stimuli, habituate to them and learn to react adequately. The serial nature of such temporal adaption could hardly be expressed in feedforward neural networks.

The obvious work-around was to represent the temporal course of an event with the dimensionality the input vector (e.g., Elman and Zipser, 1988). This spatial representation of time has the drawback that it needs a register which buffers the temporal input. Defining such a buffer at design-time of a network incorporates difficulties. Size has to be limited and thus the longest possible temporal pattern needs to be known in advance. A limited register also suggests a constant size of the input vector, and temporal interpretations of absolute and relative position in time are challenging in such a system.

Another approach to represent time in a neural network is to remember the effects of processing and use this memory as a dynamic input for the processing system. Many attempts were made to accomplish the incorporation of memory into neural networks. For example Hopfield (1982) introduced a recurrent network in which besides input and output connections recurrent connections between binary threshold units of the same layer existed. Those connections fulfilled the conditions that *1.)* for every connection a symmetric counterpart existed, and *2.)* no unit had a connection to itself. The later introduced Boltzmann machines (Hinton and Sejnowski, 1983) rely on such *Hopfield networks* but, as mentioned earlier, use stochastic update functions.

Later Jordan (1986) proposed a simple recurrent neural network (RNN) relying on multi-layer perceptron. His network incorporated one-for-one connections from output to so-called

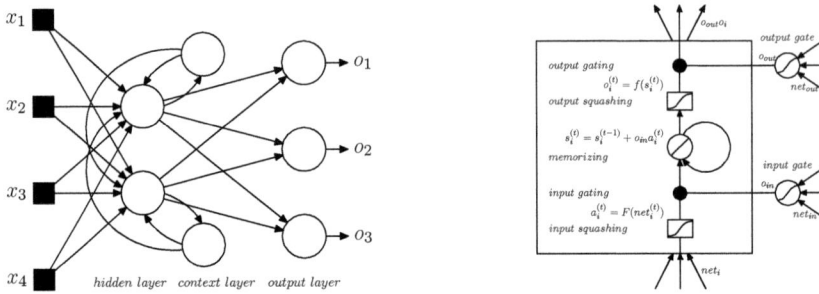

Figure 2.14: Simple Recurrent Neural Network (left), Long Short-term Memory Cell (right). (*Source*: Adapted from Elman 1990, pg. 184 (left), and Hochreiter and Schmidhuber 1997, pg. 1740 (right))

state units. State units, then, served as additional input for the units of the hidden layer. This allowed the hidden units to see their own previous output. Elman (1990) modified this approach in that way that instead of the network's output the activation values from the hidden unit were saved in a layer similar to the state layer of Jordan. Elman called this layer *context layer*. The left side of Figure 2.14 gives an impression of such a network. Backward connections from hidden layer to context layer were again one-for-one. So, the context layer had the same number of units as the hidden layer. In contrast the forward connections from context units to hidden units were fully distributed, which allowed each hidden unit to see the full context from the previous time step.

Even though simple recurrent neural networks consider temporal patterns in a time series of input vectors, a training phase is still needed to set the optimal weight configuration with respect to the training set. In *Elman networks* back-propagation in the version of Rumelhart et al. (1989a) is utilized. However, recurrent connections are not subject of optimization and, thus, keep their fixed weight[9] of 1.0.

A variation of the internal memory concept of Elman is the long short-term memory introduced by Hochreiter and Schmidhuber (1997). They replaced traditional hidden and context layer summation units by multi-part memory cells like the one on the right side of Figure 2.14. The input vector to such a cell was used as input for the cell of course and additionally to activate the input and output gating units of the cell. If those gates allowed access to the cell, then the input was processed and the activation value maintained in a simple summation unit

---

[9]Activation functions used in Elman network bound weight between 0.0 and 1.0.

*Modeling Team Intention Recognition*

with a self-recurrent link until the next input vector was allowed to access the cell. The propagation of a cell's activation value was regulated by the gating units in the same manner as the input.

**Evolving Connectionist Systems**  An approach known as the evolving connectionist system (ECoS) paradigm enhances the concepts of feedforward and recurrent neural networks by the facility to adapt the structure of a network. Ghobakhlou et al. (2003) described a simple evolving connectionist system (SECoS) relying on one of first and best known implementations of the ECoS paradigm – the evolving fuzzy neural network (EFuNN) introduced by Kasabov (1998). In contrast to EFuNN Ghobakhlou et al. omitted the fuzzified input space in their version, which led to a much plainer architecture with simple units instead of multipart cells like those mentioned above. But simultaneously the simple evolving connectionist system respected the general principle of adaptation, which was essential for this paradigm. Therefore this work explains the much simpler approach of Ghobakhlou et al..

During the training phase SECoS adapts to input data in an real-time manner using expansion and aggregation of its evolving layer. An exemplified diagram of adaptation in a SECoS network is given on the left side of Figure 2.15. Expansion works as follows; the evolving layer increases its set of units by a new unit whenever the maximum activation $a_{max}$ in the evolving layer is less than a coefficient called sensitivity threshold. In the other cases – if the sensitivity threshold was surpassed – the error between the calculated output vector and the desired output vector is evaluated. If this error is larger than an error threshold or another output unit than the desired output unit is most highly activated, then a new unit is added

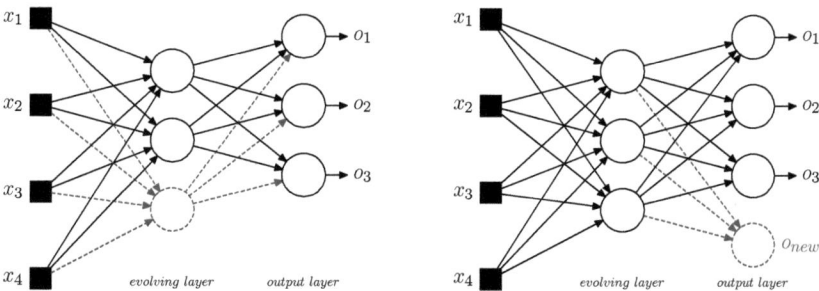

Figure 2.15: Simple Evolving Cognitive System: Expansion of Evolving Layer (left) and Addition of an Output Unit (right). (*Source*: Adapted from Ghobakhlou et al. 2003, pg. 77 (left), pg. 79 (right))

75

to the evolving layer as well. If a unit was added, then the connections are applied from the set of inputs to the new unit and thence to all output units. Incoming weights vector of the added unit is set to the input vector, and its outgoing weights are set to the desired output vector. To limit the expansion of the evolving layer after a certain number of training cycles, aggregation is utilized.

Aggregation searches for a subset of units from the evolving layer for which the Euclidian distances between 1.) entire input weight vector and subset weight vector, and 2.) entire output weight vector and subset output vector are below a specific threshold. This subset of units is then merged into one unit with averaged weights for input and output connections.

Furthermore, as Ghobakhlou et al. (2003) noted, evolving connectionist systems allow for an easier accommodation to a classification of new input classes than the networks mentioned earlier. In SECoS, for example, just a new output unit is added and supplied with zero-weighted incoming connections from the units of the evolving layer (cp., with the right side of Figure 2.15). After that training can proceed from the point before the new output unit was added with training data containing entities of the additional input class to adapt the evolving layer and the weights of its new connections to the added output unit optimally. A rewind of the training phase as common in other neural network approaches is not needed.

### 2.4.2 Temporal Probabilistic Models

Almost in parallel to the *connectionist* approach from the previous section another approach to address signal processing arose from the *control* and *statistics* community. Common to both communities is that they usually have to deal with time series of sparse and noisy perceptions as well as uncertainty about how the observed environment will change over time. Consider dynamic processes as for example navigating a robot through an unknown region that is just observable by some sensors or to forecast weather or the stock market from past observations. At each particular point in time those processes are in a certain state, which can be described by a set of causally connected random variables called *temporal probabilistic model*.

The classical problem of this approach is that not all variables' values may be known at a given time. Some may be observable, others may not. Therefore such systems apply Bayesian inference that tries to infer the probability distribution over the hidden nodes' values from the values of the known (observable) nodes. Formally speaking, let $X_t$ denote the unobservable set of variables, and $E_t$ denotes the set of observations at a certain time slice $t$. If further a sequence from $i$ to $j$ is denoted by $i{:}j$, then, following the notation of Murphy (2002), the idea of temporal probabilistic systems is to model how $X_t$ causes $E_t$ and $X_{t+1}$ and, then, to infer $X_{1:t}$ given $E_{1:t}$ by the invert mapping using Bayes' theorem.

Another challenge in temporal probabilistic systems is that, since they include new variables with every additional time step, the set of variables is virtually unrestricted. With every variable also a *conditional probability table* (CPT) or *conditional probability distribution* (CPD) respectively must be specified, which defines the conditions for a state transition of that variable. This implies that a virtually unlimited number of CPTs or CPDs might need modeling. Additionally, if there exists an unrestricted number of variables, then each may have an unbounded quantity of parents. Without constraining assumptions this quasi-infinite character would cause problems in both modeling and inference. Therefore, temporal probabilistic models include two restrictions to prevent those problems.

The first assumption, which merely facilitates modeling, is that changes over time are caused by a *stationary process*. The stationary character, i.e., assuming that the principles responsible for state transitions of variables do not alter themselves, enables for exemplary conditional probability modeling only for variables within a time slice.

Secondly, such systems must restrict their reasoning to a finite time frame to allow a constant complexity per time step. Assume a fixed lag $\ell \geq 0$ so that $t-\ell:t$ is the finite frame of time; then the performance of a system would suffer if its reasoning depended on states beyond the lag. Temporal probabilistic models address this constraint by applying the assumption that the current state of a system depends on only a constant set of previous states that contain all needed history information[10]. This belief was studied in depth by Markov (e.g., Markov, 1971) and hence is named *Markov assumption*. Similarly, processes satisfying the assertion are called *Markov processes* or *Markov chains*.

The order of a Markov chain describes how far a state's dependencies reach into the past, i.e., if the current state of a system depends on only the previous state, the system is called *first-order Markovian*. Using the formal notation, the corresponding conditional independence

---

[10]The connectionist approach suffers history information mainly. Recurrent neural networks mentioned in the previous section also incorporate history by adding internal state units, but, according to Bengio et al. (1994), those are not able to model long-term dependencies between states.

assertion of a temporal probabilistic model usually is:

$$P(X_t | X_{0:t-1}) = P(X_t | X_{t-1}), \qquad (2.14)$$

which indicates that the entire evolution of the system is enclosed in the conditional distribution $P(X_t | X_{t-1})$. This is called the *transition model*, in this case for a first-order Markov process. In higher-order processes the conditional distribution is $P(X_t | X_{t-h}, \ldots, X_{t-1})$ where $h$ is the order of the process. However, by augmenting the state-space higher-order processes can be transformed to comply to the first-order Markovian condition (cp. e.g., Murphy, 2002).

Evidence variables $E_t$ must be restricted for the same reason. Russell and Norvig (2002) stated that those typically depend only on the current state. Hence the conditional distribution called *sensor model* is:

$$P(E_t | X_{0:t}, E_{1:t-1}) = P(E_t | X_t) \qquad (2.15)$$

In addition to transition and sensor model a temporal probabilistic system must always define a *prior* probability distribution $P(X_0)$ over the state-space, which enables easy incorporation of a-priori knowledge into the model. Combined with the conditional distributions from Equations (2.14 & 2.15) the joint distribution over all variables of the complete model can be given as follows:

$$P(X_0, X_1, \ldots, X_t, E_1, \ldots, E_t) = P(X_0) \prod_{i=1}^{t} P(X_i | X_{i-1}) P(E_i | X_i) \qquad (2.16)$$

This provides the general framework for temporal probabilistic reasoning, which for now is independent of particular specifications of state-space, and prior, transition model or sensor model. More concrete models are described in the following sections.

**Hidden Markov Models**

The *hidden Markov model* (HMM) introduced by Baum and Petrie (1966) and described in detail by Rabiner (1989) and Bengio (1999) is a temporal probabilistic model with a *single*, *discrete* random variable describing the state of the modeled temporal process at a certain time. That is, the unobservable set of variables $X_t \in \{1, \ldots, S\}$, where $\{1, \ldots, S\}$ is the finite set of discrete states which the system can adopt. Usually $S$ specifies a variable with a single value, but additional values can be added by combining them into a variable of value tuples.

The state set then consists of all combinations of individual values.

With the finite set of discrete states in HMMs the transition model $P(X_t|X_{t-1})$ turns into a $S \times S$ matrix $\mathbf{T}$, where the probability of a transition from one state $i$ to another state $j$ is $\mathbf{T}_{ij} = P(X_t = j | X_{t-1} = i)$. Similar simplifications can be made for the other parameters of HMMs, namely prior turns into $\pi_i = P(X_0 = i)$ and sensor-model turns into a positive semi-definite (psd) matrix $\mathbf{O}$, where $\mathbf{O}_i = P(j | X_t = i)$ because $E_t$ is observable and, thus, known to be $j$.

In principle the evidence variables $E_t$ in HMMs are not restricted to be symbols from a discrete set $E_t \in \{1, \ldots, C\}$. So another option for $E_t$ is to form $N$-dimensional feature vectors in $\mathbb{R}^N$. For this case it is common to represent the sensor model as a Gaussian:

$$p_{E_t|X_t}(j|i) = \mathcal{N}(j; \mu_i, \Sigma_i), \tag{2.17}$$

with mean $\mu_i$ and covariance $\Sigma_i$ or as a mixture of $M$ Gaussians:

$$p_{E_t|X_t}(j|i) = \sum_{m=1}^{M} p_{M_t|X_t}(m|i) \mathcal{N}(j; \mu_{mi}, \Sigma_{mi}), \tag{2.18}$$

where $\mathcal{N}(j; \mu_{mi}, \Sigma_{mi})$ is the Gaussian density with mean $\mu_{mi}$ and covariance $\Sigma_{mi}$ evaluated at $j$:

$$\mathcal{N}(j; \mu_{mi}, \Sigma_{mi}) = \frac{1}{(2\pi)^{\frac{C}{2}} |\Sigma_{mi}|^{\frac{1}{2}}} \exp\left(-\frac{1}{2}(j - \mu_{mi})' \Sigma_{mi}^{-1} (j - \mu_{mi})\right), \tag{2.19}$$

and $M_t$ is a hidden variable that specifies which mixture component to use based on the conditional prior weight $\mathbf{W}_{im} = P(M_t = m | X_t = i)$ of each mixture component (cp. e.g., Murphy, 2002, pg. 7).

However, HMMs have one serious drawback. Due to the constraint that a complete hidden state must fit into one single variable the number of possible values grows exponentially with every addition of a new state feature. Consider the tracking (e.g., intentions) of a group $N$ of $n$ individuals. If each person is in one of $s$ possible states from the specified state set $S$, then the hidden state of the model $X_t = (X_t^1, \ldots, X_t^n) \in \{1, \ldots, S \times N\}$ can take $O(s^n)$ different values from the Cartesian product of $S$ and $N$. This leads inference as well as learning into intractable problems. Many proposals were made to overcome these problems (e.g., factorial HMM (FHMM) (Ghahramani and Jordan, 1997), coupled HMM (CHMM) (Saul and

Jordan, 1995; Brand, 1996), hierarchical HMM (HHMM) (Fine et al., 1998), or abstract HMM (AHMM) (Bui et al., 2000)). However, this work does not dig further into details of those proposals, since DBNs described in Section 2.4.2 generalize HMMs and simultaneously make improvements to the issues (see e.g., Murphy (2002) or Bengio (1999) for more insights on HMM variations).

**Kalman Filter Models**

The *Kalman filter model* (KFM) also known as *linear dynamical system* or – more informative – as *linear Gaussian model* was introduced by Kalman (1960) to provide a model which is able to describe the physical motion of objects as a temporal probabilistic process. Motion (e.g., the trajectory of an object) is usually characterized by continuity and linearity, and KFMs provide *several continuous* random variables to model this sort of problems. For the trajectory example that is, the state-space for object tracking might consist of a location $L = (A, B)$ and a velocity $V = (\dot{A}, \dot{B})$ in $\mathbb{R}^2$. Thus, the unobservable state at a given point in time is a vector of continuous random variables $X_t = (L_t, V_t) = (A_t, B_t, \dot{A}_t, \dot{B}_t) \in \mathbb{R}^4$. Note that for notation reasons the mentioned case exemplifies the general case, where the hidden state is specified by a vector of $S$ variables and thus is $X_t = (1, \ldots, S) \in \mathbb{R}^S$ and the observable evidence is $E_t = (1, \ldots, C) \in \mathbb{R}^C$.

Gaussian distributions are used to model the parameters for KFMs, which implies that the current state $X_t$ causes the next state $X_{t+1}$ with the help of a linear function plus a certain amount of Gaussian noise. This means that the hidden state is $X_t = \mathbf{T}X_{t-1} + \mathcal{N}(\mu_X, \mathbf{Q})$ and its transition is modeled as:

$$p_{X_t \mid X_{t-1}}(j \mid i) = \mathcal{N}(j; \mathbf{T}i + \mu_X, \mathbf{Q}), \tag{2.20}$$

where $\mathbf{T}$ is a $S \times S$ matrix and $\mathbf{Q}$ is a $S \times S$ psd matrix called process noise. The evidence function is specified similarly; i.e., $E_t = \mathbf{O}X_t + \mathcal{N}(\mu_E, \mathbf{R})$ and the sensor model is:

$$p_{E_t \mid X_t}(j \mid i) = \mathcal{N}(j; \mathbf{O}i + \mu_E, \mathbf{R}), \tag{2.21}$$

where $\mathbf{O}$ is a $C \times S$ matrix and $\mathbf{R}$ is a $C \times C$ psd matrix called sensor noise. According to Roweis and Ghahramani (1999), $\mu_X$ and $\mu_E$ can be added to the first columns of matrices $\mathbf{T}$ and $\mathbf{O}$ respectively and hence are set 0 within the next equations.

*Modeling Team Intention Recognition*

Returning to the above trajectory example, if a constant velocity $V = (\dot{A}, \dot{B})$ is assumed and external influences are considered, then the hidden state expands to:

$$\begin{pmatrix} a_t \\ b_t \\ \dot{a}_t \\ \dot{b}_t \end{pmatrix} = \begin{pmatrix} 1 & 0 & \delta & 0 \\ 0 & 1 & 0 & \delta \\ 0 & 0 & 1 & 0 \\ 0 & 0 & 0 & 1 \end{pmatrix} \begin{pmatrix} a_{t-1} \\ b_{t-1} \\ \dot{a}_{t-1} \\ \dot{b}_{t-1} \end{pmatrix} + \mathcal{N}(0, \mathbf{Q}), \text{ where } \mathbf{Q} = \begin{pmatrix} q_a & q_{ab} \\ q'_{ab} & q_b \end{pmatrix} \quad (2.22)$$

Then, assuming that just the position of the tracked object can be observed, the evidence is:

$$\begin{pmatrix} e_t^a \\ e_t^b \end{pmatrix} = \begin{pmatrix} 1 & 0 & 0 & 0 \\ 0 & 1 & 0 & 0 \end{pmatrix} \begin{pmatrix} a_t \\ b_t \\ \dot{a}_t \\ \dot{b}_t \end{pmatrix} + \mathcal{N}(0, \mathbf{R}), \text{ where } \mathbf{R} = \begin{pmatrix} r_a & r_{ab} \\ r'_{ab} & r_b \end{pmatrix} \quad (2.23)$$

The problem with Kalman filter models is that they only allow for linear Gaussian transition and sensor models. This always leads to a state distribution like the one on the left side of Figure 2.16 (i.e., a multivariate Gaussian with a single maximum), even if another explanation would obviously be more reasonable (e.g., the one shown on the right side of Figure 2.16).

In addition many real world applications, such as e.g., smart environments, require to incorporate nonlinearity and discontinuity into the model. Consider, for instance, inferring the location of a person in a smart meeting room where places are modeled as nodes on an undirected cycled path graph. If a single Gaussian is used to include all these places, then usually the most probable location of the person would be everywhere but not at those

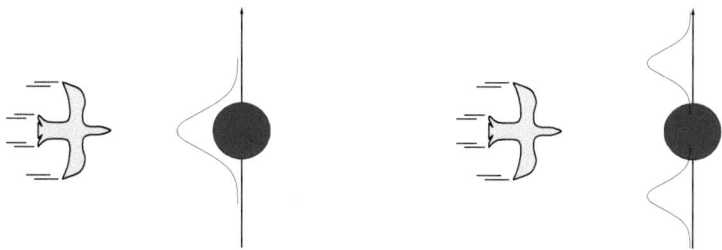

Figure 2.16: A bird flying toward an obstacle (top views). A Kalman filter will predict the location of the bird using a single Gaussian centered on the obstacle (left). A more realistic model allows for the bird's evasive action, predicting that it will fly to one side or the other (right). (*Source:* Adapted from Russell and Norvig 2002, pg. 563)

places. Some attempts were made to overcome the very strong assumptions of linearity and continuity and instead allow multimodality (e.g., extended KFM (EKF) (Bar-Shalom and Fortmann, 1988), unscented KFM (UKF) (Wan and van der Merwe, 2001), switching KFM (SKF) (Murphy, 1998)).

Again, this work does not dig further into details of those attempts, since DBNs described in the next section generalize KFMs, too. Furthermore, they allow for complex combinations of discrete and continuous variables and, thus, overcome the limitations of KFMs.

**Dynamic Bayesian Networks**

With last century's early Nineties a framework for representing temporal probabilistic models was introduced that had much more expressive power than the models mentioned so far. It is called *dynamic Bayesian network* (DBN), which is a variation of the term 'dynamic belief network' coined first by Dean and Kanazawa (1988), and reflects the use of Bayesian inference in such models. A key feature is the sparse encoding of Markov processes, which leads to slimmer modeling in comparison to, e.g., HMMs. Since their first usage by Dean and Kanazawa (1988, 1990), Nicholson (1992), and Kjærulff (1992) DBNs were used in several approaches. They became popular in various communities (e.g., computer vision (Bui et al., 2000; Duong et al., 2005)), robotics (Liao et al., 2003), activity recognition (Patterson et al., 2003), and activity monitoring (McCowan et al., 2003; Dielmann and Renals, 2004)) over the last years.

A DBN consists, as the other temporal probabilistic models, of a sequence of time slices. Each time slice describes the possible state of a system at a given time $t$. A time slice consists of a set of nodes that represent the system's state variables at that time. State variables may be connected through *directed causal links*. A connection such as $X \rightarrow Y$ means that the current value of $Y$ depends on the current value of $X$. This dependency is described by a *conditional probability distribution* (CPD).

The simplest form of CPD is a table, which is suitable when all node's variables are discrete-valued. Tabular CPDs, also called *conditional probability tables* (CPT), are denoted in the following form:

| $X$ | $P(Y=0 \mid X)$ | $P(Y=1 \mid X)$ |
|---|---|---|
| 0 | 0.9 | 0.1 |
| 1 | 0.3 | 0.7 |

(2.24)

which in this example says that, in case $X$ is 0, the value of $Y$ will be 0 with a probability of

*Modeling Team Intention Recognition*

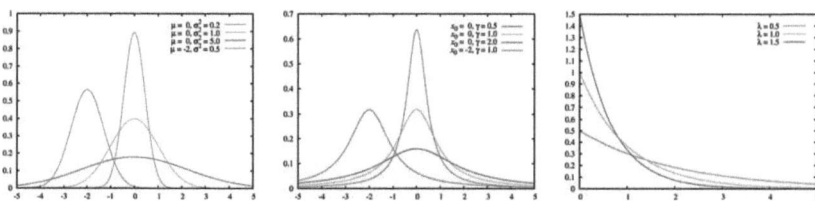

Figure 2.17: Frequently utilized probability distributions: Gaussian (left), Cauchy (center), and Exponential distribution (right) with different parameters.

0.9 and it will be 1 with a probability of 0.1. (If $X$ is 1, $Y$ will be 0 with a probability of 0.3 and 1 with a probability of 0.7.) Causal links may connect nodes within a time slice, they may also connect nodes between time slices – the latter is used to express the fact that the state at time $t$ depends on the previous state at time $t-1$. Note, as mentioned before, that this work considers only temporal probabilistic models that are first-order Markovian; i.e., DBNs where the state $t$ depends only on state $t-1$ and no previous states.

In case of continuous-valued nodes the CPD is specified by the *probability density function* (PDF) of the underlying continuous distribution. Virtually every continuous distribution could be used to describe the conditional probability of a node's value. Figure 2.17 shows some one-dimensional distribution exemplars. If, for example, the values are Exponential-distributed[11], then the CPD has the following form:

$$p_{Y|X}(j|i) = f(j; \lambda_i) = \begin{cases} \lambda_i e^{-\lambda_i j} &, j \geq 0 \\ 0 &, j > 0 \end{cases} \quad (2.25)$$

where $\lambda$ is the rate parameter[12]. In contrast, if the values are Beta-distributed the CPD looks as follows:

$$p_{Y|X}(j|i) = f(j; \alpha_i, \beta_i) = \frac{j^{\alpha_i - 1}(1-j)^{\beta_i - 1}}{\mathrm{B}(\alpha_i, \beta_i)}, \quad (2.26)$$

where $\alpha$ and $\beta$ are shape parameters and $\mathrm{B}(\alpha, \beta)$ is the *beta function* or *Euler integral*. Several other CPDs and PDFs are regularly used with DBN modeling. Murphy (2002) provides a well structured and detailed overview on this topic in his work's appendices.

---

[11] Exponential distribution can be used to model events, which take place during a fixed time span but tend to prolongations (e.g., talks, lectures).

[12] A rate parameter is the reciprocal of a scale parameter that both must affect the size of a distribution. Other parameters could be location or shape parameters that shift and reshape a distribution respectively; e.g., Gaussian and Cauchy distribution apply location and scale parameters, and others apply shape parameters.

Chapter 2

The characteristics of dynamic Bayesian networks drawn above indicate that DBNs are able to generalize the previously mentioned HMMs and KFMs. This is shown in Figure 2.18 where the HMM and KFM examples from the previous sections are depicted as DBN structures respectively. The representations follow the standard convention where shading means that a node is observed. Clear nodes represent hidden variables of the network. Two slices of the network are depicted representing the state-space of the current and the previous time slice. The directed links between nodes in combination with CPTs and CPDs describe the dependencies of discrete-valued and continuous-valued variables in the network respectively.

The difference between DBNs and HMMs is characterized by Murphy (2002, pg. 15), reporting *"that a DBN represents the hidden state in terms of a set of random variables, $X_t^1, \ldots, X_t^{N_h}$, i.e., it uses a distributed representation of state. By contrast, in an HMM, the state space consists of a single random variable $X_t$."* The DBN representation of the KFM in Figure 2.18 shows a trivial exemplar of such a distributed state representation, since it distinguishes between position $P$ and velocity $V$. The distribution has the advantage that in contrast to HMMs just the required variables and 'real' dependencies must be stored instead of the Cartesian product of variables and values (cp., Section 2.4.2). About the difference between DBNs and KFMs Murphy (2002, pg. 15) stated: *"that a KFM requires all the conditional probability distributions (CPD) to be linear-Gaussian, whereas a DBN allows arbitrary CPDs."* Generalization in DBNs overcomes the typical limitations of KFMs, i.e., linearity and continuity (cp., Section 2.4.2), and enables tracking for nonlinear discontinued real world applications, such as smart envi-

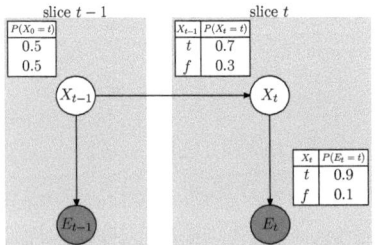 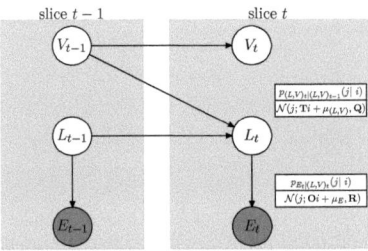

Figure 2.18: DBN structure for a HMM (left): Discrete valued conditional distributions of prior, transition model and sensor model in a HMM. A row in these CPTs must sum to 1. $P(X_0 = f)$, $P(X_t = f)$, and $P(E_t = f)$ were skipped, since those can be derived from the other values. DBN structure for a KFM (right): $X_t = (L_t, V_t) = (A_t, B_t, \dot{A}_t, \dot{B}_t)$ is the hidden state-space. The structure indicates that the velocity $\dot{V}$ just depends on its previous state but the position $P$ depends on the previous position as well as the velocity of the tracked object. Position is observed by sensors. All CPDs are linear Gaussian.

ronments. Obviously the generalization introduces additional costs in modeling and forces extended computational power, but the distributed state-space, the nonlinearity and discontinuity; all advantages, that follow not least from the less restricted topology and more general graph structure respectively, introduce a good balance between expressiveness and manageability, and make DBNs the representation of choice in the control and statistics community.

### 2.4.3 Relevant Essence

Reviewing methods for modeling in signal processing has brought the realization that the granularity of the modeling itself and the selection of an appropriate method for modeling is strongly related to the goal of modeling and the capabilities that observation of the environment can provide. The modeling may aim to exactly understand the one process that leads to an output, or the purpose is to model a process that provides an appropriate explanation and prognosis of output data respectively. Cowell et al. (2007) categorized the different purposes of modeling as *scientific* versus *technological* modeling and put a definition of both the following way:

> *Scientific modelling is concerned with attempting to understand some assumed 'true' objective process underlying the generation of data. This process, if it were known, could be used for purposes of explanation, or causal understanding, as well as prediction. By definition, there can only be one true process, and the purpose of inference is to say something about what it might be.*
>
> *Technological modelling has less grandiose aims. The purpose of such a model is to provide a good explanation of past data, and good forecasts for future data, irrespective of whether it corresponds to any underlying 'reality'. Thus, the object of inference is now the usefulness, rather than the truth, of a model. From such a viewpoint, one can allow the co-existence of several different models for the same phenomenon.* (Cowell et al., 2007, pg. 244)

In principle both 'schools' of modeling, *connectionist* as well as *probabilistic*, are equally applicable to both purposes of modeling, *scientific* as well as *technological*. However, it appears that the connectionist approach (instance-based, non-parametrizable) is more likely used for scientific modeling due to its neurobiological "brain metaphor" roots (cp. with Section 2.4.1), whereas for a technological modeling purpose the probabilistic approach (model-based, parametrizable) obviously seems reasonable because Bayesian inference on random variables provides the most probable explanation for an observation.

Another influencing question for selecting modeling methods is whether the model has to handle sequences of data (e.q., time or genome) or not. If the current state of a system depends on previous states in a sequence, then this has to be considered when choosing a modeling method. Both approaches provide methods for modeling recurrence of stationary states, but according to Bengio et al. (1994) the connectionist approach of recurrent neural networks shows amnesia to long-term dependencies, whereas probabilistic approaches avoid this problem.

Further, the amount and the quality of observation data as well as a-priori knowledge about a process may have an impact on the modeling decision. If the data is precise and covers the significant information of an operating process, then a connectionist method is probably the right choice for modeling. Also if the problem is not understood quite well but a large amount of precise data was collected such a method can yield good solutions. On the other hand, if only incomplete and noisy observations are available, but a-priori knowledge can be brought into the design, a probabilistic approach for modeling provides a better solution.

Finally, the application domain constrains which types of models are suitable for modeling the processes of the domain. If a highly dynamic environment must be observed, such as the Smart Meeting Room Environment sketched in Section 1.6, then it is mandatory to decide for flexible modeling techniques. Here, connectionist methods show a disadvantage compared to probabilistic methods due to their long training phase. Besides ECoS (cp., Section 2.4.1) all discussed neural networks must be retrained from the beginning if the structure of the network is changed.

Summarizing the section on modeling in signal processing, this subject area provides several modeling methods, connectionist as well as probabilistic. I have learned that

- modeling is driven by the overall purpose, i.e., *scientific* versus *technological*,
- sequences require special attention, since they incorporate intractable issues quickly,
- method selection is tied to process insight, available data, and observation capabilities,
- dynamic processes need modeling techniques that flexible scaling with the problem.

This knowledge in combination with the findings from the psychological areas mentioned before offers a good starting point for the conception of a model for robust and training-free prior knowledge real-time intention analysis in teams. But before starting the introduction of my concept for such a model in the next chapter I briefly summarize the current chapter.

## 2.5 Summary

The current chapter reviewed fields from psychology, namely social psychology and cognitive psychology. The review identified on the one hand social aspects from the nature of groups and on the other hand functionalities of human cognition that both exert influence on decisions to make in the design and method selection for this work's system concept. Afterwards this chapter enlightened on a selection of different methods from the signal processing field. This selection based on the findings from Section 1.5 and aimed to contrast the varying features of these methods. Pertinent aspects for each section were condensed in a *Relevant Essence* subsection (cp., with Sections 2.2.7, 2.3.6 & 2.4.3). Together these subsections provide the findings that are essential for a revision of the concept criteria. The next chapter explains in adequate detail this work's proposal for a team intention model based on the revisited criteria catalogue.

# Chapter 3

# The Team Intention Model Approach

## 3.1 Introduction

This chapter explains the concept of a robust system for real-time intention analysis in teams. It starts with the refinement of criteria based on a reworking of the scenario given in Section 1.6 and a description of the concrete lab situation in my department's SmartAppliance-Lab. Then the proposal of this work – the agenda-driven Team DBN – is introduced. It is explained which methods from the previous chapter can be utilized to structure team tasks and to design team intention models in general. A short note outlines an approach for model generation. After that inference tasks are identified that must be solved for the Team DBN and the approaches utilized for this concept are explained in detail.

To prove the proposed concept, tools and an experimental infrastructure were designed and realized. Hence, this chapter also explains requirements and architecture for the implemented experimental infrastructure. Finally, the usage of the enclosed components and modules is described. But next this chapter starts with considerations about the scenario and the lab in order to refine the criteria catalogue.

## 3.2 Instrumenting the Lab

Fields from psychology, specifically social psychology and the problem solving subfield of cognitive psychology, showed that it is possible and suitable to break down human behavior and the nature of groups into categories and that individuals as well as groups apply several correlated individual and group tasks to achieve certain team goals. If one is interested in inferring team goals to be able to offer goal oriented assistance – as my department does – a task oriented framework or lexicon seems to fit best for such a "goal–task–action" break down. Once such a lexicon of tasks – an agenda exists, a major question is how such a-priori knowledge about a team can be utilized for a team intention model.

Several pieces of information can be extracted from an agenda. First, an agenda (e.g., the one from Figure 1.3) provides a temporal sequence of a set of group tasks which will probably occur during the course of a meeting. Secondly, a person's name assigned to a task may refer to a special role of that person within the team. He adopts this role very likely, if the team intends to process this specific task. That is, 'Presentation of Proposal of Software Architect Sheldon' from the agenda example means that Sheldon has the presenter role and all other team members may adopt the listener role but at least are not presenters at the same time. Finally, a specific agenda can be split into a kind of task hierarchy. It may consist of a set of somehow related team tasks or actions that may form a tree-like hierarchy, but at least splits into a set of quasi-parallel user action sequences of the team members. Imagine the following more concrete scenario to realize how agenda information fits into the process.

### 3.2.1 Concrete Scenario

The scene starts at the 'meeting attendees entering room'-situation of the scenario given in Section 1.6: Remember *Sheldon*, *Leonard*, and *Penny*. The three staff members of an IT department enter the Smart Meeting Room to meet for a presentation and discussion session. The appliance ensemble of the room is aware of the purpose of the meeting. Preliminary agenda information was incorporated into a model that provides information about usually aspired team tasks and related user actions as a-priori knowledge. While *Sheldon*, *Leonard*, and *Penny* move within the room their motion is tracked utilizing ToA-positioning of their RF-badges. Those pieces of sensor information are not as reliable as one would expect. Sparse, intermittent, and noisy sensor readings are challenges that the model has to handle. At the beginning of the meeting the team of software architects changes the course of the appointed presentations spontaneously. *Leonard* walks to the presentation stage to give his talk. With the assistive power of the appliance ensemble this represents no problem. The incorporated

*The Team Intention Model Approach*

model provides inference mechanisms that are able to recognizes the deviation[1]. So, the appliance ensemble of the room guesses the correct team intention, brings forward the presentation of *Leonard*, and puts it onto the screen just before he enters the presentation stage. After *Leonard*'s talk, the team turns back to the agenda and *Sheldon* presents. Finally, chief architect *Penny* moves for presentation (shown in Figure 3.1 on the left side). The ensemble infers one team intention after another and every speaker is proactively provided with his particular presentation.

This description is a subset of the scenario given in Section 1.6 and contains assumptions which limit the scope that the proposed concept has to cover. Note that the limitations were made merely for experimental reasons. In summary the scenario allows 5 team intentions aka. activities or tasks (i.e., presentation of *Sheldon*, *Leonard*, and *Penny*, discussion, exit) × 2 team actions (i.e., prepare a task, and perform a task) × 3 users (*Sheldon*, *Leonard*, and *Penny*) × 4 user actions (i.e., wandering around, sit & listen, presenting slides, and leave room). Limitations that may rely on the available laboratory infrastructure are described in the next section, which gives an overview about the SmartApplianceLab.

### 3.2.2 Concrete Lab Situation

The right side of Figure 3.1 shows the built-in appliances of the SmartApplianceLab. Remember, the purpose of this laboratory is to assist teams in meeting situations. Thus, it obviously has to contain typical meeting room equipment. So, built into the lab is a battery of projectors (one of them steerable), and there are several controllable motor screens[2] and lamps. Further the lab is equipped with a few different sensor systems. These include presence sensors, RFID-based access control, and a ultra-wideband-based (UWB) indoor-positioning system called Ubisense Platform to observe users in the room. Additionally, some environment sensors (e.g. inside and outside temperature, humidity, luminosity) are available to capture the overall environments state. Note that this work exclusively utilizes sensor information from the Ubisense Platform due to two reasons: *1.*) some sensor equipment was not available in the lab as experiments took place, and *2.*) the focus of this work is rather on modeling the

---

[1] Note that *Leonard* could walk to presentation stage for other reasons (e.g. to adjust the mic or to pic some whiteboard markers). But because the inference process considers his activity not independent from the other team members' activities it is still able to recognize that an activity is going on, which is not on the agenda. In this situation the ensemble could ask the team what to do or it could show no reaction. This would be a matter of strategy planning and the available acting appliances.

[2] In both drawings of Figure 3.1 eight rather hard to recognize motor screens are depicted by slim red and gray lines; three on each side wall and two screens that simultaneously work as window blinds on the end wall above.

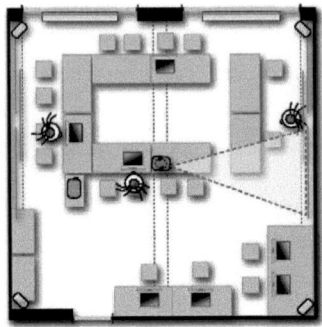 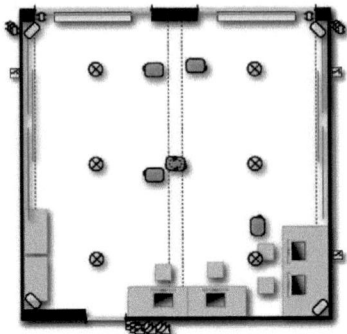

Figure 3.1: Schematic bird views of the SmartApplianceLab: A scene from the scenario described in Section 3.2.1 (left), where ○ are Ubisense Platform sensors for localizing the inherent tags worn by persons 🦞. Equipment of the laboratory (right), furthermore, includes switches ⚡, buttons ⊠, and dimmers △ to control projection surfaces (red and gray lines near the walls) and lamps ⊗ manually. ⊛ and ⊟ are stenciled projectors where the icon with arrows indicates that this projector is steerable.

negotiation process of a team about the course of their intended tasks than on fusing sensor data. Thus, in Figure 3.1 just the Ubisense Platform sensors and tags are depicted. Obviously the very existence of sensing and acting appliances or perception and motor components respectively does not lead to smart assistance of the lab's user. Reasoning components have to infer user needs, and decision making is needed to plan an appropriate strategy for assistance. Furthermore, as Coen et al. (1999) phrased it, some *"computational glue"* has to be provided for interconnecting all SmartApplianceLab components and channelling information among them.

**Ensemble Communication Framework**

Figure 3.2 shows the components of the *Ensemble Communication* (ECO) framework built for the SmartApplianceLab. The ECO framework incorporates the components needed for the software infrastructure of a smart environment in a distributed manner where no central component is required. Rather, *Zeroconf*[3] communication channels enable seamless subscription

---

[3] *"[Zeroconf is a]n IETF specification that enables devices on an IP network to automatically configure themselves and be discovered without manual intervention. If required, Zeroconf can assign an IP address and alternate host name to a device. Once assigned, Zeroconf lets users and applications readily discover the service it offers."* (TechWeb: TechEncyclopedia, 2008)

## The Team Intention Model Approach

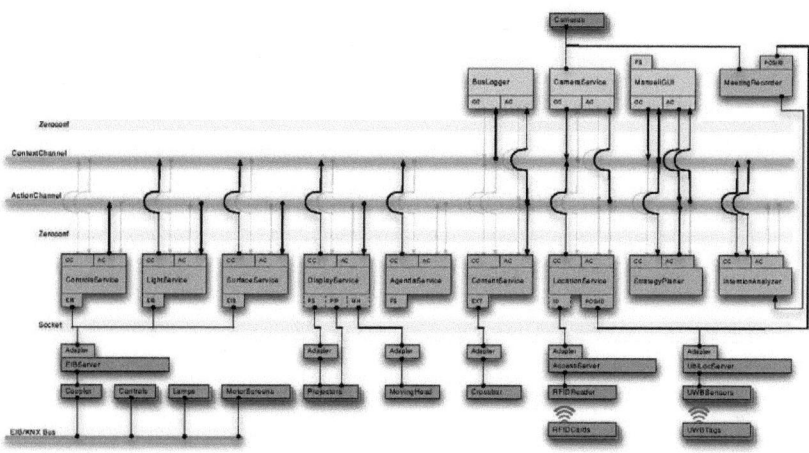

Figure 3.2: ECO framework components utilized to form an ensemble out of the equipment and optional mobile devices mentioned in Figure 3.1. Blue color in the drawing means third-party hardware and software. ECO framework components are colored red and green, where green represents test and helper components. Beige emphasizes the reasoning component the concept of this work is intended for. Socket interfaces provide homogenous access to the devices. Adapters encapsulate device specific hardware interfaces. *FS* indicates access to the file system. Other abbreviations on the socket level indicate device specific communication protocols. A device in combination with an ECO framework service forms an appliance. All appliances can interconnect via two Zeroconf channels to exchange context information and action requests. *CC* means ContextChannel and *AC* stands for ActionChannel.

of appliances and take care that sent messages get through to their addressees. As indicated by the arrows from communication channels to different appliances and vice versa, the ECO framework allows its appliances to subscribe to communication channels in various ways. Appliances can connect to each of the available channels as sender and/or as listener. Virtually every combination of subscriptions is possible, but depending on the purpose of an appliances only a certain subscription patterns may be meaningful:

- *Send to the CC* – Several appliances act as perceptual components (e.g., LightService, SurfaceService, DisplayService, AgendaService, LocationService) and thus load the ContextChannel (CC) with context, status or sensor information respectively.

- *Listen at and send to CC* – The IntentionAnalyzer is the reasoning component that subscribes to CC as listener and sender in order to read data from CC, interpret it, and upload the interpretations or predictions back to the CC.

93

- *Listen at the CC and send to the AC* – The StrategyPlaner is the decision making component that reads appliance states and intention interpretations to decide for a set of appropriate assisting actions. Then, these actions are requested via the ActionChannel (AC).

- *Listen at the AC and send to the CC* – Finally, another set of appliances, which is not inevitably disjunct from the perceptual components above, runs as motor components (e.g., LightService, SurfaceService, DisplayService, ContentService) and processes the action requests from the AC.

Virtually every component could run on its own computer, or even better, the computer itself could be integrated into the smart appliance. Thanks to Zeroconf, these smart appliances can then form and configure a smart environment in an ad-hoc manner to share their states and negotiate about user needs.

**Note on Ubisense Platform**

Ubisense is a precise real-time location system (RTLS) company, utilizing UWB technology to deliver a six-dimensional feature vector (i.e., $\{X, Y, Z, Roll, Pitch, Yaw\}$) of position in, as they claimed, *"unprecedented levels of precision, responsiveness, reliability and scalability"* (Ubisense, 2008). The frequency range for UWB is specified as between 3.1 and $10.6 GHz$. Using such extremely short pulsed signals provides mainly two advantages for position calculation: *1.)* these signals are able to pass through objects such as walls and clothing, which results in computations that are not influenced by signal covering (RFID and laser range finders suffer from this problem.) and much less affected by multi-path distortions (This is a serious problem for conventional RF technologies and ultra-sonic waves.), and *2.)* if multi-path distortions still appear (e.g., on metal surfaces or objects with high water content), then the filtering of the correct signal is much easier than with conventional RF technologies.

In addition to the advantages inherent to UWB technology itself the Ubisense Platform combines the two common methods for location calculation, namely *time difference of arrival* (TDOA) and *angle of arrival* (AOA), to get more reliable results than others. Ubisense stated that their UWB-based RTLS *"can be typically accurate to about 15cm"* (Ubisense, 2008). This was one argument to utilize Ubisense Platform in the SmartApplianceLab, because accurate

*The Team Intention Model Approach*

reliable sensor data may be crucial for learning robust model parameters[4]. Another argument was that the localization with ID-tags incorporates a simple way for identifying single users in team environments, and, thus, avoids a problem described by Schulz et al. (2003) as *track confusion*, which appears with the use of anonymous sensors such as presence sensors or pressure mats in environments where multiple users need to be tracked.

## 3.3 Criteria Revisited

After the in-depth investigations made in Chapter 2, the appropriation to a concrete scenario in Section 3.2.1 and the introduction of the SmartApplianceLab in the previous section it is reasonable to revisit the criteria catalogue for the team intention model from Section 1.7 and decide which methods fit best to the criteria and which conflict with them. Remember, the relevant criteria for the team intention model are:

- pursuance of a **training-free prior knowledge approach**,
- capability of using **various lexica of team activities** (i.e., agendas),
- allowance for **easy extensions** (e.g., to larger teams),
- support of **real-time recognition**,
- provision of **robust recognition** from simple sensor data,
- tracking of **team activity history**, and
- **separate modeling** of complex team and atomic user activities.

Several criteria indicate that a neural network approach is inadequate for team intention recognition. First of all, this is because neural networks enable hardly the integration of prior knowledge. Thus, they always need a training phase to adjust the weights of their particular neurons. This also balks the easy extension to larger teams or new sensors and inhibits the change of team activity lexica in such a model, because after every change of the network's structure the whole network must be retrained. Here, ECoS' form an exceptional case, since these networks just retrain new or changed nodes in the net. Nevertheless ECoS' need initial

---

[4]However, in fact it turned out that the claims made by Ubisense were somewhat ambitious.

training too. Finally, even a fourth criterion is an argument against a neural network approach. With a neural network it is difficult to ensure tracking of history, since this approach in some characteristics (e.g., feedforward neural nets) does not enable modeling of memory and in other characteristics (e.g., recurrent neural nets) tends to unlearn its memories.

KFMs are also unsuitable to address intention inference. Never even the people tracking issue allows the usage of a KFM approach. Various furniture in the SmartApplianceLab (cp. with left side of Figure 3.1) indicate that localization of people is not a linear tracking problem, which KFMs could handle. Besides this, modeling the system state in more than one hidden node is not allowed in KFMs, which is in contrast to the separate modeling criterion and also inhibits an easy model extension.

HMMs suffer from the same problems. In their original form they also bar modeling system states in more than one hidden node and, thus, violate the separate modeling and easy model extension criteria too. Additionally HMMs have this complexity problem mentioned in Section 2.4.2 due to their modeling restrictions. Remember that the state space grows exponentially with the number of state features.

DBNs, in contrast, fit well to the criteria catalogue. With DBNs it is easy to incorporate a-priori knowledge, which makes them usable without a training period. The state space can consist of several hidden nodes, which in fact enables separate modeling of team and user activities. A virtually unlimited number of hidden nodes provides enough space for the tracking of even large histories. Further, the first Markov assumption inherent to all mentioned temporal models combined with DBN-specific sparse encoding of node dependencies allows for a compact mapping of a temporal process on a stationary model. Combined with an approximative inference method (e.g., particle filters) such a stationary DBN can deliver robust recognition results in real-time. Finally, choosing a modular and hierarchical design for a model permits the required capabilities to change the lexica of team activities and adjust the model to different team sizes easily.

Table 3.1 again summarizes the above discussion and indicates that a DBN is the representation of choice for the concept proposed with this work, since all criteria are satisfied.

# The Team Intention Model Approach

Table 3.1: Matrix summarizing *Criteria Satisfaction* of the different modeling approaches. Gray fields mean that the approach satisfies the criterion partly; e.g., RNNs and ECoS' have a memory but tend to amnesia, or HMMs and KFMs can handle various agendas but due to the single hidden node it is hard to change them.

|  | Neural Networks | | | Probabilistic Models | | |
|---|---|---|---|---|---|---|
| **Criteria** | FNN | RNN | ECoS | HMM | KFM | DBN |
| training-free prior | ● | ● | ● |  |  |  |
| various agendas | ● | ● | ● | ◐ | ◐ |  |
| easy extension | ● | ● | ● | ● | ● |  |
| real-time recognition |  | ● | ● | ◐ | ● |  |
| robust recognition |  | ● | ● | ● | ● |  |
| history tracking | ● | ◐ | ◐ | ◐ | ◐ |  |
| separate modeling | ● | ● | ● | ● | ● |  |

## 3.4 Agenda-driven Team DBN

Now that the modeling approach is chosen, the next step is to deliberate how agenda information like that described in the scenarios (cp., Sections 1.6 & 3.2.1), can be prepared to fit into an explicit probabilistic team intention model as a-priori knowledge. As already mentioned in Section 3.2.1, the earlier review of the *social psychology* aspects regarding teams in Section 2.2 indicated that an agenda could be seen as an outline of a goal-oriented team process, which roughly describes a sequence of team tasks that a team intends to execute. And the review of problem solving strategies in Section 2.3 revealed that it is reasonable to model such a sequence as a hierarchical breakdown into atomic actions. Hence, the approach for this work is to define a *task model* that specifies the breakdown of a sequence of composite activities into individual atomic steps, between which a partial order may be defined. Roughly speaking it describes a *plan* of actions, where the term *action* will denote an atomic step in the task sequence. Remember, the concept of task models originates independently from two research areas:

In *cognitive psychology*, task models have been developed as a means for formally describing human problem solving behavior. Section 2.3 presented a set of very good examples for this class of models that are merely applied as the foundation of several proposals for *model-based adaptive user interface design* (e.g., Mori et al., 2002). These models can be used in two ways:

*1.)* for analyzing the cognitive complexity of given user interfaces or workflows, and *2.)* for designing user interfaces or workflows by first developing a model of the task at hand and then choosing appropriate (dialogue) elements for the individual atomic activities.

As introduced in Section 2.4 in *signal processing*, technological task models have been developed as a means for *estimating the actual behavior of a signal source*, for which only incomplete and noisy observations are available. The fundamental algorithmic approach is Bayesian filtering. A Bayesian filter requires a hypothesis about a signal source's behavior repertoire, a hypothesis about which behavior will cause what observation, and a set of observations. Based on this information, the filter will yield the most probable explanation for the observed data – i.e., the most probable behavior of the signal source given the observations (see e.g., Russell and Norvig (2002) for an introduction to Bayesian filtering).

However, the specific kinds of task models used for addressing the above two challenges differ significantly. In the area of adaptive user interfaces and work flows, hierarchical task graphs are used whereas for behavior inference, probabilistic temporal models – such as dynamic Bayesian networks – are employed for describing behavior by specifying the probabilities of different possible causes for a certain situation. Consequently, in both areas models are currently developed *independently*.

But, once signal sources are human users, as in the scenario described in Section 3.2.1, and the Bayesian filter wants to infer what the users probably do, then the relation between both origins for task models becomes clear. Intuitively, one would assume that a model which specifies the temporal orderings of subtasks of a team should have some relation to a model that specifies what a team of users will probably do next.

If observation data is provided by location sensors (e.g., the UbiSense Platform mentioned in Section 3.2.2 or GPS), accelerometers attached to a user's body (or his mobile phone), or information about objects touched by the user (using, e.g., RFID), then a model correctly describing a team's strategy for achieving a certain goal is an ideal hypothesis for a Bayesian filter. Given a task model and a set of sensor readings, a Bayesian filter will output the user's most probable goal.

In essence this means, that, from a viewpoint of mobile and ubiquitous computing, combining the independent developments of task models from cognitive psychology and signal processing origins for the use in smart environments has two important uses:*1.)* As a means for deriving the dialogue structure of a mobile human computer interface or the workflow of a collaborative group situation (*hierarchical tasks models*). 2.) As a means for providing activity support for users (and teams) through proactive assistance (*probabilistic behavior models*).

### 3.4.1 Structuring Team Tasks

With respect to hierarchical task models, one of the most popular notations is the CTT notation already mentioned in Section 2.3.5. In this notation, a compound activity is represented by a task-tree. Each node in the tree represents a task; composite tasks may be broken down into subtasks. For each task node it may be specified if this activity is executed by the user, by the application, or by an interaction between user and application. Remember that in addition, the possible execution sequences of a composite task's sibling nodes may be further constrained by temporal relations such as "$\alpha \mid = \mid \beta$" ($\alpha$ and $\beta$ may be executed in any sequence), "$\alpha \mid \mid \mid \beta$" ($\alpha$ and $\beta$ can be performed in any order, overlapping, or at the same time), or "$\alpha \gg \beta$" ($\alpha$ has to be executed before $\beta$).

Figure 3.3 presents typical CTTs, describing the agenda from the scenario in Section 3.2.1. The meeting consists of three talks by users A, B, C (represented by the task nodes A Presents, B Presents, and C Presents, respectively in the task tree that is labeled "Cooperative Part") and

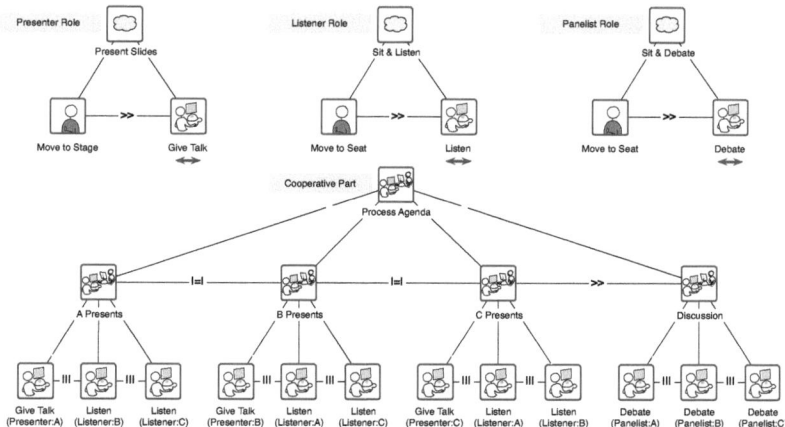

Figure 3.3: Task model in CTT notation specifying the schedule of the meeting described by the scenario in Section 3.2.1 as a cooperative composite task. Node icons correspond to the legend of Figure 2.9.

a discussion (task node Discussion in the same task tree). The talks can be given in any order, which is specified by the temporal relation *order independency* ("| = |"). But the discussion can only be performed after all talks were presented. This is specified by the *enabling* relation ("≫"), which implies that all tasks left from the operator have to be finished first.

During the meeting users can adopt three different roles, namely Presenter, Listener, and Panelist. The role task trees arrange the atomic actions that are associated with each role. In this model each role consists of a preparation stage (i.e., 'Move to Stage' or 'Move to Seat') and an acting stage (i.e., 'Give Talk', 'Listen', 'Debate'). The *enabling* relation ("≫") indicates that acting only starts if preparation is done and the bidirectional arrows expresses that the acting stage is a cooperative action where users may influence each other. How people influence each other during acting stage is communicated by the relations between the atomic action leaves of the task tree representing the cooperative part. Here, the users just act in parallel. This is indicated by the *concurrency* relation ("|||").

Typically, hierarchical task models are used to specify how users behave while interacting either with a software system or with each other in cooperative scenarios. Although they allow to describe the basic temporal structure of compound activities in smart environments, which is required for the concept proposed with this work, additional information are needed for inferring activities and intentions of users from sensor data. Methods for intention inference must know how probable at all a certain execution sequence of the agenda is, and how probable a particular team activity as a cause for a set of observations is. The next section describes the approach to address this problem.

### 3.4.2 Team DBN Proposal

As outlined above, computing a user's current activity from sensor data requires a task model that allows to make statements about the plausibility of sensor data given a specific activity. A system can then try to identify the user's current task by selecting that task whose action sequence is most plausible with respect to the observed sensor data. As the related work presented in Section 1.4 has shown, probabilistic methods for identifying a user's current task, specifically Bayesian Filtering, have been successfully used in several projects that aim at supporting user activities in classrooms, meeting rooms, and office environments (e.g., Franklin et al., 2002; Bui, 2003; Duong et al., 2005). Even offline annotation frameworks

## The Team Intention Model Approach

use Bayesian approaches to segment recorded meeting corpora into sequences of user activities (Zhang et al., 2004; McCowan et al., 2005). Projects from the application fields just mentioned increasingly investigate dynamic Bayesian networks (DBN) for modeling a user's activities (e.g., Patterson et al., 2003, 2004; Zhang et al., 2006).

As mentioned earlier, this work also proposes a DBN-based approach, but it looks at using DBNs for inferring the current activity and the intention of upcoming activities of a *team* of users. Given (noisy and intermittent) sensor readings of the *team members' positions* in a meeting room, I am interested in inferring the *team's current objective* – such as having a presentation delivered by a specific team member, or having a round table discussion, a break, or the end of the meeting. In order to define a complete probabilistic model, sub-models have to be provided for the following three aspects:

- How a team produces a sequence of joint intentions (Team model),
- Which actions a user performs in response to a joint intention (User model), and
- Which sensor data are caused by what actions (Sensor model).

Hence, the basic structure of the DBN proposed for modeling the cooperation of such a team can be given by the *directed acyclic graph* (DAG) that is shown in Figure 3.4. The principal approach is to layer the DBN into three descending levels, specifically *team level*, *user level*,

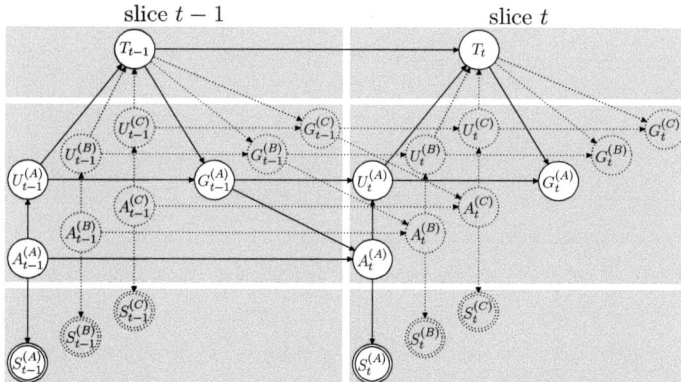

Figure 3.4: Two-sliced dynamic Bayesian network (DBN) modeling team intention inference. It shows the three levels, the intra-slice dependencies between observable (double-contoured) and hidden variables, as well as the inter-slice dependencies between consecutive states.

101

and *sensor level* that break down the complex inference task to the unit level of atomic sensor readings. Besides the team level that contains just a single node, each level consists of a set of nodes (proportional to the number of team members) that encode the current composite state of this level's variables. The depicted DBN shows how the goal-oriented behavior of a team of three users during a meeting is modeled. In order to exploit agenda information, a DBN structure is needed that is able to incorporate an explicit agenda, and that represents a technological mapping of the negotiation process between the team and its members during activity selection. In principal a team's negotiation about new activities (team and user respectively) can be put as follows:

```
done ← TRUE;
for i = 1 to #_U do
    if U_t^(i).done ≠ TRUE then
        done ← FALSE;
        return;
if done = TRUE then
    T_t.history ← T_{t-1}.history ∪ T_{t-1}.activity;
    T_t.activity ← a probable team activity from the agenda that is not in T_t.history yet;
    for i = 1 to #_U do
        intialize G_t^(i);
        G_t^(i).activity ← an user activity that is related to the selected team activity;
else
    for i = 1 to #_U do
        G_t^(i) ← U_t^(i);
```

**Team Level**

At the top level, the Team Node $T_t$ represents the current team intention. The team's intention at time $t$ depends on what the team has already achieved (i.e., Team Node $T$ at time $t-1$, $T_{t-1}$), and what the users $i$ are currently trying to achieve (the User Nodes $U_t^{(i)}$, where $i \in \{A, B, C\}$). If all users have achieved their individual assigned sequence of actions for the current team intention, the team $T$ will adopt a new intention. This may cause new assignments to the users. The User Nodes $G_t^{(i)}$ represent these – possibly new – assignments.

For decision making in this group process this means that at each time slice the team looks at what the users have achieved so far, and then decides what the users should do next. The CPT of Team Node $T$ therefore represents the negotiation process by which the team members

# The Team Intention Model Approach

Table 3.2: Conditional probability table of Team Node $T$.

| $T_{t-1}.history$ | $T_{t-1}.activity$ | $U_t^{(i)}.done, i \in \{A, B, C\}$ | $P(T_t.history = h \cup \{\alpha\} \mid T_{t-1}, U_t^{(i)})$ | $P(T_t.history = h \mid T_{t-1}, U_t^{(i)})$ | $P(T_t.activity = \alpha_T \mid T_{t-1}, U_t^{(i)})$ | $P(T_t.activity = \xi \mid T_{t-1}, U_t^{(i)}), \xi \neq \alpha_T$ |
|---|---|---|---|---|---|---|
| $h$ | $\alpha_T$ | $\forall i : U_t^{(i)}.done = true$ | 1 | 0 | 0 | $mmodel(T_t.history, \xi)$ |
| | | $\exists i : U_t^{(i)}.done = false$ | 0 | 1 | 1 | 0 |

agree on the next joint activity. For instance, if the team decides that the next activity should be the presentation of user A, it would assign to user A the presenter role with the tasks to go to the speaker stand and deliver his contribution, while users B and C would adopt the listener role, which refers to the tasks to take a seat in the audience and listen carefully.

The CPT of the Team Node $T$ in the proposed network basically looks as shown in Table 3.2. The *history* slot of the $T$ node records the team's previous activities. Given a set of team activities **A**, an *execution history* is a set of team activities that already have been performed. The set of all execution histories is the power set of **A**, which is denoted by $2^A$. Note that this model makes the simplifying assumption that the exact *sequence* of team activities is not important for recording history. However, it is easy to change the history model to a sequence model. The *activity* slot denotes the team's current goal that the users try to achieve jointly through their individual assigned sequence of atomic actions. If all users are done with their assignment, the Team Node $T$ will add the current activity $\alpha$ to its history $h$ and it will then choose a new activity $\xi$. Otherwise, it will continue its current activity.

In the depicted CPT, *mmodel* is the essential point. It is a function that, given the execution history of Team Node $T$ at current time step $t$ and a new activity $\xi$, will yield the probability that the team will choose $\xi$ as next activity. The *mmodel*-function includes a-priori information, namely the agenda, and decides from agenda and execution history about what a team will most likely do next in a certain situation. Remember the task model for the cooperative

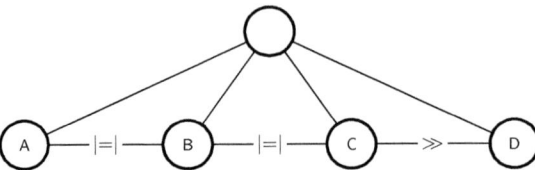

Figure 3.5: Task model specifying the schedule of a meeting.

part of the scenario from Figure 3.3 described in Section 3.2.1, a more schematic drawing of the preliminary knowledge about the meeting structure in Figure 3.5 indicates that the possible activities of the team are the elements of the *set* {A, B, C, D} and the system knows that the team has an agenda stating the *sequence* of team activities ⟨A, B, C, D⟩. Obviously, in this situation *mmodel* should return the highest probability for team activity B when given the history {A} – modeling the prejudice that a team tends to follow its agenda. However, the same function should also assign non-zero probabilities to the other actions in order to account for the possibility of deviations from an agenda.

A possible model for the simple four-step agenda from the scenario that states "A, B, C may happen in any order but most probably in the order ⟨A, B, C⟩, while D must be the last action." is given in Figure 3.6. The figure indicates that *mmodel* essentially specifies a Markov Model where the states are partial execution histories (e.g., {A}, {A, B}, etc.) and the edges are transitions between execution histories. Transitions are labeled with probabilities of how likely the team will try a certain new team activity after a particular execution history. Probability values encode the most probable execution sequence.

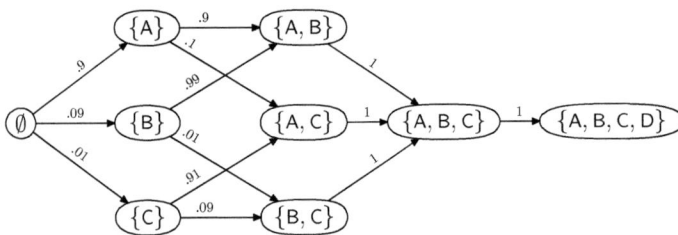

Figure 3.6: Markov model of the agenda driven team activity selection process with exemplary transition probabilities.

*The Team Intention Model Approach*

Table 3.3: Deterministic mapping of team goals to user roles and assigned action sequences for the concrete scenario.

| Team Goal | User | Role | Action Sequence | |
|---|---|---|---|---|
| A Presents | A | Presenter | Move to Stage | Give Talk |
| | B | Listener | Move to Seat | Listen |
| | C | Listener | Move to Seat | Listen |
| B Presents | A | Listener | Move to Seat | Listen |
| | B | Presenter | Move to Stage | Give Talk |
| | C | Listener | Move to Seat | Listen |
| C Presents | A | Listener | Move to Seat | Listen |
| | B | Listener | Move to Seat | Listen |
| | C | Presenter | Move to Stage | Give Talk |
| Discussion | A | Panelist | Move to Seat | Debate |
| | B | Panelist | Move to Seat | Debate |
| | C | Panelist | Move to Seat | Debate |

**User Level**

With new team activities, new user activities must be assigned to the team members, too. The negotiation about new assignments of user actions can be either deterministic or probabilistic. A probabilistic negotiation would follow the approach described above for the Team Node $T$. But in closed scenarios where team goals lead to unambiguous user goals also deterministic assignments of atomic user action sequences may be used for simplification. Staged meeting scenarios as described in Section 3.2.1 and implemented for the experiments of this work (cp., with Chapter 4) are representatives of this category. Thus, a fixed mapping between team activities and user assignments was specified for the proposed team intention model.

This mapping is shown in Table 3.3. In principle, the team members can adopt three roles, namely Presenter, Listener, Panelist. If a user adopts a particular role (e.g., Presenter), then he has to achieve a certain user goal that consists off a fixed sequence of atomic actions (e.g., ⟨'Move to Stage', 'Give Talk'⟩). Note that one would like to apply a probabilistic negotiation about atomic user actions in a specific situation, then one would have to specify a similar function as the *mmodel* function for every role that the members of a team could adopt in that certain situation.

The proposed DBN shown in Figure 3.4 models negotiation at the user level by the depen-

Table 3.4: Conditional probability table of a User Node $U$.

| $G^{(i)}_{t-1}.activity, i \in \{A, B, C\}$ | $G^{(i)}_{t-1}.done$ | $G^{(i)}_{t-1}.perform$ | $A^{(i)}_t.position$ | $A^{(i)}_t.duration$ | $P(U^{(i)}_t.perform = true\|G^{(i)}_{t-1}, A^{(i)}_t)$ | $P(U^{(i)}_t.perform = false\|G^{(i)}_{t-1}, A^{(i)}_t)$ | $P(U^{(i)}_t.done = true\|G^{(i)}_{t-1}, A^{(i)}_t)$ | $P(U^{(i)}_t.done = false\|G^{(i)}_{t-1}, A^{(i)}_t)$ | $P(U^{(i)}_t.activity = \alpha_{G^{(i)}}\|G^{(i)}_{t-1}, A^{(i)}_t)$ | $P(U^{(i)}_t.activity = \xi\|G^{(i)}_{t-1}, A^{(i)}_t), \xi \neq \alpha_{G^{(i)}}$ |
|---|---|---|---|---|---|---|---|---|---|---|
| $\alpha_{G^{(i)}}$ | false | false | $ps_{A^{(i)}} \neq atLoc(i)$ | | 0 | 1 | 0 | 1 | 1 | 0 |
| | | | $ps_{A^{(i)}} = atLoc(i)$ | | 1 | 0 | | | | |
| | | true | | $du_{A(i)} \neq atEnd(\alpha_{G^{(i)}}, t)$ | | | 0 | 1 | | |
| | | | | $du_{A(i)} = atEnd(\alpha_{G^{(i)}}, t)$ | | | 1 | 0 | | |
| | true | | | | | | | | | |

dencies around the User Node $U^{(i)}$ and $G^{(i)}$. Whether a user $i$ has achieved his assignment at time $t$ – given by User Node $U^{(i)}_t$ – depends on the user's current action $A^{(i)}_t$ and his previous assignment $G^{(i)}_{t-1}$. User Node $G$ handles the mapping of team goals to user goals and, hence, depends on the current team state $T_t$ and the status of the user's assignment $U^{(i)}_t$ that is represented by the User Node's done and perform variables. The Action Node $A^{(i)}_t$ records the current state of the user's action. Related variables can be the user's current position and velocity (in case he has to reach a certain location as for the 'Move to Stage' or 'Move to Seat' actions) or his speaking duration (in case he has to deliver his presentation as during the 'Give Talk' action). The actual action $A^{(i)}_t$ that a user is doing at time $t$ depends on his previous action and assignment – $A^{(i)}_{t-1}$ and $G^{(i)}_{t-1}$.

The corresponding CPTs and CPDs respectively are shown in the Tables 3.4 – 3.6. Essential for a User Node $U$'s CPT is the distinction between the *prepare* and *perform* stage of an assignment. As indicated by the mapping in Table 3.3 each user activity consists of a preparation and a performing action. Due to the scenario these parts are restricted to a single atomic action each. In more complex settings where a user activity includes a larger action sequence more than one action may be processed in either stage, but categorization into preparation

# The Team Intention Model Approach

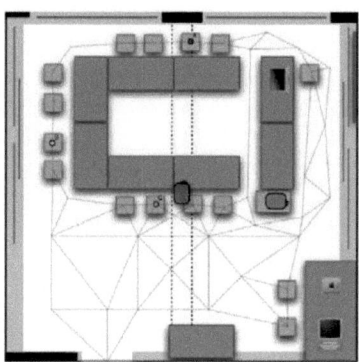

Figure 3.7: The motion graph links every relevant location to each other.

and performing remains the same. In Table 3.4 two functions control whether a user assignment has reached performing stage or goal stage respectively. The *atLoc*-function compares the actual position of a user provided by the user's Action Node $A$ with a location foreseen for the user assignment. Therefore the positions from the A node are mapped orthographically on the edges of an undirected motion graph that includes all relevant locations of the smart meeting room as nodes. Figure 3.7 shows the motion graph for the SmartAppliance-Lab. Once arrived at this location the user can start performing. During performing stage the

Table 3.5: Conditional probability table of a User Node $G$.

| $T_t.activity$ | $U_t^{(i)}.activity, i \in \{A,B,C\}$ | $U_t^{(i)}.done$ | $U_t^{(i)}.perform$ | $P(G_t^{(i)}.perform = true\|T_t, U_t)$ | $P(G_t^{(i)}.perform = false\|T_t, U_t)$ | $P(G_t^{(i)}.done = true\|T_t, U_t)$ | $P(G_t^{(i)}.done = false\|T_t, U_t)$ | $P(G_t^{(i)}.activity = a_{U^{(i)}}\|T_t, U_t)$ | $P(G_t^{(i)}.activity = \xi\|T_t, U_t), \xi \neq a_{U^{(i)}}$ |
|---|---|---|---|---|---|---|---|---|---|
| $\alpha_T$ | $\alpha_{U^{(i)}} = map(i, \alpha_T)$ | false | false | 0 | 1 | 0 | 1 | 1 | 0 |
|  |  |  | true | 1 | 0 |  |  |  |  |
|  |  | true |  |  |  | 1 | 0 |  |  |
|  | $\alpha_{U^{(i)}} \neq map(i, \alpha_T)$ |  |  | 0 | 1 | 0 | 1 | 0 | 1 |

Table 3.6: Motion model of an Action Node A.

| $G_{t-1}^{(i)}.done, i \in \{A,B,C\}$ | $G_{t-1}^{(i)}.perform$ | $A_{t-1}^{(i)}.position$ | $A_{t-1}^{(i)}.velocity$ | $A_{t-1}^{(i)}.duration$ | $A_t^{(i)}.position$ | $A_t^{(i)}.velocity$ | $A_t^{(i)}.duration$ |
|---|---|---|---|---|---|---|---|
| false | false | | | | $ps_{A^{(i)}} + A_{t-1}^{(i)}.velocity \times \delta t$ | $change(v_{A^{(i)}})$ | 0 |
| | true | $ps_{A^{(i)}}$ | $v_{A^{(i)}}$ | $du_{A^{(i)}}$ | | | $du_{A^{(i)}} + \delta t$ |
| true | | | | | $ps_{A^{(i)}}$ | $init(v_{A^{(i)}})$ | $du_{A^{(i)}}$ |

atEnd-function controls the progress of the user's performance. If the user $i$ reaches the end of his performance, then goal achievement is signaled by changing the $U_t^{(i)}.done$ variable to *true*. Essential for a User Node $G$'s CPT shown in Table 3.5 is the *map*-function that implements the above mentioned deterministic mapping of team activities to user activities (cp., with Table 3.3). If a new activity was assigned to a user $i$, then the activity progress control variables $G_t^{(i)}.done$ and $G_t^{(i)}.perform$ are reset to *false*. Table 3.6 depicts the transitions in an Action Node $G$. Depending on whether a user $i$ is done or not with his last assignments the corresponding $A_t^{(i)}.velocity$ or $A_t^{(i)}.duration$ variables are initialized (*init*-function) or updated (*change*-function) respectively. If a user is additionally in performing stage, then the duration of this action is tracked as well.

**Sensor Level**

Finally, the sensor observations of user $i$ at time $t$ – the Sensor Node $S_t^{(i)}$ – depend on the user's action at that time – $A_t^{(i)}$. Note that these sensor nodes are the *only* observable nodes in the proposed team intention model. The available sensor data – the set of $S_t^{(i)}$ values for the times up to $t$ – is utilized to find the sequence of values for $T_s, s \in \{1\ldots t\}$ that best explains the observed data. So, the team's negotiations about joint activities is estimated from the observable behavior of the team members so far. Remember the proposed DBN given in Figure 3.4, only the Sensor Node labeled $S$ are observable where all the other ones are hidden. Each of these nodes represents a sensor observation from the in Section 3.2.2 mentioned Ubisense RTLS. Data that reports just the position of a user.

Table 3.7: Conditional probability distribution for the sensor model of a Sensor Node $S$.

| $P_{S_i^{(l)}.position \mid A_i^{(l)}.position}\left(ps_{S^{(l)}}, ps_{A^{(l)}}\right)$ |
|---|
| $\mathscr{C}\left(ps_{S^{(l)}}; ps_{A^{(l)}} + x_{0_{S^{(l)}.position}}, \gamma\right)$ |

The corresponding sensor model which describes the distribution of the available data is shown in Table 3.7. In this table $\mathscr{C}$ represents the *Cauchy*-distribution, which was chosen for its heavy-tailed character. In cases where the tracked targets tend to abrupt changes of their acceleration (obviously humans show these characteristics) heavy-tailed distributions enable approximate inference algorithms, namely particle filters[5], to produce more reliable result than the Gaussian distributions usually utilized (Ikoma et al., 2001; Ichimura, 2002).

Now that a proposal for a probabilistic team intention model is available, the inference of user and team activities or intentions respectively can move into the focus. But before describing this part of the concept in Section 3.5, the next section gives a note on a challenge related to the model itself, namely the efficient synthesis of at least parts of the model.

### 3.4.3 Note on Synthesizing Team DBN

One may agree that the proposed model fits reasonably well to the concrete scenario given in Section 3.2.1, but at the same time it is also noticeable that the envisioned scenario obviously includes a rather simplistic meeting agenda[6]. Since the number of history states grows exponentially in the number of available activities, a crucial question is how such a model, especially the agenda, can be specified *efficiently*.

Sure, model generation or high-level behavior modeling respectively is not the core of this work but it might be important for the acceptance of the model introduced in the last section to provide a concept for this issue. Therefore an approach proposed in Giersich et al. (2007) is mentioned that shows one possible way to find at least naive procedures that enable the synthesis of the TeamDBN. This procedure utilizes hierarchical task models for defining the structure and transition probabilities of the team level in the proposed DBN. Specifically, an annotated CTT graph forms the basis for generating the initial proposal of the *mmodel-*

---

[5] Sections 3.5.2 & 3.5.3 will show that particle filter is the algorithm of choice for inference in a state space like the one modeled by the proposed DBN.
[6] A rather simplistic agenda was chosen merely for simplification reasons. A limited number of agenda items and user activities enable for clear model description and experiments.

function. Next, I explain how task models such as task-trees can be used to simplify the definition of the team intention model.

Consider that a task model **M** defined over a set of actions **A** basically specifies a DAG on possible execution histories $h \in 2^{\mathbf{A}}$, with the additional constraint

$$(h, h') \in \mathbf{M} \Rightarrow \exists a \in \mathbf{A} : h \cup \{a\} = h', \tag{3.1}$$

where $h$ and $h'$ are the nodes of the graph and $(h, h')$ denotes an edge. This means that in a task model **M**, a history $h'$ directly results from a history $h$ through the execution of a single activity $a$. The empty history $\emptyset$ is the root of the DAG. Note, if histories are represented by sequences instead of sets, then this graph is a tree.

For a given history $h$, the set $\mathbf{C}(h)$ denotes the set of activities that may directly follow this history. $\mathbf{C}(h)$ is defined as follows:

$$\mathbf{C}(h) = \{a \in \mathbf{A} \mid (h, h \cup \{a\}) \in \mathbf{M}\}. \tag{3.2}$$

Clearly, the graph **M** directly represents the structure of a corresponding Markov model. At this point, the question to be addressed is how to provide initial proposals for the transition probabilities of this Markov model.

The idea is to allow developers of task models to annotate their task-trees with additional information from which these initial proposals for the transition probabilities can be derived.

One straightforward approach is to annotate each sibling activity $a$ with a "priority" $prio(a)$, which is a number that indicates how important an early execution of this node is in relation to the other siblings. This is outlined schematically in Figure 3.8 for the scenario's agenda. For independently ordered tasks (temporal relation *order independency* "|=|"), the priorities indicate the probabilities of being executed first. Then, for a given history $h$ and a possible

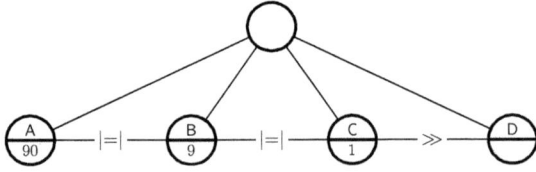

Figure 3.8: Extended task model specifying the schedule of a meeting.

110

extension $\xi \in C(h)$, the probability of a transition from $h$ to $h \cup \{\xi\}$ is calculated from the priorities by:

$$P(h \cup \{\xi\}|h) = \frac{prio(\xi)}{\sum_{\alpha \in C(h)} prio(\alpha)}. \qquad (3.3)$$

Generating *mmodel* from the hierarchical task model in Figure 3.8 using the above calculation results in a Markov model like the one shown in Figure 3.6. In this example the probability that the meeting starts with the presentation of A first is 0.9. Accordingly, it is 0.09 for presentation B. The probability that the meeting starts with the third talk C is 0.01. If the meeting has started with talk B, the probabilities for the following two possible transitions to $\{B, C\}$ and $\{A, B\}$ are given by

$$\frac{prio(C)}{prio(A) + prio(C)} \approx 0.01, \text{ and } \frac{prio(A)}{prio(A) + prio(C)} \approx 0.99.$$

Note that the most probable path through the generated Markov model is indeed the one following the agenda: $\emptyset \to A \to \{A, B\} \to \{A, B, C\} \to \{A, B, C, D\}$. Also, if an activity is taken out of order, the Markov model specifies that the team will try to *return* to the agenda. That is, e.g., when the meeting has been started with B, the most probably following activity will be to return to the planned sequence by executing A. Thus, the generated Markov model represents the intuition behind the task-tree annotations of execution priorities.

The considerations just made show at least that a proposal for a probabilistic model of user behavior can be generated from an annotated hierarchical task model. This enables the exploitation of well established user interaction design methodologies (e.g., task-tree modeling) for the purpose of model generation.

An interesting question is now *how well* the intended Markov model can be specified by the priority annotations. Not all possible distributions for the transition probabilities can be generated from these task-tree annotations (after all, the number of priority annotations is much smaller than the number of transitions in the Markov model).

However, it seems sufficient if the generated model is *approximately* correct: the exact transition probabilities are not known in advance anyway. They have to be learned from the observation of real team behavior. The generated probabilities only have to be as exact as to permit a system a *reasonable* assistance right from the start, before training data is available, but of course, the better the initial estimate, the less training data will be required. The salient point will be a useful definition of "reasonable" and "approximate" in this context. It appears to be possible to provide such definitions. However, the proposed approach is just a marking of a question, which holds research issues that are beyond the scope of this work.

So, e.g., the specific task-tree annotations and the accompanying probability computation given in Section 3.4.3 implicitly assume that the team uses a particular agenda management strategy. Specifically, the synthesized model assumes that a team prefers to execute activities in the order of their original priority, independent of the history. This is called a *return to agenda* strategy. Sometimes, teams might use other strategies. One example is to *continue with the successor*, which means that if the meeting had started with talk B, the most probable next activity would be C. In this strategy the original successor of an activity actually executed in the agenda is the most probable following activity. Another strategy of a team could be to *stick to a timetable* and execute each activity as close as possible to the original schedule.

Different strategies may require different annotations to a hierarchical task model. For instance, in case of using *continue with successor*, priority annotations must be provided at the parent task level rather than at the sibling level. In addition, it might be conceivable to provide a set of mechanisms for inheriting such annotations within a task-tree. Further a set of annotations must be identified that allows to specify the *typical* team strategies for agenda management with *sufficient precision*, whereas the set of annotation mechanisms has to be kept as small as possible.

Obviously, this list could be continued, but this section was merely intended to show that sensitive parts of the proposed Team DBN, like the *mmodel* function that tends to grow exponentially, can be generated using simple enhancements of established methodology.

## 3.5 Team Intention Inference

The previous sections described the probabilistic modeling approach of this work to infer user and team activities or intentions respectively. The choice for a DBN-based model indicates that the question of how to update the model given the sensor measurements is addressed using a Bayesian inference approach. This section identifies the basic inference tasks needed to enable reasoning as mentioned in the concrete scenario in Section 3.2.1 and describes issues of inference that arise from the proposed model. Finally, the specific particle filter approach used for inferring team intentions is explained.

# The Team Intention Model Approach

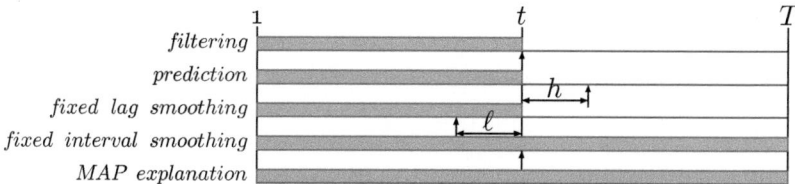

Figure 3.9: Basic inference tasks in temporal probabilistic models. Shade segments are the intervals for which observations are available. Arrows pointing up represent the time steps for which the system states are inferred. $T$ denotes the length of a complete data sequence, $t$ is the current time, $h$ represents the prediction horizon, and $\ell$ is the time lag that inference is behind current time. (*Source*: Adapted from Murphy 2002, pg. 3)

### 3.5.1 Inference Tasks

Russell and Norvig (2002) listed a number of basic inference tasks that must be solved for temporal probabilistic models like the DBN proposed as team intention model. Figure 3.9 summarizes these tasks graphically and indicates that the applicability of a certain inference task depends on the availability of observation data. Merely two categories can be distinguished: *1.*) *real-time* inference that uses data up to the current time step, and *2.*) *offline* inference that in contrast utilizes recorded complete data sequences.

The envisioned scenario requires real-time inference of actual activities and intended next activities (intentions) of a team during a meeting. The constraint that data has to be processed immediately as it arrives involves the restriction that only observations up to the current time step $t$ in the meeting are available for inference. Furthermore, the assistance is focused on present and future activities of the team so that only inference of actual and future states of the model matters. Thus, relevant corresponding inference tasks in the proposed concept are *filtering* and *prediction* respectively.

Filtering using the Bayesian approach is *"the task of computing the belief state – the posterior distribution over the current state, given all evidence to date"* (Russell and Norvig, 2002, pg. 546). In other words a filter has to estimate $p\left(\mathbf{x}_t | \mathbf{e}_{1:t}\right)$ for a continuous stream of evidences in the interval $1:t$. From using Bayes' theorem in terms of likelihood, it is known that the posterior probability is proportional to the product of the prior probability and the

113

likelihood. Hence, the belief state can be defined recursively as:

$$
\begin{aligned}
p(x_t|e_{1:t}) &= \frac{p(e_t|x_t, e_{1:t-1})\, p(x_t|e_{1:t-1})}{p(e_t|e_{1:t-1})} \\
&\propto p(e_t|x_t, e_{1:t-1})\, p(x_t|e_{1:t-1}) \\
&= p(e_t|x_t, e_{1:t-1}) \left[ \int p(x_t|x_{t-1}, e_{1:t-1})\, p(x_{t-1}|e_{1:t-1})\, dx_{t-1} \right] \\
&= p(e_t|x_t) \left[ \int p(x_t|x_{t-1})\, p(x_{t-1}|e_{1:t-1})\, dx_{t-1} \right]
\end{aligned}
\qquad (3.4)
$$

with a normalizing constant $1/\alpha_t = p(e_t|e_{1:t-1}) = \int p(e_t|x_t)\, p(x_t|e_{1:t-1})\, dx_t$. Note that the likelihood $p(e_t|x_t, e_{1:t-1})$ can be replaced immediately by $p(e_t|x_t)$ due to the first Markov assumption on evidence space. Similarly, the transition model $p(x_t|x_{t-1}, e_{1:t-1})$ can be simplified to $p(x_t|x_{t-1})$.

Prediction is *"the task of computing the posterior distribution over the* future *state, given all evidences to date"* (Russell and Norvig, 2002, pg. 546). Hence, prediction has to determine $p(x_{t+h}|e_{1:t})$ for a system state situated a horizon $h>0$ time steps in future using the evidence stream $1:t$. Using marginalization in combination with the Chapman-Kolmogorov equation for conditional probability, a formal definition for the prediction case can be put as:

$$
p(x_{t+h}|e_{1:t}) = \int p(x_{t+h}|x_{t+h-1})\, p(x_{t+h-1}|e_{1:t})\, dx_{t+h-1}. \qquad (3.5)
$$

Obviously, one-step ahead prediction, $p(x_t|e_{1:t-1})$, computed from the prior belief state $p(x_{t-1}|e_{1:t-1})$, is already enclosed in the filtering definition formulated in Equation (3.4) (cp., with terms put in square brackets).

This indicates that applying inference the Bayesian way consists of two major steps: *prediction* and *update*. First the prediction step projects the posterior probability density over the actual state of the model forward from time-step $t$ to $t+1$ using the explicitly modeled transition probabilities. And then the update step adapts the estimated posterior probability density over the future state using possibly new evidences $e_{t+1}$ from the sensor model. Speaking in terms of Equation (3.4), that is, the posterior distribution over the actual state is $p(x_t|e_{1:t})$, the transition model is $p(x_{t+1}|x_t)$, the sensor model is $p(e_{t+1}|x_{t+1})$, and the posterior distribution over the future state is represented by $p(x_{t+1}|e_{1:t+1})$.

Note, if the model has to predict a future state $h > 1$ time steps ahead, then just the $h$

transitions of the current distribution without any update from the sensor model are involved.

### 3.5.2 Bayesian Filter Approach

In principle, the inference task within the proposed team intention model can be condensed to the following line of questioning:

> Given a series of sensor readings $\mathbf{e}_{1:t}$ up to a time $t$, what is the probability distribution of the *next* system state $p\left(\mathbf{x}_{t+1}|\mathbf{e}_{1:t}\right)$, and what is the probability distribution if the "next state" becomes the actual system state $p\left(\mathbf{x}_{t+1}|\mathbf{e}_{1:t+1}\right)$ due to an observation $\mathbf{e}_{t+1}$ at time $t+1$.

First, the joint probability of the system state for a single time step of the DBN-based team intention recognition process proposed in Section 3.4.2 can be given by

$$
\begin{aligned}
p(\mathbf{x}) &= p\left(T, U^{(1)}, \ldots, U^{(N)}, G^{(1)}, \ldots, G^{(N)}, A^{(1)}, \ldots, A^{(N)}\right) \\
&= \prod_{i=1}^{N} p(T|\pi(T)) p\left(U^{(i)}|\pi\left(U^{(i)}\right)\right) p\left(G^{(i)}|\pi\left(G^{(i)}\right)\right) p\left(A^{(i)}\right),
\end{aligned}
\tag{3.6}
$$

where $T, U^{(i)}, G^{(i)}$, and $A^{(i)}$ are the hidden nodes of the proposed DBN (cp., Figure 3.4) and $\pi(\cdot)$ denotes the sets of conditioning parents for the respective nodes. Expanding this joint probability over the whole period of time leads to

$$
\begin{aligned}
p\left(\mathbf{x}_{1:T}\right) = \prod_{t=1}^{T}\prod_{i=1}^{N} & p\left(T_t|\pi(T_t), \theta(T_t)\right) p\left(U_t^{(i)}|\pi\left(U_t^{(i)}\right), \theta\left(U_t^{(i)}\right)\right) \\
& p\left(G_t^{(i)}|\pi\left(G_t^{(i)}\right)\right) p\left(A_t^{(i)}|\theta\left(A_t^{(i)}\right)\right),
\end{aligned}
\tag{3.7}
$$

where $\theta(\cdot)$ represents the particular sets of conditioning parents from the previous time step. For the particular DBN proposed in Section 3.4.2 this can be substantiated to

$$
p\left(\mathbf{x}_{1:T}\right) = \prod_{t=1}^{T}\prod_{i=1}^{N} p\left(T_t|U_t^{(i)}, T_{t-1}\right) p\left(U_t^{(i)}|A_t^{(i)}, G_{t-1}^{(i)}\right) p\left(G_t^{(i)}|T_t, U_t^{(i)}\right) p\left(A_t^{(i)}|A_{t-1}^{(i)}, G_{t-1}^{(i)}\right).
\tag{3.8}
$$

Now, let's consider that the unfolding of the system state sequence $\langle \mathbf{x}_0, \ldots, \mathbf{x}_{t+1}; t \in \mathbb{N}\rangle$ is defined recursively by a state transition function

$$
\mathbf{x}_{t+1} = f_{t+1}(\mathbf{x}_t, \mathbf{v}_t),
\tag{3.9}
$$

where $f_{t+1}(\cdot,\cdot) : \mathbb{R}^{n_x} \times \mathbb{R}^{n_v} \to \mathbb{R}^{n_x}$ is a nonlinear transformation of the $n_x$-dimensional state vector $\mathbf{x}_t$ and the $n_v$-dimensional noise vector $\mathbf{v}_t$ out of the independent and identical distributed (i.i.d.) process noise sequence $\langle \mathbf{v}_0, \ldots, \mathbf{v}_t; t \in \mathbb{N} \rangle$. Then, the recursive observation function to estimate the state $\mathbf{x}_{t+1}$ from sensor readings is given by

$$\mathbf{e}_{t+1} = h_{t+1}(\mathbf{x}_{t+1}, \mathbf{n}_{t+1}), \qquad (3.10)$$

where $h_{t+1}(\cdot, \cdot) : \mathbb{R}^{n_x} \times \mathbb{R}^{n_n} \to \mathbb{R}^{n_e}$ is a nonlinear transformation of the $n_x$-dimensional state vector $\mathbf{x}_{t+1}$ and the $n_n$-dimensional noise vector $\mathbf{n}_{t+1}$ out of the i.i.d. sensor noise sequence $\langle \mathbf{n}_0, \ldots, \mathbf{n}_{t+1}; t \in \mathbb{N} \rangle$. Obviously, estimation should be derived from the sequence of all sensor readings up to the present, denoted as $\mathbf{e}_{1:t+1}$.

Equations (3.9 & 3.10) in combination with the assumption that the initial value of the demanded posterior *probability density function* (pdf) of the state vector – $p(\mathbf{x}_0)^7$ is known in advance, in principle, enable the recursive two-stage computation of posterior pdf $p(\mathbf{x}_{t+1}|\mathbf{e}_{1:t+1})$ as a solution for the inference task. First, given the availability of posterior pdf $p(\mathbf{x}_t|\mathbf{e}_{1:t})$ and transition model $p(\mathbf{x}_{t+1}|\mathbf{x}_t)$ (defined by Equation (3.9) and the statistics of the process noise $\mathbf{v}$), a prediction of the next system state can be obtained by prior pdf

$$p(\mathbf{x}_{t+1}|\mathbf{e}_{1:t}) = \int p(\mathbf{x}_{t+1}|\mathbf{x}_t) p(\mathbf{x}_t|\mathbf{e}_{1:t}) d\mathbf{x}_t. \qquad (3.11)$$

Note that like in Equation (3.4) the first Markov assumption applies to the transition model and hence $p(\mathbf{x}_{t+1}|\mathbf{x}_t, \mathbf{e}_{1:t}) = p(\mathbf{x}_{t+1}|\mathbf{x}_t)$. Secondly, when the observation $\mathbf{e}_{t+1}$ becomes available, an update of the prior pdf can be gained using Bayes' rule, i.e. the posterior pdf can be given by

$$p(\mathbf{x}_{t+1}|\mathbf{e}_{1:t+1}) = \frac{p(\mathbf{e}_{t+1}|\mathbf{x}_{t+1}) p(\mathbf{x}_{t+1}|\mathbf{e}_{1:t})}{\int p(\mathbf{e}_{t+1}|\mathbf{x}_{t+1}) p(\mathbf{x}_{t+1}|\mathbf{e}_{1:t}) d\mathbf{x}_{t+1}}, \qquad (3.12)$$

which obviously denotes the same as Equation (3.4) but one step further in time.

A related question arising from the described two-stage process of *prediction* and *update* is how to calculate the transition model $p(\mathbf{x}_{t+1}|\mathbf{x}_t)$? Given the transition function $\mathbf{x}_{t+1} = f_{t+1}(\mathbf{x}_t, \mathbf{v}_t)$ and process noise density $p(\mathbf{v}_t)$ the objective is to obtain $p(\mathbf{x}_{t+1}|\mathbf{x}_t)$.

---

[7] $p(\mathbf{x}_0|\mathbf{e}_0) \equiv p(\mathbf{x}_0)$, because $\mathbf{e}_0$ is the set of no observation.

First, the sum rule is utilized to expand the transition model:

$$\begin{aligned} p\left(\mathbf{x}_{t+1}|\mathbf{x}_{t}\right) &= \int p\left(\mathbf{x}_{t+1}|\mathbf{x}_{t},\mathbf{v}_{t}\right) p\left(\mathbf{v}_{t}\right) d\mathbf{v}_{t} \\ &= \int p\left(\mathbf{x}_{t+1}=f_{t+1}\left(\mathbf{x}_{t},\mathbf{v}_{t}\right)|\mathbf{x}_{t},\mathbf{v}_{t}\right) p\left(\mathbf{v}_{t}\right) d\mathbf{v}_{t}. \end{aligned} \quad (3.13)$$

Clearly, it must apply here that

$$\forall\, \mathbf{x}_{t+1} \neq f_{t+1}\left(\mathbf{x}_{t},\mathbf{v}_{t}\right):\; p\left(\mathbf{x}_{t+1}=f_{t+1}\left(\mathbf{x}_{t},\mathbf{v}_{t}\right)|\mathbf{x}_{t},\mathbf{v}_{t}\right)=0.$$

The Dirac delta measure $\delta(\cdot)$ complies with this constraint. Hence, Equation (3.13) can be written as

$$p\left(\mathbf{x}_{t+1}|\mathbf{x}_{t}\right) = \int \delta\left(\mathbf{x}_{t+1}=f_{t+1}\left(\mathbf{x}_{t},\mathbf{v}_{t}\right)\right) p\left(\mathbf{v}_{t}\right) d\mathbf{v}_{t}. \quad (3.14)$$

Now considering a function $s(e,v)$ that solves an equation $e$ for a variable $v$ and is utilizing convolution characteristic of the Dirac delta measure $\int \delta\left(\mathbf{x}=\mathbf{x}_{0}\right) f\left(\mathbf{x}\right) d\mathbf{x} = f\left(\mathbf{x}_{0}\right)$, then Equation (3.14) can be updated and further substituted to

$$\begin{aligned} p\left(\mathbf{x}_{t+1}|\mathbf{x}_{t}\right) &= \int \delta\left(\mathbf{v}_{t}=s\left(\mathbf{x}_{t+1}=f_{t+1}\left(\mathbf{x}_{t},v\right),v\right)\right) p\left(\mathbf{v}_{t}\right) d\mathbf{v}_{t} \\ &= p\left(s\left(\mathbf{x}_{t+1}=f_{t+1}\left(\mathbf{x}_{t},v\right),v\right)\right). \end{aligned} \quad (3.15)$$

The observation model $p\left(\mathbf{e}_{t+1}|\mathbf{x}_{t+1}\right)$ can be calculated analogously:

$$p\left(\mathbf{e}_{t+1}|\mathbf{x}_{t+1}\right) = p\left(s\left(\mathbf{e}_{t+1}=h_{t+1}\left(\mathbf{x}_{t+1},v\right),v\right)\right). \quad (3.16)$$

In general, the calculation of an optimal Bayesian solution which would provide the exact posterior probability density is intractable due to the unrestricted complexity of the density function. This issue could be addressed specifying restrictive constraints (e.g. Gaussian distributed noise densities, linear transition and observation functions, or discrete state space) to allow to use optimal algorithms such as Kalman filters or Grid-based methods (see Arulampalam et al. 2002 for details).

However, the scenario of this work describes a situation where those constraints are not valid. Hence, a suboptimal algorithm like an approximative nonlinear Bayesian filter must be applied to the proposed team intention model.

### 3.5.3 Particle Filter Approach

For doing inference on the DBN proposed in this work the particle filter algorithm is used. A particle filter is a *Monte Carlo* (MC) method which represents a complex posterior pdf by a set of weighted samples that approximate this demanded pdf. Formally speaking, if $\left\{ \mathbf{x}_{t+1}^{(i)}, w_{t+1}^{(i)} \right\}_{i=1}^{N}$ is a random set of $N$ particles with associated weights, then the posterior pdf at time $t+1$ can be approximated by

$$p\left(\mathbf{x}_{t+1} | \mathbf{e}_{1:t+1}\right) \approx \sum_{i=1}^{N} w_{t+1}^{(i)} \delta\left(\mathbf{x}_{t+1} = \mathbf{x}_{t+1}^{(i)}\right), \tag{3.17}$$

where $\sum_{i=1}^{N} w_{t+1}^{(i)} = 1$. In order to enable an appropriate approximation, weights of the particles must be chosen proportional to the importance of a particular sample for the demanded pdf. Since it is usually difficult to draw samples from $p(\cdot)$, a common practice is to select an easy to sample *importance density function* (idf) $q(\cdot)$ from which the particles are drawn. Arulampalam et al. (2002) described the importance sampling approach in detail. Samples are obtained by $\mathbf{x}_{t+1}^{(i)} \sim q\left(\mathbf{x}_{t+1} | \mathbf{x}_{t}^{(i)}, \mathbf{e}_{t+1}\right)$ so that the weighting procedure can be given recursively by

$$w_{t+1}^{(i)} \propto w_{t}^{(i)} \frac{p\left(\mathbf{e}_{t+1} | \mathbf{x}_{t+1}^{(i)}\right) p\left(\mathbf{x}_{t+1}^{(i)} | \mathbf{x}_{t}^{(i)}\right)}{q\left(\mathbf{x}_{t+1}^{(i)} | \mathbf{x}_{t}^{(i)}, \mathbf{e}_{t+1}\right)}. \tag{3.18}$$

Besides the number of particles[8], an adequate choice for the idf is essential for the quality of approximation. For pragmatical reasons the particle filter used in this work applies the obvious approach to select the prior pdfs $\forall i : p\left(\mathbf{x}_{t+1}^{(i)} | \mathbf{x}_{t}^{(i)}\right)$ as importance densities, because this yields a simplified equation for the weighting

$$w_{t+1}^{(i)} \propto w_{t}^{(i)} p\left(\mathbf{e}_{t+1} | \mathbf{x}_{t+1}^{(i)}\right). \tag{3.19}$$

Other more sophisticated methods to find a near optimal idf, can be found in literature (e.g., Doucet et al. 2000b; Arulampalam et al. 2002).

Another common issue while using particle filter is the degeneracy phenomenon, where after a few iterations, all but one particle will have negligible weight (Arulampalam et al., 2002). Usually, this problem is addressed by a resampling step in the particle filter algorithms that

---

[8]The larger the set of random samples with associated weights becomes, the closer the approximation gets to the functional description of the posterior pdf.

## The Team Intention Model Approach

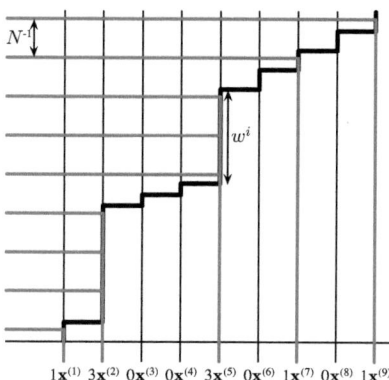

Figure 3.10: Example of the *systematic resampling* procedure introduced by Kitagawa (1996).

is executed, if the effective particle number $N_{eff}$ drops below a certain threshold. Different approaches exist to estimate $N_{eff}$, but this work employs a variant of the *sampling importance resampling* (SIR) filter introduced by Gordon et al. (1993) as *bootstrap* filter, where resampling is implemented independent of $N_{eff}$ in every time step.

A new set of samples $\left\{ \mathbf{x}_{t+1}^{*(i)}, w_{t+1}^{*(i)} \right\}_{i=1}^{N}$ is generated from the filtered posterior probability density function introduced in Equation (3.17) so that $Pr\left(\mathbf{x}_{t+1}^{*(i)} = \mathbf{x}_{t+1}^{(j)}\right) = w_{t+1}^{(j)}$. The associated weights are reset to $w_{t+1}^{(i)} = N^{-1}$, because the resampled particles are now i.i.d. samples of the posterior pdf. Figure 3.10 shows the procedure of resampling as a sample-raster representation. The cumulative weights of particles $\mathbf{x}_{t+1}^{(1)}$ up to $\mathbf{x}_{t+1}^{(N)}$ are stored in a sequence $\langle c_1, \ldots, c_N \rangle$. Starting at a random position drawn from the interval $\left[0, N^{-1}\right]$, the resampling algorithm walks along this sequence with a step width of $N^{-1}$ and decides, whether to generate a copy of the currently indexed particle or to increase the particle index accordingly and copy the new representative. This is done until $N$ new particles are generated. At the bottom line of Figure 3.10 is denoted how often each particle was replicated for the new sample set.

Figure 3.11 depicts the overall operation of a SIR filter. Starting with a sample set drawn from the idf $p\left(\mathbf{x}_t | \mathbf{x}_{t-1}\right)$ at time $t$, first, the importance weights are computed for each particle. This results in a set of samples with associated weights. Then, the resampling step replicates the most vital particles in the replacing particle set $\left\{\mathbf{x}_t^{*(i)}, N^{-1}\right\}$. Finally, the prediction of the next time step $t + 1$ is made by drawing a new set of samples that now approximates $p\left(\mathbf{x}_{t+1} | \mathbf{x}_t\right)$.

Although the introduction of a resampling step decreases degeneracy of samples, it brings

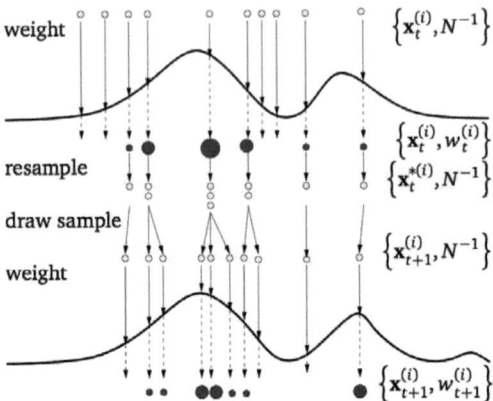

Figure 3.11: Operation of a particle filter. (*Source*: Adapted from Doucet et al. 2001, pg. 12)

in a new issue called *sample impoverishment*, which is a problem especially for systems with rather small process noise $v_{1:t+1}$. The smaller the process noise is, the faster the particle population will lump in a single system state. Obviously in such a situation the particles hardly approximate the demanded posterior pdf.

A SIR filter is sensible to small process noise merely due to its idf. The choice of $p\left(x_{t+1}^{(i)}|x_t^{(i)}\right)$ as importance density for an $i$th particle implies that first a process noise sample $v_t^{(i)} \sim p(v_t)$ is generated and then the new particle $x_{t+1}^{(i)}$ follows from $x_{t+1}^{(i)} = f_{t+1}\left(x_t^{(i)}, v_t^{(i)}\right)$. In combination with the application of resampling during each time step this can imply – if process noise is small – a nearly instant erosion of particle diversity. Nevertheless, if the amount of process noise is not critical, then Arulampalam et al. (2002) recommended a SIR filter because of its rather easy weight evaluation and sampling procedures. For the other case they identified two alternatives, namely the *auxiliary sampling importance resampling* (ASIR) filter introduced by Pitt and Shephard (1999) and the *regularized particle filter* (RPF) proposed by Musso et al. (2001). Here, just the ASIR approach is explained, because this method and the SIR filter are the two algorithms, which are exemplarily used by the tools of the experimental infrastructure that is described in the next section.

The idea of an ASIR filter to address the sample impoverishment phenomenon is to re-weight particles of the previous time step in order to support particles in likely states of the current time step. Therefore Pitt and Shephard added an auxiliary variable $k$ to the process that works as an index to the previous particle set. Thus a joint posterior pdf can be given similar to Equation (3.17) by

$$
\begin{aligned}
p\left(\mathbf{x}_{t+1}, k | \mathbf{e}_{1:t+1}\right) &\approx w_{t+1}^{(k)} \delta\left(\mathbf{x}_{t+1} = \mathbf{x}_{t+1}^{(k)}\right) \\
&\propto \left[w_t^{(k)} p\left(\mathbf{e}_{t+1} | \mathbf{x}_t^{(k)}\right)\right] \delta\left(\mathbf{x}_{t+1} = \mathbf{x}_{t+1}^{(k)}\right) \\
&= \left[w_t^{(k)} \int p\left(\mathbf{e}_{t+1} | \mathbf{x}_{t+1}\right) p\left(\mathbf{x}_{t+1} | \mathbf{x}_t^{(k)}\right) d\mathbf{x}_{t+1}\right] \delta\left(\mathbf{x}_{t+1} = \mathbf{x}_{t+1}^{(k)}\right).
\end{aligned}
\tag{3.20}
$$

The part of the right-hand side term in square brackets describes $p\left(k | \mathbf{e}_{1:t+1}\right)$ and can usually not be evaluated exactly. Thus a *simulation step* was included to approximate it.

This step includes 1.) the selection of a characterizing value $\mu_{t+1}^{(k)}$ from distribution $p\left(\mathbf{x}_{t+1} | \mathbf{x}_t^{(k)}\right)$ (e.g., mean or expectation were suggested as appropriate values in literature), and 2.) the computation of the simulation weight $\lambda_t^{(k)}$ for $k$ using

$$
\lambda_t^{(k)} \propto \frac{w_t^{(k)} p\left(\mathbf{e}_{t+1} | \mu_{t+1}^{(k)}\right)}{\sum_{i=1}^N w_t^{(i)} p\left(\mathbf{e}_{t+1} | \mu_{t+1}^{(i)}\right)}.
\tag{3.21}
$$

Using these weights the joint idf can be put as

$$
q\left(\mathbf{x}_{t+1}, k | \mathbf{e}_{1:t+1}\right) = \lambda_t^{(k)} q\left(\mathbf{x}_{t+1} | \mathbf{x}_t^{(k)}, \mathbf{e}_{t+1}\right),
\tag{3.22}
$$

and thus, samples are obtained by $\mathbf{x}_{t+1}^{(i)} \sim \sum_{k=1}^N \lambda_t^{(k)} q\left(\mathbf{x}_{t+1} | \mathbf{x}_t^{(k)}, \mathbf{e}_{t+1}\right)$ so that the weighting procedure can be given recursively by

$$
w_{t+1}^{(i)} \propto \frac{\sum_{k=1}^N w_t^{(k)^{(i)}} p\left(\mathbf{e}_{t+1} | \mathbf{x}_{t+1}^{(i)}\right) p\left(\mathbf{x}_{t+1}^{(i)} | \mathbf{x}_t^{(k)^{(i)}}\right)}{\sum_{k=1}^N \lambda_t^{(k)^{(i)}} q\left(\mathbf{x}_{t+1}^{(i)} | \mathbf{x}_t^{(k)^{(i)}}, \mathbf{e}_{t+1}\right)}.
\tag{3.23}
$$

Besides these approaches and the RPF other widely known methods exist (e.g., see Doucet et al. 2000a; van der Merwe et al. 2000), and various slightly different particle filter algorithms were introduced recently (e.g., see Klaas et al. 2005; Saboune and Charpillet 2005). But those (including RPF) were not incorporated into the tools of the experimental infrastructure yet. Hence, these approaches are not an object of this work.

The next section describes the tools and experimental infrastructure just mentioned which were developed to enable evaluating experiments on the proposed concept.

### 3.5.4 Core Tools and Team Intention Tracker

As mentioned earlier one aim of this work, besides the conceptual part, was to provide tools and an experimental infrastructure, which on the one hand enable rapid development and evaluation of different models, model parameters, or algorithms and on the other hand fit into the ECO framework mentioned in Section 3.2.2. This section gives insight into the *Intention Analyzer* component (cp., with Figure 3.2) that was developed to achieve this objective. First, requirements are deduced from the identified constraints and the consequent architecture for this component is explained. And subsequent to this projecting section, two major modules, namely *Core Tools* and *Team Intention Tracker*, are described in more detail.

**Requirements and Architecture**

Chiefly, three aspects influenced requirements for the Intention Analyzer component. The rather commonplace need is that the component must fit into a framework, in this case the ECO framework. Therefore, it is required that communication channels demanded for ECO framework components must be implemented within the Intention Analyzer.

In principle the ECO framework's communication channels provide all required data for team intention inference (i.e., team members' positions and preliminary meeting agenda). But at the same time the Intention Analyzer component should function as an experimental infrastructure, where the inference process for different models and model parameters respectively can be tested and evaluated. Obviously, an adequate architecture addressing such a requirement should facilitate a rather simple replacement of the Team Intention Model and must allow direct tapping and inserting of data in virtually every stage of the inference pipeline.

Figure 3.12 shows the architecture of the Intention Analyzer component. The core of the component consists of four modules, namely an *Adapter*, the *Learner*, the *Filter*, and the *Team DBN* plugin. These modules form a pipeline that channels the inference process. First, the Adapter module reads available sensor observations (i.e., a position update of a particular team member) and wraps it into a specific team observation message. Then, the Filter module uses this message to update the posterior pdf for the connected model. Computations of the Filter module are influenced by its customization through the Team DBN plugin module and its associated parameter sets. The message is extended to hold the posterior pdf of the current model state and, then, piped to the *Team Intention Tracker* module. This module includes a

*The Team Intention Model Approach*

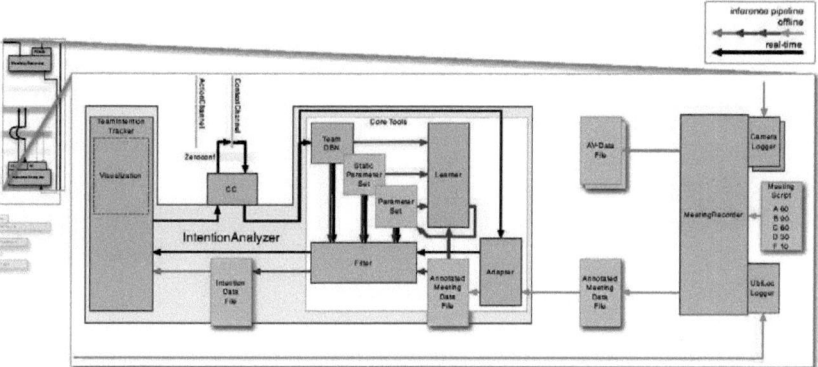

Figure 3.12: Experimental infrastructure. This enlargement of a part of Figure 3.2 shows the Meeting Recorder component on the right and the architecture of the Intention Analyzer component on the left, where beige boxes indicate modules of the Intention Analyzer and gray boxes depict observed and processed data files as well as configuration files. The arrows represent the data flow through the inference process, where black arrows show the real-time inference pipeline and colored arrows stand for the offline mode.

visualization engine. So it can either visualize probability distributions of team and user intentions that are encoded in the posterior pdf, or it only broadcasts the most probable team intention over the context channel. This procedure describes the *real-time* inference process and can be comprehended in Figure 3.12 by following the black arrows from the lower left to the context channel.

The Learner module is used by the *offline* inference pipeline. The offline mode[9] is intended to record meetings (scripted as well as in situ) in order to 1.) learn optimal parameter settings for a model, or 2.) evaluate different models and model parameters. Note that learning in this context does not mean that the real-time mode cannot be done without a trained parameter setting. Quite the contrary, the Intention Analyzer can start directly with an training-free prior knowledge-based parameter set and the Learner module provides an additional chance to refine these a-priori parameters.

Therefore, a *Meeting Recorder* component enables the recording of available sensor data. Additionally, tracking of the intention truth is available in cases of scripted meetings (orange arrows). Then, after transformation into team observation messages the recorded meeting data can be used by the Learner module to adjust model parameters (red arrows). Finally,

---

[9]In Figure 3.12 offline mode is indicated by the colored arrow starting with orange via red and blue to green.

123

the Filter module uses the same data to compute the posterior pdf for the connected model (blue arrows). The final data set can be evaluated by standard tools to compare expediences of certain models and model parameters (green arrow).

The next two sections describe the modules used during the inference process a bit more detailed, list their features, and explain the usage of each module. Further it is shown how to encode the Team DBN and how to read the visualization of Team Intention Tracker.

**Core Tools**

The Adapter, Filter, and Learner modules are stand-alone command-line tools subsumed under the term *Core Tools*. The Team DBN and its parameter sets are linked to the modules at runtime. The Adapter module is a flexible converter that reads in sensor data either from a data file recorded by the Meeting Recorder component or from the context channel, which holds the position information that was provided by the LocationService (cp., with Figure 3.2). This module provides various options to prepare data for a filtering or learning process[10].

One sort of options enables the Adapter module to eliminate several sorts of data entries from the conversion. User positions outside of a bounding box can be skipped ('-b' option) as well as data observed during the first $s$ seconds ('-f <s>' option) or data that arrives after a certain point of time $s$ ('-p <s>' option). Additionally, it is possible to erase truth data entries (i.e., 'i <time> <state> <action>' records) from files recorded by the Meeting Recorder component using a predefined Meeting Script. Then, the Adapter module provides a few mapping options, where e.g., the different tag identifications a server might produce can be mapped explicitly to internal indices ('-l <nr>=<id>' option). Furthermore some switching options cause minor changes to the output of Adapter module.

The Filter module gets its data either from a file or from a direct coupling with the Adapter module via a (network) socket. In order to use the Filter module, some options are mandatory. These options are used to define the model and model parameters utilized by the Filter module[11]. The '-X <dir>' option provides the Filter module with a location where the source of the desired model can be found and related executables can be put. The '-M <name>' option specifies the name of the desired model's main source file and the '-P <name>' option refers to the name of a file containing the corresponding parameter set.

---

[10]The interface of the Adapter module is shown by its usage listing in Figure A.1.
[11]The usage listing for the Filter module is shown in Figure A.2.

The other options can be divided into two categories, options that change default settings of the Filter module and options that route the different kinds of statistical output data. Options changing particle filter settings include capabilities to change the number of particles used in the filter (the '-n <np>' option), the resampling threshold (the '-r <thr>' option), the minimal particle weight threshold (the '- b <num>' option), and the relative weighting of sensor data (the '-a <num>' option). Further, it is possible to change the default inference mode of the Filter module by the '-f <mode>' option. Besides real-time forward filtering (the 'forward' mode), one can select offline 'viterbi' mode to get the most probable state sequence given a full observation data sequence (i.e., MAP explanation), or offline 'smoothing' mode to get a smoothed probability distribution for a particular state given an observation sequence (i.e, fixed lag smoothing or fixed interval smoothing respectively).

Output routing options contain abilities to dump full particle data (the '-d <path>' option) or just intention votes (the '-v <path>' option), to collect effective particle statistics (the '-e <path>' option), to list filter parameters (the '-l' option), and to save sensor data (the '-s <path>' option).

The Learner module provides in principle similar options as the Filter module[12]. The Learner modules provides the same capital letter options to specify the desired model and model parameters. Likewise output routing options and options changing particle filter settings built into the Learner module are a subset of the options that the Filter module makes available. Unique additional options in the Learner module are related to its iterative character. So the number of learning cycle iterations can be specified (the '-i <nr>' option) and intermediate statistic parameters for each cycle can be collected using the '-s <path>' option.

Besides Adapter, Filter and Learner module at least one model must be specified as part of the Core Tools. As mentioned above the model is provided as source code and then compiled and linked into the particular module at runtime. Listing 3.1 shows essential parts of the $C++$ style model definition, here the proposed Team DBN for the scenario specified in Section 3.2.1. The $C++$ template approach chosen for the implementation of the modules was mainly selected for performance reasons. As each particle of the particle filter that is utilized for inference includes an instance of the whole Team DBN, a large amount of data must be processed by the modules with every single time step, and the realized $C++$ solution is optimized for speed.

The basic DBN structure for the Team DBN case is always the same and hence can be included

---

[12]The Learner module's usage listing is depicted in Figure A.3.

Listing 3.1: Excerpt of the *C++* style model definition of Team DBN for the specified scenario.

```cpp
//*****
//*   model.cpp
//*****
...
//***** BASIC DBN STRUCTURE
#include "AgendaTeamDBN.h"
...
//***** TEAM SIZE
#define TSS 3

//***** AVAILABLE TEAM ACTIVITIES AND TITLES
typedef enum TeamAction {PresentA, PresentB, PresentC, Discuss, Exit, MaxTeamAction};
char *actnames[MaxTeamAction+1] =
          {"Present A", "Present B", "Present C", "Discussion", "Exit", "Wander"};

//***** DETERMINISTIC MAPPING OF TEAM ACTIVITIES TO USER ACTION SEQUENCES
template<bool B, int TSize, typename TeamState, typename TeamAction, TeamState MaxTeamState,
    TeamAction MaxTeamAction, int NumAgendaItems> TeamGoal<TSize>
    AgendaTeam<B, TSize, TeamState, TeamAction, MaxTeamState, MaxTeamAction, NumAgendaItems>
    ::preparegoals[MaxTeamAction] = {
          {Goal(Astage), Goal(Bseat), Goal(Cseat)},     // Present A: Goto
          {Goal(Aseat), Goal(Bstage), Goal(Cseat)},     // Present B: Goto
          {Goal(Aseat), Goal(Bseat), Goal(Cstage)},     // Present C: Goto
          {Goal(Aseat), Goal(Bseat), Goal(Cseat)},      // Discussion: Goto
          {Goal(TheDoor), Goal(TheDoor), Goal(TheDoor)} // Exit: Goto
    };
template<bool B, int TSize, typename TeamState, typename TeamAction, TeamState MaxTeamState,
    TeamAction MaxTeamAction, int NumAgendaItems> TeamGoal<TSize>
    AgendaTeam<B, TSize, TeamState, TeamAction, MaxTeamState, MaxTeamAction, NumAgendaItems>
    ::performgoals[MaxTeamAction] = {
          {Goal(Atime), Goal(), Goal()},                // Present A: Present + Listen
          {Goal(), Goal(Btime), Goal()},                // Present A: Present + Listen
          {Goal(), Goal(), Goal(Ctime)},                // Present A: Present + Listen
          {Goal(Dtime), Goal(Dtime), Goal(Dtime)},      // Discussion: Debate
          {Goal(), Goal(), Goal()}                      // Exit: Finish
    };

//***** AGENDA DEFINITION
template<bool B, int TSize, typename TeamState, typename TeamAction, TeamState MaxTeamState,
    TeamAction MaxTeamAction, int NumAgendaItems> TeamAction
    AgendaTeam<B, TSize, TeamState, TeamAction, MaxTeamState, MaxTeamAction, NumAgendaItems>
    ::actionmap[] =
#if USE_AGENDA
          {PresentA, PresentB, PresentC, Discuss, Exit};
const int AGENDA_ITEMS = 5;
#else
          {Exit};
const int AGENDA_ITEMS = 0;
#endif
...
//***** TRACKER PARAMETERS
//**    MARKOV MODEL
//*       PRIOR PROBABILITIES - {Preparing, Acting, Wandering, Wrapup}
double teamInitial[MaxTeamState] = {0.6, 0.0, 0.4, 0.0};
//*       TRANSITION PROBABILITIES
double teamTransit[MaxTeamState][MaxTeamState] = {
          {0.0, 1.0, 0.0, 0.0},                         // from Preparing
          {0.6, 0.0, 0.4, 0.0},                         // from Acting
          {0.0, 0.0, 0.4, 0.6},                         // from Wandering
          {1.0, 0.0, 0.0, 0.0},                         // from Wrapup
    };
template<> MarkovPDF<MaxTeamState>
    AgendaTeam<false, TSS, TeamState, TeamAction, MaxTeamState, MaxTeamAction, AGENDA_ITEMS>
    ::mm(teamInitial, teamTransit);
//**    PROBABILITY THAT THE TEAM WILL FOLLOW THE AGENDA
template<> AgendaPDF
    AgendaTeam<false, TSS, TeamState, TeamAction, MaxTeamState, MaxTeamAction, AGENDA_ITEMS>
    ::agenda(0.8);
```

from elsewhere. So, in a typical file just those parts of the model must be specified that are subject to regular change. Obviously, these include the team size and a set of the possible team activities that the inference process should be able to distinguish. Further, such a file has to define how the team activities can be brought into relation to individual user roles and action sequences. In case of Listing 3.1 team intentions are mapped deterministically to two-stage *prepare-perform*-sequences of user actions for each team member. Here, with a preparing action a user attempts to achieve his goal to bring himself into the appropriate position for his performance. Afterwards he aims at acting for a certain amount of time to achieve the performing goal.

Moreover the model file must contain an agenda. The agenda definition is basically a list containing a sequence of team activities. In addition, a set of tracker parameters must be specified, namely the prior and transition probabilities for the Markov model and a value for the probability that the team will follow its preliminary agenda during the course of the meeting. As described above these parameters can be changed via command-line options of Filter or Learner module respectively.

**Team Intention Tracker**

The Team Intention Tracker module was developed for two purposes. First, it is used by the Intention Analyzer component of the ECO framework to get a reliable estimation of the current team intention. The Intention Analyzer, then, provides this estimation via the ECO Context Channel to appliances of my department's prototype smart meeting room ensemble (cp. with Figures 1.1 & 3.1). Different research approaches rely on this context information, e.g., the team intention is used for a computer controlled multi-display environment (Heider, 2006; Heider et al., 2006) as well as light and air condition control.

The second purpose of the Team Intention Tracker is the realtime visualization of the actual inference process. The GUI that encloses a set of important statistics is shown in Figure 3.13. The large area named *Bird View* on the left side of the screenshot depicts our smart meeting room as a schematic 2D-map. It shows one possible room topology – adequate for the meeting scenario described in Section 3.2.1. Dark grey and black areas represent obstacles, e.g., walls or furniture like chairs and tables. Furthermore, this area pictures the location estimates of the particle filter for each team member. The location estimates are drawn as a curve of the last ten estimation updates. A longer tail indicates a faster moving. The color encoding represents

*Chapter 3*

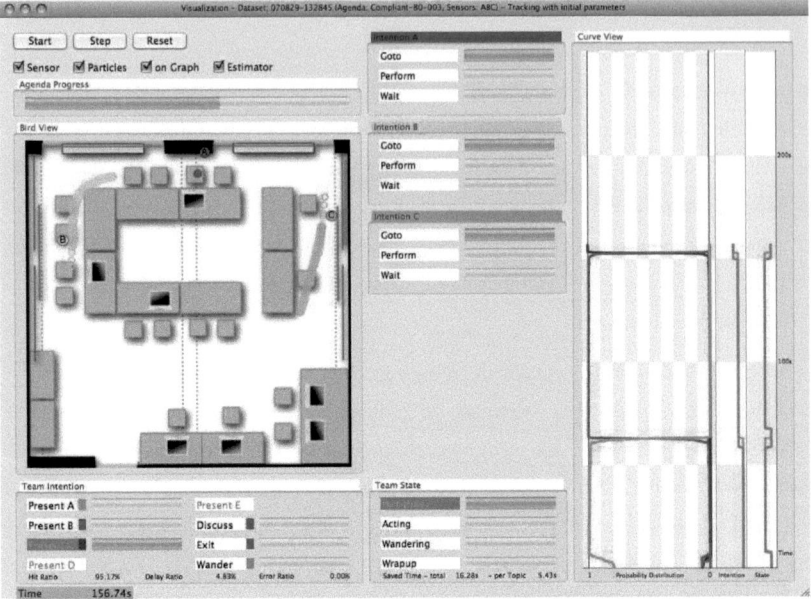

Figure 3.13: Team Intention Tracker visualization.

the affiliation to a particular team member. The actual sensor observation for the same person is depicted as a black contoured labeled circle filled with the same color as the estimation tail. Finally, the remaining particles are drawn using a transparency value proportional to the number of particles used by the particle filter. This makes accumulations of particles more noticeable than single occurrences. Note that if graph-based probabilistic location estimation is used all particles are located on an invisible graph (cp., with Figure 3.7).

In the lower part of Figure 3.13 two areas, named *Team Intention* and *Team State*, depict the probability distributions for the current team intention. The Team Intention area holds the possible high-level team activities. The level meters indicate how the particles' opinions about the current team intention are distributed. High-level team activities break down into a sequence of atomic team actions. The distribution of currently inferred team actions is encoded in the level meters of the Team State area. Finally, the visualization shows the probability distributions of associated user actions for team members A, B and C in the center of Figure 3.13. In the situation shown the currently inferred team intention is Present C. The team members are currently in Preparing state and thus user C is on his way to the presenting

## The Team Intention Model Approach

stage while user B walks back to take a seat to listen. Accordingly, the assigned user action is Goto for all team members[13].

Based on the team objective inferred, a room as my department's prototype smart meeting room may automatically configure itself to support this goal (e.g., the current speaker's presentation is mapped to one of the displays and the lighting is adjusted). In the shown case a rather rigid model was used, i.e., the state transition probabilities of the Markov model (cp., with Figure 3.6) represent a strong probability that the team will follow the agenda.

Those team activity that is deduced from particles as the estimate is highlighted in the Team Intention area by a green label. Analogously the estimated action appears with green label in the Team State area. If corresponding truth data is available, then truth is represented by a red label background for the respective activity or action. Colors used for truth and estimate labeling and those that are assigned to each activated activity recur in the *Curve View* area on the right side of Figure 3.13. This area shows how the posterior probability distribution of the system develops over time and draws true and estimated team activities and actions for every single time step.

Rough statistics about the congruity of truth and estimate in percentages and seconds is given by the *Hit Ratio*, the *Delay Ratio*, the *Error Ratio*, and in total as well as per topic the *Saved Time* values in the lower part of Figure 3.13. The Hit Ratio counts the rate of time in percentage that truth and estimate are equal. The remaining time divides into delay (i.e., the rate of time that the estimation needs to recognize new intentions) and error (i.e., the rate of time that a wrong intention is estimated). These rates are represented by the Delay Ratio and the Error Ratio respectively.

The Saved Time values count the amount of time that an inferred team intention is recognized in advance of the actual performing action of that team activity. One sums up the seconds to a total amount of saved time and one averages the time by the number of agenda topics. Note that this Saved Time value is interesting, because it would enable a smart meeting room to plan and perform strategies for the team assistance before the performing stage was reached by the team itself.

---

[13] Even A gets a Goto assigned. But as he is obviously arrived at his target location he is already done with the Preparing activity and waits to get a new activity assigned.

## 3.6 Summary

The current chapter proposed the concept of a team intention analysis system. Based on a concrete scenario and the concrete lab situation criteria for the modeling approach were revised in order to allow robust inference of team activities in real smart meeting environments. Then the procedure was explained that enables flexible structuring of team intentions for agenda-driven meeting situations. All of this was incorporated into the general design of the Team DBN. Afterwards the chapter outlined an approach for model generation and elaborated on the inference processes used with the concrete model. It provided a proof of concept for the proposed Team DBN by sketching an architecture for an implementation. The implementation of the proposed concept was on the one hand integrated in the ECO framework and on the other hand designed to serve simultaneously as a stand-alone experimental infrastructure. Finally, the usage of the implementation's components and modules was clarified. Now that the proof of concept for the Team DBN is given, the next chapter addresses the question how valuable this concept is.

# Chapter 4

# Experiments and Conclusions

## 4.1 Introduction

This final chapter substantiates my concept for a robust and training-free probabilistic system for real-time intention analysis in teams. Therefore, two experiments are introduced that utilize the particular Team DBN within the experimental infrastructure mentioned in the previous section. In the first instance a simulation study based on an early version of the Intention Analyzer was developed. Then, after a phase of redesign a second in situ study was performed in my department's prototype SmartApplianceLab with a group of volunteers. This chapter describes the study methodologies and discusses results of both experiments in separate sections. Finally it summarizes this work and draws the conclusions from it.

## 4.2 Experiment #1: Simulation Study

The first experiment that was conducted with the proposed Team DBN studies whether incomplete, unreliable, and hence sometimes misleading knowledge about the needs of a team of users (i.e., a preliminary agenda) can be used to improve the quality of intention recognition. Specifically, attention is focused on the usefulness of an unreliable agenda for improving the recognition of team activities during a meeting. Before the results of this first exploration are presented, the next part first explains the overall setup of the simulation experiment, namely questioning, procedure, and particular tools used. Afterwards follows an analysis of the findings.

## 4.2.1 Study Methodology

The simulation study that based on the Bayesian filtering approach and an early version of the explicit probabilistic team behavior model described in the previous chapter was carried out to find answers to the following questions:

- How accurate and how fast can cooperative behavior of a team be predicted with an agenda assumption and history knowledge?

- What influence do deviations of the team from the planned agenda assumption have on the prediction quality, i.e., does a wrong a-priori agenda degrade the quality of intention recognition?

- When does an explicit agenda improve prediction quality, and where are the drawbacks?

- How flexible does an agenda assumption need to be in order to optimally predict team behavior?

In the early stages of work when this experiment took place a simulation of data was chosen over real world data. This enabled a configuration of the simulated sensor model's parameters, such that different probability distributions of sensor readings could be examined. The setting includes Gaussian and Cauchy distributed sensor readings with a variety of different parameter sets to study the influence of the sensor model on the prediction quality.

As the aim of the experiments in this chapter is to analyze my approach of agenda-supported team intention recognition the basis for all evaluations is the scenario given in Section 3.2.1 of a staged meeting, where users will adopt different roles within the team. In the meeting that was described there, someone who is actually involved[1], will adopt both listener role and speaker role during the course of the track. If the team wants a certain team member to give a presentation he will adopt the objective to go to the presentation stage. Otherwise he will sit in the circle of attendees and listen. The drawing in the upper-left quarter of Figure 4.1 shows a snapshot of such a situation.

It is common sense that meetings should have structure or agendas in order to be effective (e.g., Carnes, 1980). However, meeting attendees usually follow these a-priori agendas in a more or less reliable manner only. Nevertheless these agendas obviously denote the prior

---
[1] Involvement of a person is easily derived from an agenda.

*Experiments and Conclusions*

hints about the intention of the team and the course of the event. As already mentioned in Section 3.4.2, due to the straight relation between team and user intentions, in reality the staged meeting scenario enables a deterministic assignment of user actions to team activities. Remember that this simplifying assumption is incorporated into the Team DBN. Thus, the use of the proposed Team DBN combined with location and motion observations from simulated sensors provides excellent information for inference of team intentions.

**Experimental Design**

Obviously, agenda information should improve the quality of team intention recognition if a team follows its agenda. However, as soon as a team deviates from the a-priori agenda, recognition quality may drop. The recognizer may draw wrong conclusions from misleading a-priori information that potentially defeat the expected benefit completely. The objective of this first evaluation is to investigate whether a-priori agenda information can be used to improve recognition quality in case the team complies to a certain agenda, **without** sacrificing recognition quality in the case of non-compliance with that agenda.

The main interest of this first experiment is shown in two questions:

- How **reliable** is agenda-based team intention recognition in case of compliance and non-compliance, compared to an agenda-free team activity tracking?

- How **fast** will an agenda-based team intention recognizer identify a change in the team objective (Again, in relation to agenda-free team activity tracking for compliant and non-compliant teams)?

So to assess the usefulness of this work's approach using a probabilistic behavior model that incorporates agenda and history knowledge, a simulation experiment series was set up to answer these questions. The answers, then, enable a statement about how *rigid* an agenda assumption must be to optimally predict team activities (at least for the staged meeting scenario), where rigid means that the state transition probabilities of the Markov model (cp., with Figure 3.6) represent a high probability that the team will follow the agenda.

For this experiment three different meeting sequence truths (one compliant, two non-compliant) were chosen to analyze the effect of an agenda on reliability and speed of intention recognition in case of compliance and non-compliance. First, it is assumed that the users

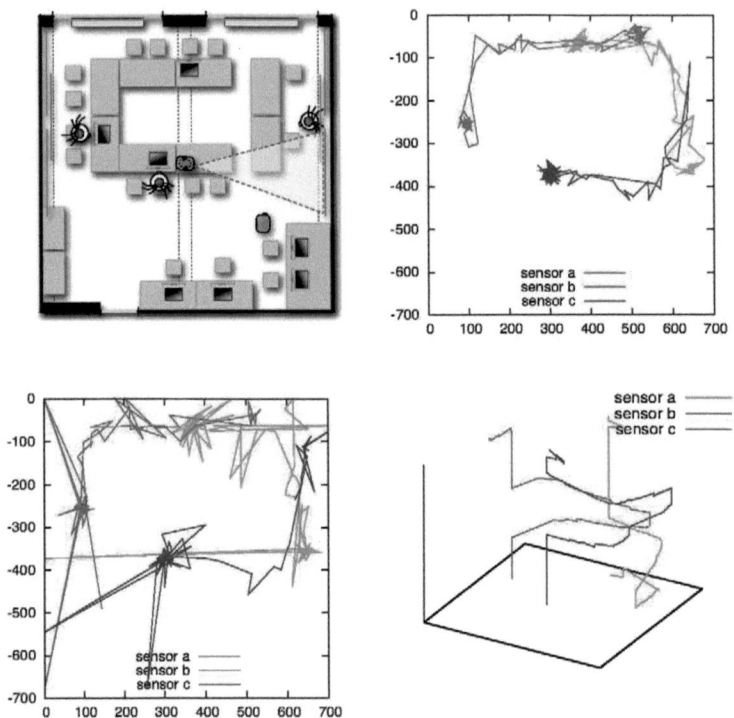

Figure 4.1: Experimental setup: Snapshot from the staged meeting scenario (upper-left); Spatial distributions of sensor readings of a $\langle A, B, C, D \rangle$ sequence with Gaussian ($\mathcal{N}$, upper-right) and Cauchy ($\mathcal{C}$, lower-left) sensor model with parameters: delay 0.15, error 15.0; Temporal distribution for the simulated truths (lower-right), where notable spots with long residence times are places as seats and presenting stages.

follow the agenda and deliver their contributions in the sequence $\langle A, B, C, D \rangle$. In the second version the sequence is slightly changed where user C presents before B $\langle A, C, B, D \rangle$. And a third course is the reverse sequence $\langle C, B, A, D \rangle$.

Further four different parameter settings were used for the sensor model. In two settings the sensor data was simulated to be Gaussian ($\mathcal{N}$) distributed. In the two other settings sensor data was generated to follow the Cauchy ($\mathcal{C}$) distribution. The settings for each distribution differed in delay between consecutive sensor readings and sensor error. Figure 4.1 shows typical simulation data sets generated from these sensor models. Simulation changed with the modification of the sensor model parameters. Gaussian distributed sensor data is closer to the

Table 4.1: Summary of experimental design: 12 different truth sequences, 4 different tracker configurations, 6 runs in any combination, 288 simulation data logs.

---

A-priori agenda:

($P_{follow}$ = probability that the team will choose the next objective on the agenda)

($n$ = number of agenda items)

We tested three tracker models $T_{P_{follow}}$ with different agenda strengths. Probabilities used for $P_{follow}$ are $\{0.6, 0.8, 0.95\}$.

$$T_{P_{follow}} = P(\xi'|\xi) = \begin{cases} P_{follow} & \text{if } \xi' \text{is next agenda item after } \xi \\ \frac{(1-P_{follow})}{n-1} & \text{otherwise} \end{cases}$$

We compared these to the tracker model $T_{uniform}$ without any agenda information.

$$T_{uniform} = P(\xi'|\xi) = \frac{1}{n}$$

3 different truth agendas:   4 different truth sensor models (columns):

$\langle A, B, C, D \rangle$,
$\langle A, C, B, D \rangle$,
and $\langle C, B, A, D \rangle$

| $\mathcal{N}$ | | $\mathcal{C}$ | | |
|---|---|---|---|---|
| 0.15 | 0.25 | 0.15 | 0.25 | sensor delay |
| 15.0 | 30.0 | 5.0 | 10.0 | sensor error |

---

real path of the user as shown in the lower right quarter of Figure 4.1, but the Cauchy model relates closer to the real sensor data provided by the Ubisense Platform UWB positioning system of my department's prototype smart meeting room.

Finally, four different models for a-priori agenda information were used for the evaluation of recognition accuracy: a random model, where every activity has the same probability and the history is not tracked, and three models that correspond to the model in Figure 3.6 with different probabilities that the users will follow their a-priori agenda $\{0.6, 0.8, 0.95\}$. For every tracker model six filter runs with 5.000 particles were logged. Table 4.1 provides an overview of the entire setup.

### 4.2.2 Results

The illustrations of two typical representatives of model $T_{.8}$ and model $T_{uniform}$ simulation runs in Figure 4.2 show that the main uncertainty about the teams objective prevails during

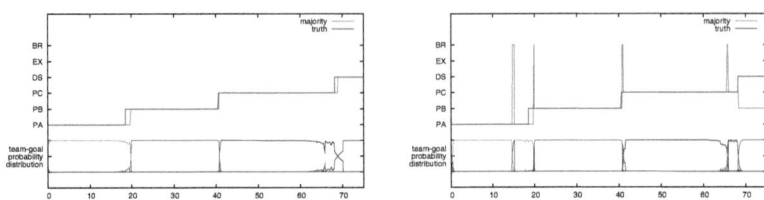

Figure 4.2: Inference of a $\langle A, B, C, D \rangle$ truth from Cauchy distributed sensor data (delay 0.25, error 10.0) with the trackers $T_{.8}$ (left) and $T_{uniform}$ (right).

the phase of an objective shift. The left picture shows the advantage of agenda knowledge. For instance the objective shift from user B presents (PB) to C presents (PC) around time slice 40 is recognized faster and more reliable than in the right picture. Further it shows that agenda knowledge leads to less misinterpretation of sensor readings. Thus the overall error rate shrinks.

Figure 4.3 shows two cases where actual team behavior is non-compliant to the a-priori agenda $\langle A, B, C, D \rangle$. The true course of the meeting is the reverse agenda $\langle C, B, A, D \rangle$. The comparsion of the depicted representatives of model $T_{.8}$ and model $T_{uniform}$ tracking runs show that despite an outlier the overall inference accuracy and speed using the agenda-driven model looks very reasonable. Comparing these particular two examples, the inference of the model with the misleading agenda does indeed even better than the agenda-free model. Obviously already the information which agenda items are about to appear and what the team has done so far is some practical knowledge for the inference of the next team intention. This information is not available from an agenda-free random model, whereby its inference accuracy suffers.

The average results over the 6 simulation runs for the 48 different parameter settings (12

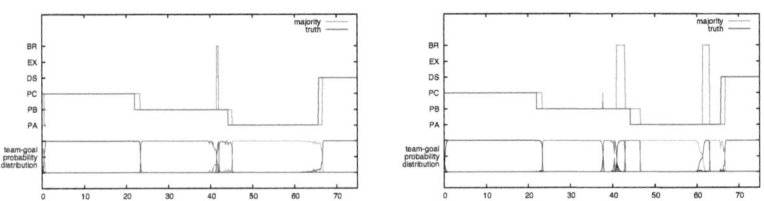

Figure 4.3: Inference of the non-compliant truth $\langle C, B, A, D \rangle$ from Cauchy distributed sensor data (delay 0.25, error 10.0) with the trackers $T_{.8}$ (left) and $T_{uniform}$ (right).

Experiments and Conclusions

Table 4.2: Average accuracy: where the rows hold the targets that the trackers $T_{.6}$, $T_{.8}$, $T_{.95}$ and $T_{uniform}$ had to predict. The accuracy values are averaged over the six runs each. $T_{.8}$ improves accuracy about 10% over $T_{uniform}$.

|  |  |  |  | $T_{.6}$ | $T_{.8}$ | $T_{.95}$ | $T_{uniform}$ |
|---|---|---|---|---|---|---|---|
| ⟨A, B, C, D⟩ | $\mathcal{N}$ | 0.15 | 15.0 | 91.657 | 91.853 | 84.620 | 75.163 |
|  |  | 0.25 | 30.0 | 90.745 | 89.812 | 90.278 | 83.867 |
|  | $\mathcal{C}$ | 0.15 | 5.0 | 96.893 | 96.893 | 96.847 | 95.740 |
|  |  | 0.25 | 10.0 | 97.045 | 96.983 | 97.202 | 89.903 |
| ⟨A, C, B, D⟩ | $\mathcal{N}$ | 0.15 | 15.0 | 96.118 | 95.917 | 95.918 | 94.453 |
|  |  | 0.25 | 30.0 | 84.198 | 82.645 | 81.935 | 79.362 |
|  | $\mathcal{C}$ | 0.15 | 5.0 | 93.075 | 93.055 | 95.583 | 80.937 |
|  |  | 0.25 | 10.0 | 89.283 | 89.258 | 70.993 | 75.922 |
| ⟨C, B, A, D⟩ | $\mathcal{N}$ | 0.15 | 15.0 | 88.700 | 88.837 | 86.618 | 73.368 |
|  |  | 0.25 | 30.0 | 76.743 | 87.440 | 73.260 | 84.685 |
|  | $\mathcal{C}$ | 0.15 | 5.0 | 88.105 | 88.372 | 78.673 | 83.888 |
|  |  | 0.25 | 10.0 | 90.857 | 92.988 | 83.687 | 79.915 |
| all agendas | $\mathcal{N}$ | 0.15 | 15.0 | **92.158** | **92.202** | **89.052** | **80.995** |
|  |  | 0.25 | 30.0 | **83.895** | **86.632** | **81.824** | **82.638** |
|  | $\mathcal{C}$ | 0.15 | 5.0 | **92.691** | **92.773** | **90.368** | **86.855** |
|  |  | 0.25 | 10.0 | **92.395** | **93.046** | **83.961** | **81.913** |
| average accuracy over all takes |  |  |  | 90.285 | 91.163 | 86.301 | 83.100 |

sensor model parameters × 4 tracker parameters) are shown in Tables 4.2 & 4.3. Here, Table 4.2 gives the team intention recognition reliability (in % correct). Therefore accuracy is measured by the percentage of time where the team intentions recognized by the trackers equal those team activities given by the simulated truth sequences. The average delay between true objective shifts of the team (i.e., where a team starts with preparing a new activity) and the trackers' recognitions of these shifts is given in Table 4.3 (in seconds $s$ behind true shift).

The comparison of the reliability values for $T_{.8}$ and $T_{uniform}$ gives the most important result of this first study:

> It is possible to improve the recognition accuracy for the compliant case by using an agenda, **without** sacrificing recognition accuracy for the non-compliant case.

Therefore, it always pays to include available a-priori agenda information into the recognition

137

Table 4.3: Average delay: where the rows hold the targets that the trackers $T_{.8}$ and $T_{uniform}$ had to predict. The time values in seconds are averaged over the six runs each. $T_{.8}$ recognizes ca 33% faster then $T_{uniform}$.

| | | | | $T_{.8}$ | | | | $T_{uniform}$ | | | |
|---|---|---|---|---|---|---|---|---|---|---|---|
| ⟨A,B,C,D⟩ | $\mathcal{N}$ | 0.15 | 15.0 | 0.00 | 4.20 | 0.30 | 1.57 | 0.08 | 4.20 | 0.40 | 13.98 |
| | | 0.25 | 30.0 | 0.00 | 2.50 | 1.32 | 0.00 | 0.20 | 2.50 | 3.13 | 0.20 |
| | $\mathcal{E}$ | 0.15 | 5.0 | 0.00 | 0.10 | 0.90 | 1.33 | 0.07 | 0.33 | 0.92 | 1.52 |
| | | 0.25 | 10.0 | 0.00 | 1.30 | 0.20 | 0.80 | 0.08 | 1.40 | 0.38 | 4.65 |
| ⟨A,C,B,D⟩ | $\mathcal{N}$ | 0.15 | 15.0 | 0.00 | 0.72 | 0.47 | 2.00 | 0.37 | 0.80 | 0.55 | 2.00 |
| | | 0.25 | 30.0 | 0.00 | 1.27 | 0.85 | 10.03 | 0.42 | 1.38 | 1.77 | 11.70 |
| | $\mathcal{E}$ | 0.15 | 5.0 | 0.00 | 2.17 | 1.00 | 0.48 | 0.00 | 0.23 | 1.00 | 7.60 |
| | | 0.25 | 10.0 | 0.00 | 5.65 | 1.05 | 1.38 | 0.00 | 5.68 | 1.22 | 11.15 |
| ⟨C,B,A,D⟩ | $\mathcal{N}$ | 0.15 | 15.0 | 0.60 | 1.00 | 1.50 | 4.80 | 0.50 | 1.00 | 1.50 | 15.13 |
| | | 0.25 | 30.0 | 0.4 | 5.60 | 1.90 | 0.90 | 0.17 | 5.73 | 2.83 | 1.08 |
| | $\mathcal{E}$ | 0.15 | 5.0 | 0.20 | 0.90 | 5.50 | 2.10 | 0.15 | 0.92 | 8.80 | 2.33 |
| | | 0.25 | 10.0 | 0.55 | 1.45 | 1.52 | 0.90 | 0.03 | 1.43 | 6.33 | 3.57 |
| all | $\mathcal{N}$ | 0.15 | 15.0 | 0.20 | 1.97 | 0.76 | 8.37 | 0.32 | 2.00 | 0.82 | 10.37 |
| agendas | | 0.25 | 30.0 | 0.13 | 3.12 | 1.36 | 3.64 | 0.26 | 3.20 | 2.58 | 4.33 |
| | $\mathcal{E}$ | 0.15 | 5.0 | 0.07 | 1.06 | 2.47 | 1.30 | 0.07 | 0.49 | 3.57 | 3.82 |
| | | 0.25 | 10.0 | 0.18 | 2.80 | 0.92 | 1.03 | 0.04 | 2.84 | 2.64 | 6.46 |
| average delay over all takes | | | | 0.15 | 2.24 | 1.38 | 3.59 | 0.17 | 2.13 | 2.40 | 6.25 |
| | | | | | Σ | 7.36 | | | Σ | 10.95 | |

system, even if the correlation between the agenda sequence and the true activity sequence is not very strong in every case. Consider that inference with an agenda-free model tends to select agenda items plurally on a random basis. This is prevented by agenda-based models with inherent history tracking.

However, as can be seen by comparing the results of the agenda-driven models $T_{.6}$, $T_{.8}$, and $T_{.95}$, it is important to assign a suitable probability to the agenda's preferred sequence. On the one hand, if this value is too high (e.g., .95), then the agenda becomes too rigid. Thus, the system will tend to assume that the team follows the agenda, even if the observation data from the sensors tell a different story. On the other hand, a further increasing of the looseness of an agenda (e.g., to .6) does not imply a further improvement in recognition of especially the non-compliant action sequences. It seems that unnecessary looseness will presumably degrade

*Experiments and Conclusions*

recognition capability. But even though the data shows appropriate indications supporting this guess, those do not significantly substantiate it.

Finally, by looking at the delay data, it becomes visible that an agenda reduces the delay, specifically for the later team actions. As already mentioned in the context of Figure 4.3 that compares the most accurate tracker configuration $T_{.8}$ with the agenda-free model $T_{uniform}$ this is due to the agenda model specific history tracking. An agenda-driven model like $T_{.8}$ will not reconsider items already worked off. In comparison to the agenda-free variant $T_{uniform}$ this aspect, clearly, reduces the degrees of freedom for decision making on the next team intention with every completed agenda topic .

**Conclusion**

The results of this first experiment regarding intention recognition for cooperative teams, namely inference accuracy and speed, show that despite noisy observable sensor data and a rather ad hoc prior probability distribution for the occurrence of agenda items a precise and robust inference is possible. Adding agenda knowledge to a team behavior model is identified as an improvement for the compliant cases and as non-disturbing for the non-compliant cases. This supports the claim that even unreliable agendas have positive effects on inferring intentions of cooperative teams.

The promising findings from the first experiment encouraged a further in-depth development of the team intention model to cover the "team meeting" domain appropriately. A distinction between the preparing and performing stages was added to the model and an ability to learn adequate probability distributions for the agenda compliance and state changes as well as sensor model and timer model parameters using the expectation maximization (EM) algorithm was incorporated into the experimental infrastructure. The second experiment described in the next section evaluates how these enhancements influence in-situ recognition in my department's SmartApplianceLab.

## 4.3 Experiment #2: Instrumented Field Study

The second experiment carried out with the proposed Team DBN determines how this approach handles real sensor data. Using a corpus of instrumented meeting recordings it studies whether the results of experiment #1 that even unreliable agenda knowledge improves recognition quality can be repeated in an in-situ setting. Another question of interest is, if the added division of a team activity into two team actions, i.e., a preparing stage and an acting stage, involves a more reliable recognition of the current team intentions. This experiment investigates the robustness of intention analysis using the proposed Team DBN in case of incomplete sensor observations. And it examines incidentally whether the quality of agenda-driven team intention recognition can be improved by learning adequate sensor model and timer model parameters using the methods implemented in the experimental infrastructure so far. Again, before the results of this second exploration are presented and the findings are analyzed, the overall setup of the in-situ experiment is described, namely questioning, procedure, and particular tools used.

### 4.3.1 Study Methodology

The instrumented field study was again based on the Bayesian filtering approach and used the final version of the explicit probabilistic team behavior model proposed in Section 3.4.2, which includes the two stages approach that distinguishes between a preparation and a performance phase. The questioning of this experiment #2 is similar to the first exploration just for a real world setting. It tries to find answers to the queries:

- How accurate and how fast can cooperative behavior of a team be predicted with an agenda assumption and history knowledge using real sensor data?
- What influence do deviations of the team from the planned agenda assumption have on the prediction quality in an in-situ setting?
- When does an explicit agenda improve prediction quality, and where are the drawbacks?

In addition to the first experiment's queries it addresses the following questions:

- How robust can cooperative behavior of a team be recognized if sensor data of single team members is lacking?
- Does recognition using an explicit agenda improve prediction robustness over the agenda-free approach?
- Is learning of the sensor model and timer model parameters a way to better results?

*Experiments and Conclusions*

For this experiment an in-situ setting was chosen to enable statements about the proposed approach that are based on real world data. Therefore a corpus of instrumented meetings was set up to provide a collection of data that was gathered in a controlled environment to allow a comparison of the demanded measures.

**Experimental Design**

The basis for the structure of the instrumented meetings is the staged meeting scenario given in Section 3.2.1, where the team members will perform different activities and adopt different roles within the group. In the run-up of the experiment a preliminary agenda for the meetings was defined that corresponds to the scenario. The durations of the presentations of the different team members in the agenda were set to the following values: A presents 60$s$, B presents 90$s$, and C presents 60$s$, too. The discussion is scheduled with 30$s^2$. Accordingly, the preliminary agenda for all instrumented meetings recorded for the corpus lists as follows:

```
60 seconds     Presentation of the proposal of person A
90 seconds     Presentation of the proposal of person B
60 seconds     Presentation of the proposal of person C
30 seconds     Discussion of the proposals
End of the meeting
```

All scripts for the instrumented meetings follow the ⟨Present, Present, Present, Discuss⟩ structure described in the scenario, but only a part of the recorded meetings are compliant with the agenda ⟨A, B, C, D⟩ outlined. The other recorded courses deviate from the meeting agenda randomly. All in all, 7 compliant and 13 non-compliant of a total of 20 meetings were recorded by a semi-automatic meeting recorder. Therefore three-person teams of volunteers acted on the audio instructions of the meeting recorder and an observer annotated every transition from the preparing stage to the performing stage by clicking a button in the application. Then, the meeting recorder writes all sensor readings together with the observed state transitions into a file. This file represents the truth for the recorded meeting. Figure 4.4 gives an impression how the recorded data looks like. Here the sensor footprints of all recorded meetings are lapped. The drawing on the right side indicates the sequence of data occurrence.

---

[2]Obviously the durations selected here are rather short, but the interest in this experiment was merely on the transition phases of the meeting.

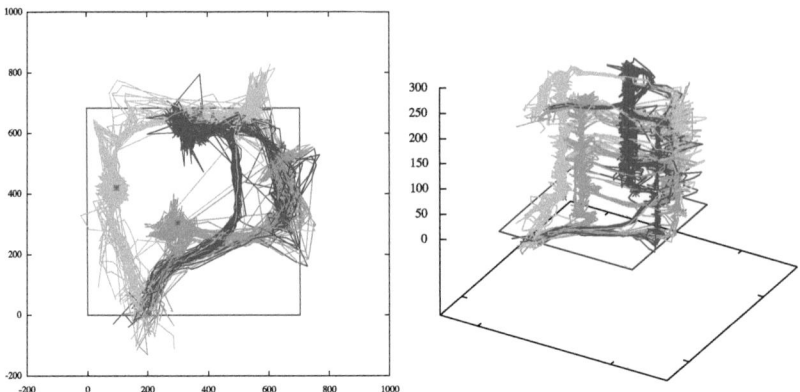

Figure 4.4: Recorded sensor footprints lapped for all recordings of instrumented meetings. Colors encode the different team members A (green), B (yellow), and C (blue). Red stars indicate the related locations on the path graph (see, Figure 3.7).

The structure of this experiment has three parts. First is the precision test. To analyze the precision of the team intention recognition two different settings of the sensor model and two different settings of the timer model were combined with three different configurations of $P_{follow}$ (i.e., the probability that the team will follow the agenda). The resulting tracker setups ($T_{.6}$, $T_{.8}$, $T_{.95}$) are used to filter the 20 different recorded meetings. These filter runs[3] are compared to the according filter runs using the agenda-free tracker $T_{uniform}$. In summary, each of the four parameter configurations is filtered 20 times for each of the four trackers.

As second part a reliability test was added to emphasize the reliability of the result from the precision test. Therefore two of the recorded meetings (a compliant one and a non-compliant one) were selected randomly. These two meetings were filtered 10 times with each of the 16 parameter×tracker combinations to enable a statement about the variation in result of the precision test.

The third part of the experiment was the robustness test. This was set up to examine how the precision of the recognition changes if some of the observation data is not available. Therefore the recorded meeting data was slightly modified. For each of the recorded meetings three additional data sets were produced where the data of one of the three team members A, B, and C was skipped. Now the same procedure as for the precision test was applied to the modified data set. Table 4.4 provides an overview of the entire setup.

---

[3]Again, filtering was done with a number of 5.000 particles.

Table 4.4: Summary of experimental design: 20 different recorded truth sequences (7 compliant, 13 non-compliant), 4 different tracker configurations, 1 filter run per parameter set over each of the 20 recorded meetings for precision and robustness, 10 filter runs per parameter set over 2 randomly selected meetings for reliability.

---

**A-priori agenda:**
Settings are analogous to the settings in Table 4.1.

**Precision**

20 different recorded meetings:
- 7 compliant,
- 13 non-compliant

4 different initial parameter settings (columns):

| $\mathcal{N}$ | | $\mathcal{E}$ | | sensor model |
|---|---|---|---|---|
| 150, 150 | | 9.75 | | |
| $\mathcal{N}$ | $\mathcal{E}$ | $\mathcal{N}$ | $\mathcal{E}$ | timer model |
| 85 | 85 | 85 | 85 | |

**Robustness**

20 recordings lacking data of A:
20 recordings lacking data of B:
20 recordings lacking data of C:
- 7 compliant,
- 13 non-compliant

4 different initial parameter settings (columns):

| $\mathcal{N}$ | | $\mathcal{E}$ | | sensor model |
|---|---|---|---|---|
| 150, 150 | | 9.75 | | |
| $\mathcal{N}$ | $\mathcal{E}$ | $\mathcal{N}$ | $\mathcal{E}$ | timer model |
| 85 | 85 | 85 | 85 | |

**Reliability**

10 × 2 different recorded meetings:
- 1 compliant,
- 1 non-compliant

4 different initial parameter settings (columns):

| $\mathcal{N}$ | | $\mathcal{E}$ | | sensor model |
|---|---|---|---|---|
| 150, 150 | | 9.75 | | |
| $\mathcal{N}$ | $\mathcal{E}$ | $\mathcal{N}$ | $\mathcal{E}$ | timer model |
| 85 | 85 | 85 | 85 | |

---

Remember that this study also asked the question if learning of sensor model and timer model parameters can yield better results in team intention analysis than the a-priori parameter settings provides anyway. Hence the precision test was rerun with learned parameter settings as soon as the learner had determined the values for the parameter setting by iterating the data of each recorded meeting for every parameter×tracker combination 5 times. The result of the parameter learning are mentioned in a separate section later on. Next section focuses on the results of the precision, reliability and robustness tests.

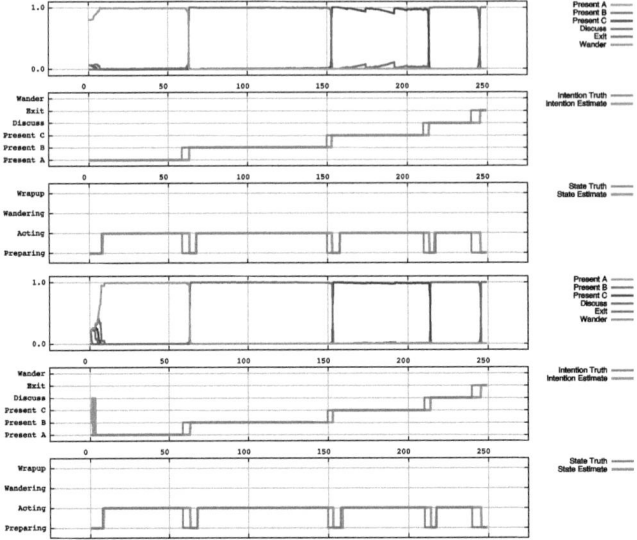

Figure 4.5: Inference of a compliant truth with the initial $\mathcal{N}_{sensor} \times \mathcal{N}_{timer}$ configuration. The three top rows show the distribution of the particle votes for team intentions as well as the estimates for the objective and the stage of the team in comparison to the true team objective and stage for the tracker $T_{.8}$. The three bottom rows depict the same for the tracker $T_{uniform}$.

### 4.3.2 Results

The illustrations of the $T_{.8}$ and $T_{uniform}$ tracker results of the best recognized agenda-compliant meeting truth in Figure 4.5 show similar characteristics as the results of the simulation experiment explained in Section 4.2.2. Again, the uncertainty about the team's objective rises in the phases of transition from one intention to another. The three top drawings illustrating tracker $T_{.8}$ indicate the advantage of agenda knowledge. Compared to the three bottom drawings that are related to the $T_{uniform}$ tracker they show that with the use of an agenda a more reliable inference of the team's objective is possible, especially at the beginning of a meeting.

Further it can be noticed that the decisions of both trackers for an intention transition lag a certain amount of time behind the true team objective shift. This is similar to the result of the simulation study, too. But thanks to the enhancement of the Team DBN, which in the current version can distinguish between the preparation and the performance of an activity, it can be seen at the same time that the trackers decide on a new team intention noticeable prior to the

*Experiments and Conclusions*

start of the acting stage of a team activity. Table 4.5 indicates that the delay just mentioned depends on the existence of an agenda and on the parameterization of the tracker. This table breaks down the portion of the meeting filtering results where truth and estimation differ. The rows hold the results for the different parameter settings, i.e., all combinations of *1.* the agenda compliance, *2.* the Gaussian sensor model, and *3.* the timer model – Gaussian $\mathcal{N}$ or Exponential $\mathcal{E}$.

The values of a row encode from left to right the *delay rate* (i.e., the percentage of the meeting time that the estimation needs to shift to new team intentions), the *total error rate* (i.e., the percentage of the meeting time that the estimation decides for wrong team intentions), and the *acting error rate* (i.e. same as the total error rate, but for the acting time only), first for the agenda-driven tracker $T_{.8}$ and second for the agenda-free tracker for $T_{uniform}$.

From the first values of the table it can be seen that on the one hand for agenda compliant meetings a delay rate of a tracker using an agenda is on average smaller than the delay rate of an agenda-free tracker. On the other hand for non-compliant meetings it is just the other way round. Obviously, this indicates that for compliant cases an agenda-driven model is closer to the truth and for non-compliant cases an agenda-free model might be favorable. But with dropping the agenda the chance for tracking history is lost, too. This can be seen from the second values: the error rates. These increase dramatically for the agenda-free model, even for non-compliant meetings. So using a list of things to do (e.g. a preliminary agenda) and keeping track of what has been done so far (i.e., using a history) seems a good idea for a team intention model, even if the team deviates from the order in the list. The third values, i.e., the acting error rates, finally indicate when recognition errors mainly occur. They demonstrate

Table 4.5: Average delay and error: The values encode LTR the delay rate, the total error rate, and the acting error rate for the different setting parameter×tracker values.

|  |  |  | $T_{.8}$ | | | $T_{uniform}$ | | |
|---|---|---|---|---|---|---|---|---|
| compliant | $\mathcal{N}$ | $\mathcal{N}$ | 6.064 | 0.606 | 0.000 | 6.484 | 2.639 | 0.587 |
|  |  | $\mathcal{E}$ | 5.897 | 1.750 | 1.147 | 6.242 | 2.436 | 0.000 |
| non-compliant | $\mathcal{N}$ | $\mathcal{N}$ | 6.406 | 1.053 | 0.000 | 5.899 | 2.597 | 0.261 |
|  |  | $\mathcal{E}$ | 6.337 | 1.060 | 0.000 | 5.522 | 2.551 | 0.248 |
| all agendas | $\mathcal{N}$ | $\mathcal{N}$ | 6.235 | 0.829 | 0.000 | 6.192 | 2.618 | 0.424 |
|  |  | $\mathcal{E}$ | 6.117 | 1.405 | 0.573 | 5.882 | 2.494 | 0.124 |

Table 4.6: Average accuracy: The values encode the accuracy results for all tested parameter×tracker configurations. The accuracy figures list the mean filtering accuracies of the respective meeting recordings. According to paired t-Tests over the results the agenda-driven trackers $T_{.6}$, $T_{.8}$, and $T_{.95}$ outperformed the agenda-free tracker $T_{uniform}$ significantly.

|  |  |  | $T_{.6}$ | $T_{.8}$ | $T_{.95}$ | $T_{uniform}$ |
|---|---|---|---|---|---|---|
| compliant | $\mathcal{N}$ | $\mathcal{N}$ | 93.047 | 93.330 | 93.497 | 90.876 |
|  |  | $\mathcal{E}$ | 92.081 | 92.353 | 92.295 | 91.322 |
|  | $\mathcal{C}$ | $\mathcal{N}$ | 84.732 | 87.352 | 86.556 | 64.759 |
|  |  | $\mathcal{E}$ | 85.032 | 86.255 | 84.744 | 73.187 |
| non-compliant | $\mathcal{N}$ | $\mathcal{N}$ | 92.466 | 92.541 | 92.324 | 91.504 |
|  |  | $\mathcal{E}$ | 92.215 | 92.603 | 92.037 | 91.927 |
|  | $\mathcal{C}$ | $\mathcal{N}$ | 67.088 | 65.969 | 67.930 | 69.555 |
|  |  | $\mathcal{E}$ | 70.445 | 67.765 | 69.700 | 71.461 |
| all agendas | $\mathcal{N}$ | $\mathcal{N}$ | 92.756 | **92.935** | 92.910 | **91.190** |
|  |  | $\mathcal{E}$ | 92.148 | **92.478** | 92.166 | **91.624** |
|  | $\mathcal{C}$ | $\mathcal{N}$ | **75.910** | 76.660 | **77.243** | 67.157 |
|  |  | $\mathcal{E}$ | **77.738** | 77.010 | **77.222** | 72.324 |

that the usage of an agenda-driven tracker reduces the vulnerability to errors in recognition during the acting stages of the team activities in all meeting types in comparison to trackers without agenda knowledge.

The averaged accuracy figures for filter runs with initial parameter values are shown in Table 4.6. The table lists the results for all parameter configurations of 1. the agenda compliance, 2. the sensor model – Gaussian $\mathcal{N}$ or Cauchy $\mathcal{C}$, and 3. the timer model – Gaussian $\mathcal{N}$ or Exponential $\mathcal{E}$ combined with the trackers $T_{.6}$, $T_{.8}$, $T_{.95}$ and $T_{uniform}$. As in the simulation study, the tracker $T_{.8}$ shows the most promising results. Especially in combination with the $\mathcal{N}_{sensor} \times \mathcal{N}_{timer}$ and $\mathcal{N}_{sensor} \times \mathcal{E}_{timer}$ configurations it significantly improves recognition quality over the agenda-free tracker $T_{uniform}$. The Box-Whisker plots in Figure 4.6 illustrate these improvements. The left side of this figure compares the filter results of the two variants of tracker $T_{.8}$ with the two variants of tracker $T_{uniform}$ for agenda-compliant meeting recordings, whereas the right side of the figure compares the results for the meeting recordings that are not compliant with the preliminary agenda.

In order to allow a statement about how reliable these accuracy results are a reliability test was

*Experiments and Conclusions*

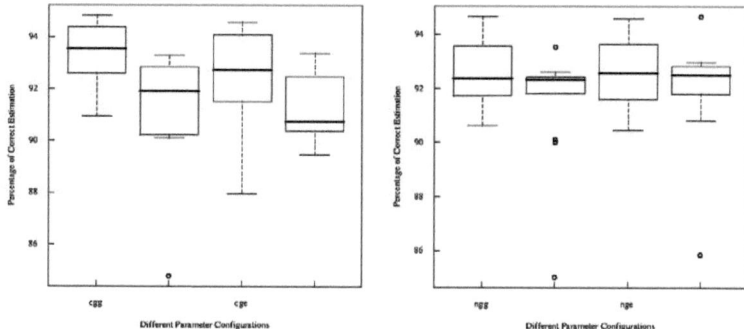

Figure 4.6: Accuracy: These Box-Whisker plots depict the median and the mean variation in the accuracy results of the different filter runs for the recorded meetings. The drawings show the comparisons of differently parametrized $T_{.8}$ and $T_{uniform}$ trackers using initial parameter values. In this context *cgg* means: compliant, $\mathcal{N}_{sensor} \times \mathcal{N}_{timer}$ and *nge* stands for: non-compliant, $\mathcal{N}_{sensor} \times \mathcal{E}_{timer}$. The other abbreviations *cge* and *ngg* are respective combinations of these meanings.

performed. For this test two representatives of the meeting recordings were chosen randomly, one from the agenda-compliant meetings and one from the non-compliant cases. 10 filter runs were performed with each representative to examine how the filtering results vary. The results related to the $\mathcal{N}_{sensor} \times \mathcal{N}_{timer}$ and $\mathcal{N}_{sensor} \times \mathcal{E}_{timer}$ configurations of the trackers $T_{.8}$ and $T_{uniform}$ are shown in Figure 4.7. The left side of the figure compares the reliabilities of the filtering accuracy of the compliant representative, and the right side of the figure shows a comparison of the results when using the non-compliant meeting.

From these plots it can be seen that the accuracy results from the agenda-driven trackers are far more reliable than the results from the agenda-free tracker. Furthermore they state that using an agenda leads to more consistent filtering results than using an agenda-free tracker. This shows again that incorporating an agenda into the team intention model and keeping track of the history improves the quality of team intention recognition.

The introduction of the two phases of a team activity (i.e., preparation and performance) into the team intention model reveals another interesting result. Remember, while recording the meetings for the experimentation corpus an observer annotated the transition between preparing stage and acting stage by clicking a button on the meeting recorder. The preparation phase is typically the time frame a smart environment has to recognize the situation and must

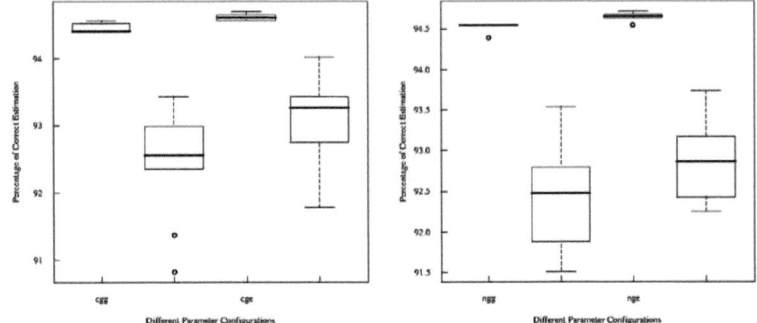

Figure 4.7: Reliability: These Box-Whisker plots depict the median and the mean variation in the accuracy results of the 10 filter run iterations of two randomly selected meeting recordings, one from compliant meetings (left) and one from non-compliant meetings (right). Again, the drawings show the comparisons of differently parametrized $T_{.8}$ and $T_{uniform}$ trackers using initial parameter values. The abbreviations encode the same meanings as in Figure 4.6.

provide appropriate assistance. Table 4.7 shows when the $T_{.8}$ and $T_{uniform}$ trackers decide for new team objectives. The values encode from left to right the saved time per topic (i.e., the averaged time frame from an estimator's transition to a correct new team intention up to the truth's transition from preparing to acting), the percentage of saved time on the entire meeting, and percentage of saved time on the preparation phases of the meetings.

The table indicates that the trackers always recognize the objective shift before the team starts performing its current activity. Again, agenda-driven trackers in all cases decide significantly

Table 4.7: Average saved time: The values encode LTR the saved time per topic, the percentage of saved time on the entire meeting, and percentage of saved time on the preparation phases of the meetings for the different setting parameter×tracker values.

| | | | $T_{.8}$ | | | $T_{uniform}$ | | |
|---|---|---|---|---|---|---|---|---|
| compliant | $\mathcal{N}$ | $\mathcal{N}$ | 3.783 | 7.613 | 53.301 | 3.058 | 6.155 | 41.896 |
| | | $\mathcal{E}$ | 3.814 | 7.675 | 54.145 | 3.160 | 6.359 | 42.289 |
| non-compliant | $\mathcal{N}$ | $\mathcal{N}$ | 4.068 | 8.204 | 52.378 | 3.764 | 7.592 | 47.969 |
| | | $\mathcal{E}$ | 4.113 | 8.296 | 52.864 | 3.907 | 7.878 | 50.169 |
| all agendas | $\mathcal{N}$ | $\mathcal{N}$ | 3.925 | 7.908 | 52.819 | 3.411 | 6.874 | 45.046 |
| | | $\mathcal{E}$ | 3.964 | 7.986 | 52.472 | 3.533 | 7.119 | 46.314 |

Table 4.8: Exemplary results of the Paired $t$-Test emphasizing that time savings with model $T_{.8}$ are statistically significant in comparsion to the agenda-free model $T_{uniform}$. In this example the compliant, $\mathcal{N}_{sensor} \times \mathcal{N}_{timer}$ configurations of both models were compared.

**P value and statistical significance:**

The two-tailed $P$ value equals 0.0037

By conventional criteria, this difference is considered to be very statistically significant.

**Confidence interval:**

The mean of $T_{.8}$ minus $T_{uniform}$ equals 0.90750

95% confidence interval of this difference: From 0.33297 to 1.48203

**Intermediate values used in calculations:**

$t = 3.3061$

$df = 19$

standard error of difference = 0.274

|  | $T_{.8}$ | $T_{uniform}$ |
|---|---|---|
| Mean | 7.99690 | 7.08940 |
| SD | 1.13296 | 1.66723 |

faster on a new team objective than the agenda-free tracker. On average the decision is made in the first half of the preparing stage. Note that the moment when all team members arrived at their associated location was selected for the observer's annotation of the preparing-acting transition. In typical meeting situations this is the time when the struggle with the presentation hardware really begins. Thus the proposed agenda-driven team intention model provides enough reserves to configure the room, even more than an agenda-free approach.

A final question was how the different trackers behave in cases lacking sensor data. Therefore the sensor readings of one team member at a time was erased from the meeting recordings and then the same filter runs as for the precision test were performed. The Box-Whisker plots in Figure 4.8 show selected results of this robustness test (i.e., trackers $T_{.8}$ and $T_{uniform}$). Not only that agenda-driven trackers obviously demonstrate a stronger robustness than the agenda-free trackers. They also achieve similar accuracy results as in the precision test, at least when filtering agenda-compliant meetings. For non-compliant meetings mean variation rises and the filtering results depend strongly on the quality of the remaining sensor data. Agenda-free trackers demonstrate even worse behavior. Thus this test demonstrated clearly that the robustness of a team intention model profits from incorporation of agenda knowledge.

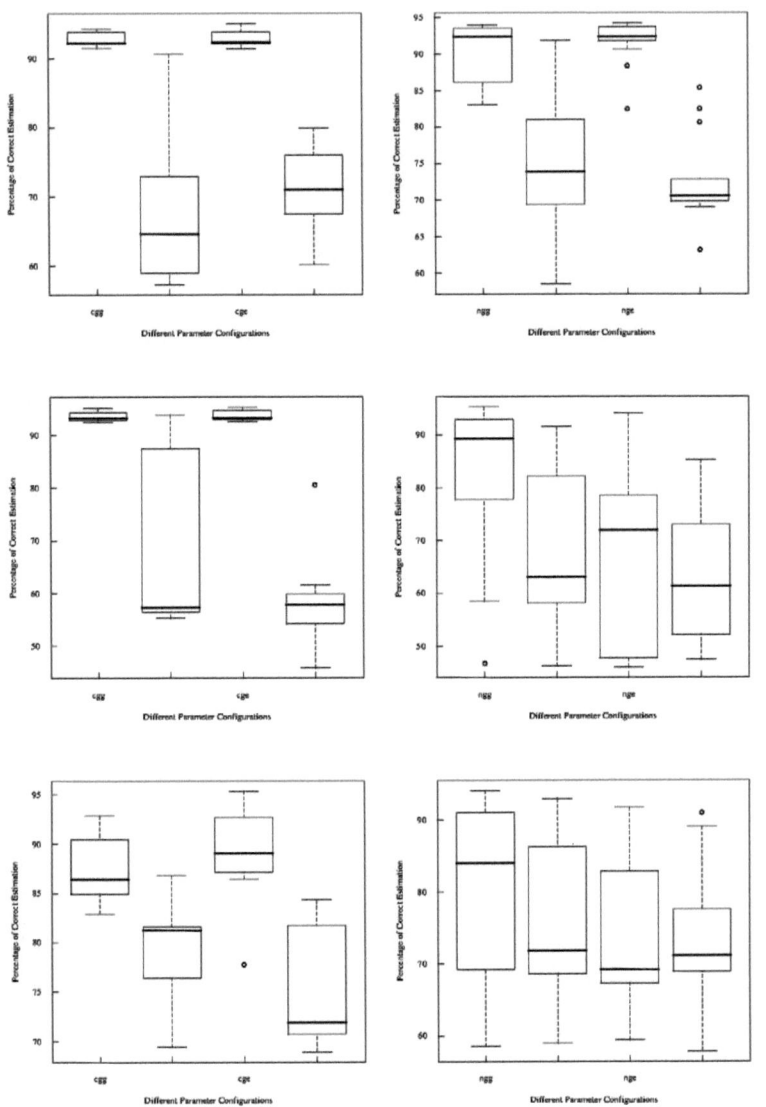

Figure 4.8: Robustness: These Box-Whisker-plots depict the results from runs where the recorded data of one team member at a time was dropped. Set up as in Figures 4.6 & 4.7, in the runs shown by the first row drawings sensor data from A was dropped. The runs shown in the second row lack B's data, and in the runs in third row data from C was dropped.

*Experiments and Conclusions*

**Note on Parameter Learning**

Up to this point this work did not made any attempt to describe the learning approach used in the experimental infrastructure that may enable the refinement of a-priori parameter settings. This is simply due to the fact that the implementation of learning algorithms in the experimental infrastructure was not completed. It was planned to implement the expectation maximization (EM) method introduced by Dempster et al. (1977) for parameter learning. The operation of algorithms of this category is as follows:

Given a joint probability distribution $p\left(\mathbf{e}_{1:T}, \mathbf{x}_{1:T}|\theta\right)$ over observed variables $\mathbf{e}_{1:T}$ and hidden variables $\mathbf{x}_{1:T}$, controlled by the parameters $\theta$, the objective is to maximize the likelihood $p\left(\mathbf{e}_{1:T}|\theta\right)$, and therefore

1. Select the initial parameters $\theta^{old}$.
2. Evaluate $p\left(\mathbf{x}_{1:T}|\mathbf{e}_{1:T}, \theta^{old}\right)$ and calculate the Expectation

$$\mathscr{Q}\left(\theta, \theta^{old}\right) = \int_{\mathbf{x}_{1:T}} p\left(\mathbf{x}_{1:T}|\mathbf{e}_{1:T}, \theta^{old}\right) \ln p\left(\mathbf{e}_{1:T}, \mathbf{x}_{1:T}|\theta\right).$$

3. Determine the revised parameters $\theta^{new}$ by **Maximizing** the function

$$\theta^{new} = \arg\max_{\theta} \mathscr{Q}\left(\theta, \theta^{old}\right).$$

4. Check for convergence. If the convergence criterion is not satisfied, then let $\theta^{old} \leftarrow \theta^{new}$ and reiterate by returning to step 2.

Again, the virtually indefinite complexity of the density function makes a calculation of the optimal parameter setting for the proposed team intention model intractable (cp. with Section 3.5.2). Therefore the idea was to realize two approximative Bayesian smoothing approaches within the parameter learning environment, namely the forward-backward smoother and the maximum a-posteriori (MAP) smoother described in detail e.g., by Klaas et al. (2006). But the implementation was not finished in time to be evaluated during this second experiment. At this stage of work only a simple forward smoother could be utilized that adopts the filtering step of the particle filter for smoothing. This obviously includes merely the observations up to the current time step instead of the knowledge from the complete timeframe observed. Hence different sources warn that it may fail to converge (Bishop, 2006) and can perform poorly (Klaas et al., 2006) due to the lack of hindsight. However, utilizing the for-

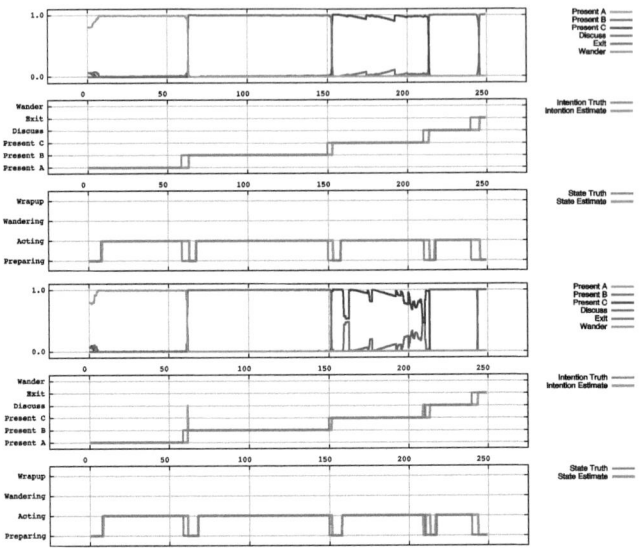

Figure 4.9: Inference of a compliant truth with the initial $\mathcal{N}_{sensor} \times \mathcal{N}_{timer}$ configuration. The three top rows show the distribution of the particle votes for team intentions as well as the estimates for the objective and the stage of the team in comparison to the true team objective and stage for the tracker $T_{.8}$. The three bottom rows depict the same for the tracker $T_{.8}$ with trained parameters.

ward learner was the only way to address the last question of this experiment: Is learning of the sensor model and timer model parameters a way to better results?

Figure 4.9 shows the $T_{.8}$ representative from Figure 4.5 in comparison to the trained version's result. The learning of the parameters of the sensor model resulted in tighter scale parameters (i.e., a scale of $\{150, 150\}$ vs. a scale of $\{61.8, 57.6\}$). The direct comparison shows that this led to a faster but more error-prone recognition of the team objectives. Despite this tendency to more errors in recognition the accuracy in fact increased for the depicted case. This is mainly a result of the rather good availability of sensor data. The phase of the meeting where C holds his presentation indicates what happens if sensor observations get sparser or respectively noisier. In these cases a tighter scale compromises the viability of potentially important particles of the filter. Not all meeting recordings provide the same quality of sensor data as the representative depicted in Figure 4.9. Thus, the over-all results of this first test on how learning could help to refine a-priori parameter settings are moderate. The Box-Whisker

## Experiments and Conclusions

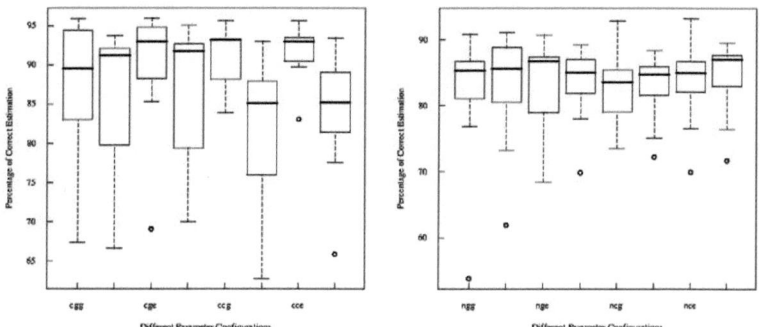

Figure 4.10: Accuracy: These Box-Whisker plots depict the median and the mean variation in the accuracy results of the different filter runs for the recorded meetings. The drawings display the comparisons of differently parametrized $T_{.8}$ and $T_{uniform}$ trackers using trained parameter values. In this context cgg means: compliant, $\mathcal{N}_{sensor} \times \mathcal{N}_{timer}$ and ngg stands for: non-compliant, $\mathcal{E}_{sensor} \times \mathcal{E}_{timer}$. The other abbreviations cge, ccg, cce, ngg, nge, and ncg are respective combinations of these meanings.

plots shown in Figure 4.10, which summarize the accuracy results of the different $T_{.8}$ trackers in comparison to the respective $T_{uniform}$ trackers, indicate this phenomenon. The variation of the accuracy results heavily increased after refining the sensor model parameters with the mentioned forward learner. Even though especially compliant meetings filtered with agenda-driven trackers tend to a better recognition with learned parameters (medians of these runs gather around 92% correct), the number of unsubstantial recognized meetings increased, too.

### Conclusion

Despite the rather awkward results of the learning test that need further investigation the experiment #2 showed once again that the proposed approach of agenda-driven team intention recognition based on a Team DBN is a preeminent idea that can pass in a real world setting, too. The important result from the first study that *it is possible to improve the recognition accuracy for the compliant case by using an agenda,* **without** *sacrificing recognition accuracy for the non-compliant case,* also holds for the in-situ experiment. Again, the accuracy and reliability results of the different variants of the agenda-driven trackers outperform the results of the agenda-free $T_{uniform}$ tracker versions. This statement that adding agenda knowledge to a team behavior model is an improvement holds for the average error rate, too, but in this case the advance is made at the expense of recognition speed, especially while filtering non-compliant meetings. On the other hand the analysis of experiment #2 showed that the time savings that can be realized with trackers using agenda knowledge are larger than the savings of cases where no agenda information was used. This compensates for the speed drawback.

The second important finding is that the additional knowledge of an unreliable a-priori agenda dramatically improves recognition quality in cases of missing sensor data, no matter if the meeting has an agenda-compliant course or a non-compliant course. Thus an agenda-driven Team DBN is a real improvement for the robustness of team intention recognition. Finally, the experiment showed that appropriate initial parameters for the sensor model and the timer model enable very reasonable recognition results without any help of parameter learning. Nevertheless parameter learning provides a way to optimize the recognition results but simultaneously involves the danger of the memorization of training data at the expense of flexibility and robustness.

In summary, the results of this second experiment regarding intention recognition for cooperative teams show that a precise and robust inference in a real world situation is possible. Adding agenda knowledge to a team behavior model is again identified as an improvement for the compliant cases and as non-disturbing for the non-compliant cases. The excellent findings on precision and robustness support the claim that even unreliable agendas have positive effects on inferring intentions of real cooperative teams. The findings about time savings indicate the usefulness of team intention models in assistive smart environments. And, the rather moderate findings on learning should encourage further in-depth research on appropriate learning strategies for the team intention model.

## 4.4 Summary and Outlook

Smart Environments as representatives of the ubiquitous computing paradigm are a promising approach to assist users with their real world problems. In the surroundings of a real world scenario it is valuable to provide user assistance in an unobtrusive implicit manner. Especially in team situations a deducible objective of the team might provide a solid base for a Smart Environment to decide on an assistance strategy. This work determined how such a system for the intention analysis in teams could be designed.

Therefore, a criteria catalogue was developed by means of a typical ubiquitous computing scenario. The relevant criteria that were identified for the team intention model are *1.*) pursuance of a **training-free prior knowledge approach,** *2.*) capability of using **various lexica of team activities** (i.e., agendas), *3.*) allowance for **easy extensions** (e.g., to larger teams), *4.*) support of **real-time recognition,** *5.*) provision of **robust recognition** from simple sensor data, *6.*) tracking of **team activity history,** and *7.*) **separate modeling** of complex team and atomic user activities. Simultaneously, the related ubiquitous computing projects were examined to identify appropriate methods by which the criteria related problems of team intention analysis could be addressed.

Considering the constraints from the scenario and the respective criteria, it turned out that the concept of choice is a probabilistic model for real-time team intention recognition. The evaluation of the state of the art in ubiquitous computing showed that so far very few attempts have been made to model a team's negotiation process on a future team objective. Besides considerations by Zhang et al. (2004) and McCowan et al. (2005), which are interested in the subsequent annotation of meetings, to the best of my knowledge no other approach is known that complies with the identified criteria for team intention recognition in smart environments. Nevertheless other research directions exist that already studied the behavior of groups and teams. In order to learn from these interdisciplinary findings this work reviewed research on human behavior in a group and as an individual made by social psychologists and cognition psychologists respectively and identified ideas that might help to model a team negotiation process as desired.

Reviewing the field of social psychology provided valuable insights into the "nature of groups". These clearly influenced the design decisions regarding the team intention model. The review showed that *1.*) if a group is a team in terms of collaboration a task or respectively **goal-oriented acting** of the team members can be presumed, *2.*) interdependences and structures in groups can exist, where group members have equal rights and, thus, the behavior of the different members of a team can be **modeled equally,** and *3.*) the **sensor observation** of the team is an adequate technique that, combined **with a coding scheme** (e.g., an a-priori agenda), allows an objective and systematic recognition of team events.

In addition to the findings from reviewing social psychology research the evaluation of the cognitive psychology field showed that especially *reasoning* and *problem solving* aspects as part of the cognitive psychology subfield *thinking* promise insights into human behavior that are constructive with respect to the design of a team intention model. The fundamental statement here is that human reasoning and problem solving is goal oriented. People tackle a certain goal in a "divide & conquer" manner. Abstracting this behavior, that is, they try to find an efficient transformation from an initial state to a desired goal state by subdividing the possibly composite activity into a set of atomic actions. The different models from cognitive research typically enable a hierarchical formulation of the individual user goal. Here, the CTTE was the most interesting approach with respect to the design of a team intention model as it allows to subdivide cooperative multi-user tasks into individual subtasks for the persons involved in a team. In summary, the review of this research field showed that *1.)* cooperative behavior of individuals can be modeled by **hierarchical structures** that reflect typical problem solving strategies, *2.)* the temporal sequence of certain activities is tied to observable **preconditions and effects** of the underlying actions, and *3.)* the knowledge for solving problems can be derived from **perception, memory**[4], or reasoning.

The reviews of the social and cognitive psychology fields clearly influenced the design of the team intention model's structure and the description of temporal dependencies of compound activities. Nevertheless these research areas provided few information about how input stimuli (sensor data) are related to a certain output (execution sequence). This question is rather a matter of signal processing research that develops scientific as well as technological models as a means for estimating the actual behavior of an observed signal source. Two fundamental approaches from the signal processing area were examined with respect to their usefulness in the scenario specified for this work. The selection of the methods was derived from the criteria catalogue. Hence this work **compared** the **connectionist** approach with the **probabilistic** method only. And, the purpose for modeling was rather technological than scientific because this work was interested in a model that explains a certain state in the team negotiation process on the basis of sensor observations. Hence the focus of this work was limited to **technological modeling**.

The in-depth interdisciplinary recherche of the several different aspects in team behavior recognition provided a solid knowledge base of criteria that contribute to an easier but sound decision on an appropriate modeling approach for team behavior recognition. Combined with the revised criteria catalogue and based on the concrete scenario in this work the recherche led to the decision to utilize the temporal probabilistic modeling approach for the design of the proposed team intention model.

---

[4]That are, in context of temporal probabilistic models sensor observations, preliminary agenda knowledge and history tracking.

*Experiments and Conclusions*

The development of the agenda-driven Team DBN for real-time intention analysis in teams is a second contribution of this work. After the recherche part the considerations made during the design process and the model itself were described in detail. The core of the DBN-based model is the two-stage team negotiation on new team objectives. The two-way interaction introduced between the Team Node $T$ and the User Nodes $U^{(i)}$ was to the best of my knowledge never proposed this way before. This specific design shows several advantages. The unbundling of the team level and the user level enables a flexible extensibility of the model to larger teams than in the specific scenario. Furthermore it provides an easy way to synchronize different user activities that are related to the same compound team activity.

Obviously, the decision to use a hierarchical structure to model the team negotiation on new team objectives was derived from the in-depth recherche. And this might be seen as benefit, too, because the similarity to hierarchical task models additionally incorporates the chance for an effective automatic generation of team intention models from team task specifications even though the proposed Team DBN was handcrafted. The inference in the proposed model follows an approximative approach as usual for DBNs, namely MCMC. Therefore the particles of the utilized particle filter hold a copy of the Team DBN each. The DBN states of the particles propagate in time and with every sensor reading the particle states are evaluated, weighted, and resampled.

An experimental infrastructure that enables the evaluation of the particular model and the particular inference process is a further contribution. Here, the reason for a customized solution was twofold. First an own solution enables full control on every single parameter or respectively every single probability distribution. And secondly, the tools that were implemented should be used beyond the experimental evaluation of this work in my department's prototypical SmartApplianceLab.

But with respect to this work the experimental infrastructure was merely used to carry out experiments on the team intention model. Two studies were executed to evaluate the proposed concept of a Team DBN. The simulation study in the early stage of this work was intended to prove that the ideas for the model design head in the right direction. The in-situ experiment was meant as test of the intention recognition concept with real sensor data occurring from a real meeting situation.

In combination both experiments showed the overall feasibility of team intention recognition using the proposed approach. The introduced probabilistic team intention model performs impressingly well with an ad-hoc a-priori setting of the transition probabilities of the model. Further it turned out that it was a good idea to incorporate a-priori agenda knowledge into the model even though this does not imply a guarantee that a team indeed would follow this included agenda. Both experiments showed that it is possible to improve the recognition accuracy for the compliant case by using an agenda, **without** sacrificing recognition accuracy for the non-compliant case. Furthermore they showed that built-in agenda knowledge has a positive effect on the robustness of the system. On average the accuracy of agenda-driven trackers is significantly higher than the accuracy of the agenda-free versions even in cases of non-compliant meeting courses and lacking sensor data.

In summary, this work outlined that the development of explicit team behavior models is a challenging issue for providing proactive assistance in smart environments. Even though the selected methods and the considered design have been developed into a concept that has been proven as appropriate, more work needs to be done to exploit the full potential of the proposed agenda-driven DBN-based team intention model.

Speaking in terms of the efficient development of team intention models, it makes sense to dedicate further research to the methodology and the tools that enable an easy generation of sufficiently precise models. Such a research must consider the correct declaration of the overall team intentions for a certain domain and the appropriate representation of the problem solving strategies of specific team members. Then, it must find a suitable process to translate such a description into a customized team intention model with appropriate model parameters and agenda entries.

Regarding the recognition of the system state, more effort should be spent on incorporating a more complex sensor landscape. Heterogeneous sources of sensor data could provide the ability to detect a wider range of activities and this in turn could lead to a more reliable inference of team activities or might enable the recognizability of more complex cooperative activities and team behavior.

From the model optimization point of view, the briefly discussed learning aspect should be examined further in future research. Obviously, in the first instance the learner tool of the experimental infrastructure must be finished to enable forward-backward and MAP smoothing. Simultaneously it would be sensible to extend the existing corpus of meeting recordings or to set up corpora for other smart environment scenarios. These could then be used to optimize the quality of the model's inference by learning the optimal parameter settings. Maybe it could even be valuable to determine if the learning of the team intention model's structure promises further improvements regarding the recognition of a team's current intention.

Finally, it can be stated that the concept of a robust and training-free probabilistic system as introduced in this thesis is an appropriate and useful basis for expocauchy intention analysis in teams. The proof of the concept is given by this work. But to take the full benefit from this concept, at least some of the mentioned issues must be addressed. In short term, the smoother implementation and the parameter learning study could be tackled. The model generation and the extension to other sensors are rather mid-term issues, whereas structural learning of the team intention model is a long-term challenge.

## 4.5 Acknowledgement

Finally, I would like to express my deeply gratefulness to all the people who helped me conduct this work. Special thanks go to my supervisor Prof. Dr.-Ing. Thomas Kirste. He gave me the opportunity to work as a researcher at his chair of Mobile Multimedia Information Systems. His guidance, his support and the constructive criticism were very encouraging to the progress of this work. A special thank you goes to Prof. Dr.-Ing. Peter Forbrig, who directed me to interesting aspects of Software Engineering that were a useful pillar to this work. I also want to thank Prof Dr sc nat Christopher Lueg from University of Tasmania for his support. I am very grateful to Prof. Dr.-Ing. Alke Martens for her comments on the psychological part of this work. Thanks go to my colleagues Petra, Thomas, Christian, Albert, and Christoph for your inspiring advices and exciting time it was. Especially, I would like to thank Christiane and Sebastian for proofreading this work. Most importantly, I want to thank my parents and my beloved girlfriend Claudia for their understanding, patience, and encouragement when it was most required. This work could not have been done without your support.

This work was financially supported by the Landesforschungsförderprogramm of the LMB Mecklenburg-Vorpommern and the DFG Graduiertenkolleg MuSAMA.

# Bibliography

Abowd, G., Atkeson, C., Feinstein, A., Hmelo, C., Rob, K., Long, S., Sawhney, N., Tani, M., November 18–22 1996. Teaching and Learning as Multimedia Authoring: The Smart Classroom 2000 Project. In: Proceedings of the 4th ACM International Conference on Multimedia, MM. ACM Press, Boston, MA, USA, pp. 187–198.

Al-Hames, M., Rigoll, G., July 6–8 2005. A Multi-Modal Mixed-State Dynamic Bayesian Network for Robust Meeting Event Recognition from Disturbed Data. In: Proceedings of the 6th IEEE International Conference on Multimedia and Expo, ICME. IEEE Press, Amsterdam, Netherlands, pp. 45–48.

Anderson, J. R., 1976. Language, Memory, and Thought. Erlbaum, Hillsdale, NJ, USA.

Anderson, J. R., 1983. The Architecture of Cognition. Harvard University Press, Cambridge, MA, USA.

Anderson, J. R., 1990. The Adaptive Character of Thought. Erlbaum, Hillsdale, NJ, USA.

Anderson, J. R., 1993. Rules of the Mind. Erlbaum, Hillsdale, NJ, USA.

Anderson, J. R., April 1996. ACT: A Simple Theory of Complex Cognition. American Psychologist 51 (4), pp. 355–365.

Anderson, J. R., Bower, G. H., 1973. Human Associative Memory. Winston and Sons, Washington, DC, USA.

Arulampalam, S., Maskell, S., Gordon, N., Clapp, T., February 2002. A tutorial on particle filters for on-line non-linear/non-gaussian bayesian tracking. IEEE Transactions of Signal Processing 50 (2), 174–188.

Bales, R. F., 1950. Interaction Process Analysis: A Method for the Study of Small Groups. Addison-Wesley, Reading, MA, USA.

Bales, R. F., 1965. The Equilibrium Problem in Small Groups. In: Hare, A. P., Borgatta, E. F., Bales, R. F. (Eds.), Small Groups: Studies in Social Interaction, 2nd Edition. Knopf, New York, NY, USA, pp. 444–476.

Bales, R. F., 1970. Personality and Interpersonal Behavior. Holt, Rinehart and Winston Inc., New York, NY, USA.

Bales, R. F., Cohen, S. P., Williamson, S. A., 1979. SYMLOG: A System for the Multiple Level Observation of Groups, Klett-Cotta German Edition. Free Press, New York, NY, USA.

Bar-Shalom, Y., Fortmann, T. E., 1988. Tracking and Data Association. Academic Press, San Diego, CA, USA.

Baum, L. E., Petrie, T., 1966. Statistical Inference for Probabilistic Functions of Finite State Markov Chains. Annals of Mathematical Statistics 37, 1554–1563.

Bengio, Y., 1999. Markovian Models for Sequential Data. Neural Computing Surveys 2, 129–162.

Bengio, Y., Simard, P., Frasconi, P., March 1994. Learning Long-term Dependencies with Gradient Descent is Difficult. IEEE Transactions on Neural Networks 5 (2), 157–166.

Benne, K., Sheats, P., 1948. Functional Role of Group Members. Journal of Social Issues 4 (2), pp. 41–49.

Berger, J., Wagner, D., Zelditch Jr., M., 1992. A Working Strategy for Constructing Theories: State Organizing Processes. In: Ritzer, G. (Ed.), Studies in Metatheorizing in Sociology. Sage, Thousand Oaks, CA, USA, pp. 107–123.

Bhattacharya, A., Das, S. K., August 15–19 1999. LeZi-Update: An Information-Theoretic Approach to Track Mobile Users in PCS Networks. In: Proccedings of the 5th Annual ACM/IEEE International Conference on Mobile Computing and Networking, MOBICOM. ACM Press, Seattle, WA, USA, pp. 1–12.

Bishop, C. M., August 2006. Pattern Recognition and Machine Learning (Information Science and Statistics). Springer.

Bobick, A. F., Ivanov, Y. A., 1998. Action Recognition Using Probabilistic Parsing. In: Proceedings of the IEEE Computer Society Conference on Computer Vision and Pattern Recognition, CVPR. IEEE Computer Society, Washington, DC, USA, pp. 196–202.

# BIBLIOGRAPHY

Brand, M., 1996. Coupled Hidden Markov Models for Modeling Interacting Processes. Technical Report 405, MIT Media Lab.

Brooks, R., August 25–28 1997. The Intelligent Room Project. In: Proceedings of the 2nd International Cognitive Technology Conference, CT. Aizu, Japan, pp. 271–278.

Brotherton, J. A., Abowd, G. D., 2004. Lessons Learned from eClass: Assessing Automated Capture and Access in the Classroom. ACM Transactions on Computer-Human Interaction 11 (2), pp. 121–155.

Brumitt, B., Meyers, B., Krumm, J., Kern, A., Shafer, S. A., September 25–27 2000. EasyLiving: Technologies for Intelligent Environments. In: Proceedings of the 2nd International Symposium on Handheld and Ubiquitous Computing, HUC. Springer-Verlag, Bristol, UK, pp. 12–29.

Brumitt, B., Shafer, S., February 2001. Better Living through Geometry. Journal for Ubiquitous Computing 5 (1), pp. 42–45.

Bui, H. H., November 15-17 2002. Efficient Approximate Inference for Online Probabilistic Plan Recognition. In: Intent Inference for Users, Teams, and Adversaries: Papers from the AAAI Fall Symposium. AAAI Press, North Falmouth, MA, USA, pp. 1–18.

Bui, H. H., August 9–15 2003. A General Model for Online Probabilistic Plan Recognition. In: Gottlob, G., Walsh, T. (Eds.), Proceedings of the 18th International Joint Conference on Artificial Intelligence, IJCAI. Morgan Kaufmann, Acapulco, Mexico, pp. 1309–1315.

Bui, H. H., Venkatesh, S., West, G. A. W., July 30–August 3 2000. On the Recognition of Abstract Markov Policies. In: Proceedings of the Seventeenth National Conference on Artificial Intelligence and Twelfth Conference on Innovative Applications of Artificial Intelligence. AAAI Press / The MIT Press, Austin, TX, USA, pp. 524–530.

Burger, S., Yu, H., April 28 2002. The ISL Meeting Corpus: The Impact of Meeting Type on Speech Style. In: Proceedings of the 7th International Conference on Spoken Language Processing, ICSLP. Denver, CO, USA, pp. 301–304.

Card, S. K., Moran, T. P., Newell, A., 1983. The Psychology of Human-Computer Interaction. Lawrence Erlbaum Associates, Mahwah, NJ, USA.

Carnes, W. T., January 1980. Effective Meetings for Busy People: Let's Decide It and Go Home. McGraw Hill, New York, NY, USA.

Chen, A., Muntz, R. R., Yuen, S., Locher, I., Park, S. I., Srivastava, M. B., 2002. A Support Infrastructure for the Smart Kindergarten. IEEE Pervasive Computing 1 (2), 49–57.

Coen, M., Phillips, B., Warshawsky, N., Weisman, L., Peters, S., Finin, P., December 13–14 1999. Meeting the Computational Needs of Intelligent Environments: The Metaglue System. In: Proceedings of the 1st International Workshop on Managing Interactions in Smart Environments, MANSE. Springer-Verlag, Dublin, Ireland, pp. 201–212.

Coen, M. H., July 26–30 1998. Design Principles for Intelligent Environments. In: Proceedings of the 15th National Conference on Artificial Intelligence and 10th Innovative Applications of Artificial Intelligence Conference, AAAI, IAAI. AAAI Press / The MIT Press, Madison, WI, USA, pp. 547–554.

Coie, J. D., Dodge, K. A., Kupersmidt, J. B., 1990. Peer Group Behavior and Social Status. In: Asher, S. R., Coie, J. D. (Eds.), Peer Rejection in Childhood. Cambridge University Press, New York, NY, USA, pp. 17–59.

Cook, D., Huber, M., Gopalratnam, K., Youngblood, M., 2003a. Learning to Control a Smart Home Environment. [online], (Accessed: February 22, 2008).
URL http://www-cse.uta.edu/~holder/courses/cse6362/pubs/Cook03.pdf

Cook, D., Youngblood, M., Heierman, E., Gopalratnam, K., Rao, S., Litvin, A., Khawaja, F., March 23–26 2003b. MavHome: An Agent-Based Smart Home. In: Proceeding of the 1st IEEE International Conference on Pervasive Computing and Communications, PERCOM. IEEE Computer Society Press, Fort Worth, TX, USA, pp. 521–524.

Cook, D. J., Das, S. K., March 2007. How Smart are our Environments? An Updated Look at the State of the Art. Pervasive Mobile Computing 3 (2), pp. 53–73.

Cowell, R. G., Dawid, A. P., Lauritzen, S. L., Spiegelhalter, D. J., 2007. Probabilistic Networks and Expert Systems: Exact Computational Methods for Bayesian Networks, twelfth Edition. Information Science and Statistics. Springer.

Das, S. K., Cook, D. J., Bhattacharya, A., Heierman III, E. O., Lin, T.-Y., December 2002. The Role of Prediction Algorithms in the MavHome Smart Home Architecture. IEEE Wireless Communications 9 (6), pp. 77–84.

# BIBLIOGRAPHY

Dean, T., Kanazawa, K., 1988. Probabilistic temporal reasoning. In: Proceedings of the American Association for Artificial Intelligence Conference, AAAI. AAAI, MIT Press, Cambridge, MA, USA, pp. 524–528.

Dean, T., Kanazawa, K., 1990. A Model for Reasoning about Persistence and Causation. Computational Intelligence 5 (3), 142–150.

Dempster, A. P., Laird, N. M., Rubin, D. B., 1977. Maximum Likelihood from Incomplete Data via the EM Algorithm. Journal of the Royal Statistical Society B 39 (1), 1 – 38.

DeVaul, R. W., Sung, M., Gips, J., Pentland, A., October 21–23 2003. MIThril 2003: Applications and Architecture. In: Proceedings of the 7th IEEE International Symposium on Wearable Computers, ISWC. IEEE Computer Society, White Plains, NY, USA, pp. 4–12.

Dielmann, A., Renals, S., May 17–21 2004. Dynamic Bayesian Networks for Meeting Structuring. In: Proceedings of the IEEE International Conference on Acoustics, Speech, and Signal Processing, ICASSP. Montreal, QC, Canada, pp. 629–632.

Dion, K., March 2000. Group Cohesion: From "Field of Forces" to Multdimensional Construct. Group Dynamics: Theory, Research, and Practice 4 (1), pp. 7–26.

Dix, A. J., Finlay, J., Abowd, G. D., Beale, R., 2004. Human-Computer Interaction, 3rd Edition. Pearson Prentice-Hall, Harlow, UK.

Doctor, F., Hagras, H., Callaghan, V., 2005. A Fuzzy Embedded Agent-Based Approach for Realizing Ambient Intelligence in Intelligent Inhabited Environments. IEEE Transactions on Systems, Man, and Cybernetics, Part A 35 (1), pp. 55–65.

Doreian, P., September 1986. Measuring Relative Standing in Small Groups and Bounded Social Networks. Social Psychology Quarterly 49 (3), pp. 247–259.

Doucet, A., de Freitas, N., Gordon, N. J., 2001. Sequential Monte Carlo Methods in Practice. Springer, Berlin, Germany, Ch. 1 Introduction: An Introduction to Sequential Monte Carlo Methods, pp. 4 – 14.

Doucet, A., de Freitas, N., Murphy, K. P., Russell, S. J., 2000a. Rao-blackwellised particle filtering for dynamic bayesian networks. In: UAI '00: Proceedings of the 16th Conference on Uncertainty in Artificial Intelligence. Morgan Kaufmann Publishers Inc., San Francisco, CA, USA, pp. 176–183.

Doucet, A., Godsill, S., Andrieu, C., 2000b. On Sequential Monte Carlo Sampling Methods for Bayesian Filtering. Statistics and Computing 10, 197–208.

Duong, T. V., Bui, H. H., Phung, D. Q., Venkatesh, S., June 20–25 2005. Activity Recognition and Abnormality Detection with the Switching Hidden Semi-Markov Model. In: Proceedings of the IEEE Computer Society Conference on Computer Vision and Pattern Recognition, CVPR. Vol. 1. IEEE Computer Society Press, San Diego, CA, USA, pp. 838–845.

Elman, J. L., 1990. Finding Structure in Time. Cognitive Science 14 (2), 179–211.

Elman, J. L., Zipser, D., 1988. Discovering the Hidden Structure of Speech. Journal of the Acoustical Society of America 83, 1615–1626.

Feldman, J. A., 1985. Connectionist Models and their Applications: Introduction. Cognitive Science 9, 1–2.

Feldman, J. A., Ballard, D. H., 1982. Connectionist Models and their Properties. Cognitive Science 6, 205–254.

Fikes, R. E., Nilsson, N. J., 1990. STRIPS: A New Approach to the Application of Theorem Proving to Problem Solving. In: Allen, J., Hendler, J., Tate, A. (Eds.), Readings in Planning. Kaufmann, San Mateo, CA, USA, pp. 88–97.

Fine, S., Singer, Y., Tishby, N., 1998. The Hierarchical Hidden Markov Model: Analysis and Applications. Machine Learning 32 (1), 41–62.

Forsyth, D. R., 2006. Group Dynamics, 4th International Students Edition. Thomson Wadworth, Belmont, CA, USA.

Fox, A., Johanson, B., Hanrahan, P., Winograd, T., 2000. Integrating Information Appliances into an Interactive Workspace. IEEE Computer Graphics and Applications 20 (3), pp. 54–65.

Fox, D., Hightower, J., Liao, L., Schulz, D., Borriello, G., July-September 2003. Bayesian Filtering for Location Estimation. IEEE Pervasive Computing 02 (3), pp. 24–33.

Franklin, D., July 26–30 1998. Cooperating with People: The Intelligent Classroom. In: Proceedings of the 15th National Conference on Artificial Intelligence and 10th Innovative Applications of Artificial Intelligence Conference, AAAI, IAAI. AAAI Press / The MIT Press, Madison, WI, USA, pp. 555–560.

# BIBLIOGRAPHY

Franklin, D., Budzik, J., Hammond, K., January 13–16 2002. Plan-Based Interfaces: Keeping Track of User Tasks and Acting to Cooperate. In: Proceedings of the 7th International Conference on Intelligent User Interfaces, IUI. ACM Press, San Francisco, CA, USA, pp. 79–86.

Franklin, D., Hammond, K., May 28–June 1 2001. The Intelligent Classroom: Providing Competent Assistance. In: Proceedings of the 5th International Conference on Autonomous Agents, AGENTS. ACM Press, Montreal, Canada, pp. 161–168.

Ghahramani, Z., Jordan, M. I., 1997. Factorial Hidden Markov Models. Machine Learning 29 (2-3), 245–273.

Ghobakhlou, A., Watts, M., Kasabov, N., 2003. Adaptive Speech Recognition with Evolving Connectionist Systems. Information Science 156, 71–83.

Gick, M. L., Holyoak, K. J., 1980. Analogical Problem Solving. Cognitive Psychology 12, pp. 306–355.

Giersich, M., Forbrig, P., Fuchs, G., Kirste, T., Reichart, D., Schumann, H., July 22–27 2007. Towards an Integrated Approach for Task Modeling and Human Behavior Recognition. In: Jacko, J. A. (Ed.), Proceedings of the 12th Human-Computer Interaction International Conference, HCII. Springer-Verlag, Bejing, China, pp. 1109–1118.

Gordon, N. J., Salmond, D. J., Smith, A. F. M., April 1993. Novel Approach to Nonlinear/Non-Gaussian Bayesian State Estimation. IEE Proceedings-F Radar and Signal Processing 140 (2), 107–113.

Gray, W. D., John, B. E., Atwood, M. E., 1993. Project Ernestine: A validation of GOMS for Prediction and Explanation of Real-World Task Performance. Human Computer Interaction 8 (3), pp. 237–309.

Grossberg, S., 1976. Adaptive Pattern Classification and Universal Recoding: I. Parallel Development and Coding of Neural Feature Detectors. Biological Cybernetics 23, 121–134.

Grudin, J., 2002. Group Dynamics and Ubiquitous Computing: From "Here and Now" to "Everywhere and Forever". Communications of the ACM 45 (12), 74–78.

Hamid, R., Huang, Y., Essa, I. A., June 2003. ARGMode – Activity Recognition using Graphical Models. Proceedings of the IEEE Workshop on Event Mining: Detection and Recognition of

Events in Video at IEEE Conference on Computer Vision and Pattern Recognition, CVPR 4, 38–44.

Hayne, S. C., Smith, C. A. P., Vijayasarathy, L., December 14 2003. Chunking and Team Patten Recognition. In: Proceedings of the 3rd Annual Information Systems – Cognitive Research Exchange: Pre International Conference on Information Systems Workshop, IS-CoRE: Pre-ICIS. Seattle, WA, USA, pp. 1–24.

Hebb, D. O., 1949. The Organization of Behavior. Wiley, New York, NY, USA.

Heider, T., September 17 2006. Assigning Documents to Displays in Ad-Hoc Multiple Display Environments. In: Ubicomp 2006 Workshop Proceedings on Usable Ubiquitous Computing in Next-Generation Conference Rooms: Design, Evaluation, and Architecture. Orange County, CA, USA, pp. 1–2, [online], (Accessed: February 22, 2008).
URL http://www.fxpal.com/UbiComp2006/ThomasHeider.pdf

Heider, T., Giersich, M., Kirste, T., September 19–22 2006. Resource Optimization in Multi-Display Environments with Distributed GRASP. In: Proceedings of the 1st International Conference on Ambient Intelligence Developments, AmI.d. Springer-Verlag, Sophia Antipolis, France, pp. 60–76.

Heierman III, E. O., Cook, D. J., Das, S. K., Holder, L. B., 2001. Moving from Internet Appliances to Internet Intelligent Environments: Challenges and Directions. Tech. rep., MavHome, SmartHome, Department of Computer Science and Engineering, University of Texas at Arlington, Arlington, TX, USA.

Hightower, J., Borriello, G., 2001a. Location systems for ubiquitous computing. Computer 34 (8), 57–66.

Hightower, J., Borriello, G., 2001b. A Survey and Taxonomy of Location Sensing Systems for Ubiquitous Computing. Technical Report UW CSE 01-08-03, University of Washington, Department of Computer Science and Engineering, Seattle, WA.

Hightower, J., Borriello, G., September 7–10 2004. Particle Filters for Location Estimation in Ubiquitous Computing: A Case Study. In: Davies, N. (Ed.), Proceedings of the 6th International Conference on Ubiquitous Computing, Ubicomp. Springer-Verlag, Nottingham, UK, pp. 88–106.

# BIBLIOGRAPHY

Hightower, J., Brumitt, B., Borriello, G., June 20–21 2002. The Location Stack: A Layered Model for Location in Ubiquitous Computing. In: Proceedings of the 4th IEEE Workshop on Mobile Computing Systems and Applications, WMCSA. IEEE Computer Society, Callicoon, NY, USA, pp. 22–29.

Hightower, J., Consolvo, S., LaMarca, A., Smith, I., Hughes, J., September 11–14 2005. Learning and Recognizing the Places We Go. In: Proceedings of the 7th International Conference on Ubiquitous Computing, Ubicomp. Springer-Verlag, Tokyo, Japan, pp. 159–176.

Hightower, J., Fox, D., Borriello, G., 2003. The Location Stack. Technical Report UW CSE 03-07-01, University of Washington, Department of Computer Science and Engineering, Seattle, WA.

Hinton, G. E., Dayan, P., Frey, B. J., Neal, R. M., April 1995. The Wake-sleep Algorithm for Unsupervised Neural Networks. Sience 268, 1158–1161.

Hinton, G. E., Sejnowski, T. J., June 19–23 1983. Optimal Perceptual Inference. In: Proceedings of the IEEE Computer Society Conference on Computer Vision and Pattern Recognition, CVPR. IEEE Computer Society Press, Washington, DC, USA, pp. 448–453.

Hochreiter, S., Schmidhuber, J., 1997. Long short-term memory. Neural Computation 9 (8), 1735–1780.

Hopfield, J. J., April 1982. Neural Networks and Physical Systems with Emergent Collective Computational Abilities. Proceedings of the National Academy of Sciences of the USA 79 (8), 2554–2558.

Ichimura, N., August 11–15 2002. Stochastic filtering for motion trajectory in image sequences using a monte carlo filter with estimation of hyper-parameters. In: Proceedings of the 16th International Conference on Pattern Recognition (ICPR). Québec, QC, Canada, pp. 68–73.

Ikoma, N., Ichimura, N., Higuchi, T., Maeda, H., July 25–28 2001. Maneuvering Target Tracking by Using Particle Filter. In: Joint Proceedings of the 9th IFSA World Congress and 20th NAFIPS International Conference. Vol. 4. Vancouver, BC, Canada, pp. 2223–2228.

Inoue, K., 1996. Trainable Vision-based Recognizer of Multi-person Activities. Master's thesis, Massachusetts Institute of Technology Artificial Intelligence Lab, Cambridge, MA, USA.

Ivanov, Y. A., Bobick, A. F., 2000. Recognition of Visual Activities and Interactions by Stochastic Parsing. Transactions on Pattern Analysis and Machine Intelligence 22 (8), 852–872.

Johanson, B., Fox, A., Winograd, T., 2002a. The Interactive Workspaces Project: Experiences with Ubiquitous Computing Rooms. IEEE Pervasive Computing 1 (2), pp. 67–74.

Johanson, B., Hutchins, G., Winograd, T., Stone, M., October 27–30 2002b. PointRight: Experience with Flexible Input Redirection in Interactive Workspaces. In: Proceedings of the 15th Annual ACM Symposium on User Interface Software and Technology, UIST. ACM Press, Paris, France, pp. 227–234.

John, B. E., April 1–5 1990. Extensions of GOMS Analyses to Expert Performance Requiring Perception of Dynamic Visual and Auditory Information. In: Proceedings of the SIGCHI Conference on Human Factors in Computing Systems, CHI. ACM Press, Seattle, WA, USA, pp. 107–116.

John, B. E., Vera, A. H., Matessa, M., Freed, M., Remington, R. W., April 20–25 2002. Automating CPM-GOMS. In: Proceedings of the SIGCHI Conference on Human Factors in Computing Systems, CHI. ACM Press, Minneapolis, MN, USA, pp. 147–154.

Jordan, M. I., 1986. Serial Order: A Parallel Distributed Processing Approach. Technical Report 8604, University of California, Institute for Cognitive Science.

Kalman, R. E., 1960. A New Approach to Linear Filtering and Prediction Problems. Transaction of the ASME – Journal of Basic Engineering 82 (Series D), 35–45.

Kasabov, N., 1998. Evolving Fuzzy Neural Networks: Theory and Applications for On-line Adaptive Prediction, Decision Making and Control. Australian Journal of Intelligent Processing Systems 5 (3), 154–160.

Kasabov, N., 2002. Evolving Connectionist Systems: Methods and Applications in Bioinformatics, Brain Study and Intelligent Machines. Springer-Verlag, London, UK.

Kautz, H., Arnstein, L., Borriello, G., Etzioni, O., Fox, D., July 28–August 1 2002. An Overview of the Assisted Cognition Project. In: Proceedings of the Eighteenth National Conference on Artificial Intelligence and Fourteenth Conference on Innovative Applications of Artificial Intelligence, AAAI, Workshop on Automation as Caregiver: The Role of Intelligent Technology in Elder Care. AAAI Press / The MIT Press, Edmonton, AB, Canada, pp. 60–65.

# BIBLIOGRAPHY

Kidd, C. D., Orr, R., Abowd, G. D., Atkeson, C. G., Essa, I. A., MacIntyre, B., Mynatt, E. D., Starner, T., Newstetter, W., October 1–2 1999. The Aware Home: A Living Laboratory for Ubiquitous Computing Research. In: Proceedings of the 2nd International Workshop on Cooperative Buildings, Integrating Information, Organization, and Architecture, CoBuild. Springer-Verlag, Pittsburgh, PA, USA, pp. 191–198.

Kieras, D. E., 1988. Towards a Practical GOMS Model Methodology for User Interface Design. In: Helander, M. (Ed.), Handbook of Human-Computer Interaction. Elsevier Science Publishers, Amsterdam, Netherlands, pp. 135–158.

Kieras, D. E., 1997. A Guide to GOMS Model Usability Evaluation Using NGOMSL. In: Helander, M., T., L., P., P. (Eds.), Handbook of Human-Computer Interaction, 2nd Edition. Elsevier Science Publishers, Amsterdam, Netherlands, pp. 733–766.

Kieras, D. E., Meyer, D. E., 1995. An Overview of the EPIC Architecture for Cognition and Performance with Application to Human-Computer Interaction. EPIC Report No. 5 (TR-95/ONR-EPIC-5), University of Michigan, Ann Arbor, MI, USA.

Kieras, D. E., Polson, P. G., 1985. An Approach to the Formal Analysis of User Complexity. International Journal of Man-Machine Studies 22 (4), 365–394.

Kitagawa, G., 1996. Monte Carlo Filter and Smoother for Non-Gaussian Nonlinear State Space Models. Journal of Computational and Graphical Statistics 5 (1), 1–25.

Kjærulff, U., June 17–19 1992. A Computational Scheme for Reasoning in Dynamic Probabilistic Networks. In: Proceedings of the Eighth Annual Conference on Uncertainty in Artificial Intelligence. Morgan Kaufmann Publishers Inc., San Mateo, CA, USA, pp. 121–129.

Klaas, M., Briers, M., de Freitas, N., Doucet, A., Maskell, S., Lang, D., July 26–29 2005. Toward Practical $N^2$ Monte Carlo: The Marginal Particle Filter. In: Proceedings of the 21th Conference on Uncertainty in Artificial Intelligence (UAI). Edinburgh, Scotland, UK, pp. 308–315.

Klaas, M., Briers, M., de Freitas, N., Doucet, A., Maskell, S., Lang, D., 2006. Fast particle smoothing: if i had a million particles. In: ICML '06: Proceedings of the 23rd international conference on Machine learning. ACM Press, New York, NY, USA, pp. 481–488.

Krumm, J., Harris, S., Meyers, B., Brumitt, B., Hale, M., Shafer, S., July 1 2000. Multi-Camera Multi-Person Tracking for EasyLiving. In: Proceedings of the 3rd IEEE International Workshop on Visual Surveillance, VS. IEEE Computer Society Press, Dublin, Ireland, pp. 3–10.

Laird, J. E., Newell, A., Rosenbloom, P. S., September 1987. SOAR: An Architecture for General Intelligence. Artificial Intelligence 33 (1), pp. 1–64.

LaMarca, A., Chawathe, Y., Consolvo, S., Hightower, J., Smith, I., Scott, J., Sohn, T., Howard, J., Hughes, J., Potter, F., Tabert, J., Powledge, P., Borriello, G., Schilit, B., May 8–13 2005. Place Lab: Device Positioning Using Radio Beacons in the Wild. In: Proceedings of the 3rd International Conference on Pervasive Computing, PERVASIVE. Springer-Verlag, Munich, Germany, pp. 116–133.

Le Gal, C., Martin, J., Lux, A., Crowley, J. L., 2001. Smart Office: Design of an Intelligent Environment. IEEE Intelligent Systems 16 (4), 60–66.

Liao, L., Fox, D., Hightower, J., Kautz, H., Schulz, D., October 27–31 2003. Voronoi Tracking: Location Estimation Using Sparse and Noisy Sensor Data. In: Proceedings of the IEEE/RSJ International Conference on Intelligent Robots and Systems, IROS. Vol. 1. IEEE Computer Society Press, Las Vegas, NV, USA, pp. 723–728.

Liao, L., Fox, D., Kautz, H., 2005a. Location-based Activity Recognition. In: Weiss, Y., Schölkopf, B., Platt, J. (Eds.), Advances in Neural Information Processing Systems: Proceedings of the 18th Conference on Neural Information Processing Systems: Natural and Synthetic, NIPS. MIT Press, Cambridge, MA, USA, pp. 787–794.

Liao, L., Fox, D., Kautz, H., July 30–August 5 2005b. Location-based Activity Recognition using Relational Markov Networks. In: Proceedings of the Nineteenth International Joint Conference on Artificial Intelligence, IJCAI. Edinburgh, Scotland, UK, pp. 773–778.

Liao, L., Fox, D., Kautz, H., 2007. Extracting Places and Activities from GPS Traces using Hierarchical Conditional Random Fields. International Journal of Robotics Research 26 (1), 119–134.

Liao, L., Fox, D., Kautz, H. A., July 25–29 2004. Learning and Inferring Transportation Routines. In: Proceedings of the 19th National Conference on Artificial Intelligence and 16th Conference on Innovative Applications of Artificial Intelligence, AAAI, IAAI. AAAI Press / The MIT Press, San Jose, CA, USA, pp. 348–353.

## BIBLIOGRAPHY

Maier, N. R. F., August 1931. Reasoning in Humans. II. The Solution of a Problem and its Appearance in Consciousness. Journal of Comparative Psychology 12 (2), pp. 181–194.

Markov, A. A., 1971. Extensions of the Limit Theorems of Probability Theory to a Sum of Variables Connected in a Chain. reprinted in Appendix B of: Howard, Ronald A. Dynamic Probabilistic Systems vol I: Markov Models, John Wiley & Sons Ltd..

McClelland, J. L., Rumelhart, D. E., the PDP Research Group, 1988. Parallel Distributed Processing: Exploration in the Microstructure of Cognition, eighth Edition. Vol. 2: Psychological and Biological Models. MIT Press, Cambridge, MA, USA.

McCowan, I., Gatica-Perez, D., Bengio, S., Moore, D., Bourlard, H., November 3–4 2003. Towards Computer Understanding of Human Interactions. In: Procceedings of the 1st European Symposium on Ambient Intelligence, EUSAI. Springer-Verlag, Eindhoven, Netherlands, pp. 235–251.

McCowan, L., Gatica-Perez, D., Bengio, S., Lathoud, G., Barnard, M., Zhang, D., 2005. Automatic Analysis of Multimodal Group Actions in Meetings. IEEE Transactions on Pattern Analysis and Machine Intelligence 27 (3), pp. 305–317.

McGrath, J. E., 1984. Groups: Interaction and Performance. Prentice Hall, Upper Saddle River, NJ, USA.

Merriam–Webster Medical Online Dictionary, 2008. Definition of *"Cognitive Psychology"* [online], (Accessed: January 25, 2008).
URL http://medical.m-w.com/medical/Cognitive%20Psychology

Merriam–Webster Online Dictionary, 2008a. Definition of *"Persona"* [online], (Accessed: April 11, 2008).
URL http://www.m-w.com/dictionary/Persona

Merriam–Webster Online Dictionary, 2008b. Definition of *"Social Psychology"* [online], (Accessed: December 7, 2007).
URL http://www.m-w.com/dictionary/Social%20Psychology

Merriam–Webster Online Dictionary, 2008c. Definition of *"Connectionism"* [online], (Accessed: March 19, 2008).
URL http://www.m-w.com/dictionary/Connectionism

Minsky, M. L., Papert, S. A., 1969. Perceptrons: An Introduction to Computational Geometry. MIT Press, Cambridge, MA, USA.

Moore, D. J., Essa, I. A., July 28–August 1 2002. Recognizing Multitasked Activities from Video using Stochastic Context-free Grammar. In: Proceedings of the Eighteenth National Conference on Artificial Intelligence and Fourteenth Conference on Innovative Applications of Artificial Intelligence. AAAI Press / The MIT Press, Edmonton, AB, Canada, pp. 770–776.

Moreland, R. L., Levine, J., 1982. Socialization in Small Groups: Temporal Changes in Individual-Group Relations. Advances in Experimental Social Psychology 15, pp. 137–192.

Moreno, J. L., 1934, revised 1953. Who Shall Survive?, 2nd Edition. Beacon-House, Beacon, NY, USA, [online] <http://www.asgpp.org/docs/WSS/WSS.html> (Accessed: January 9, 2008).

Mori, G., Paternò, F., Santoro, C., 2002. CTTE: Support for Developing and Analyzing Task Models for Interactive System Design. IEEE Transactions on Software Engineering 28 (8), pp. 797–813.

Mozer, M. C., March 23–25 1998. The Neural Network House: An Environment that adapts to its Inhabitants. In: Proceedings of the American Association for Artificial Intelligence Spring Symposium. AAAI Press, Palo Alto, CA, USA, pp. 110–114.

Mozer, M. C., 2005. Lessons from an Adaptive House. In: Cook, D. J., Das, S. K. (Eds.), Smart Environments: Technologies, Protocols, and Applications. John Wiley & Sons Ltd, Hoboken, NJ, USA, pp. 273–294.

Mozer, M. C., Dodier, R. H., Anderson, M., Vidmar, L., Cruikshank III, R. F., Miller, D., 1995. The Neural Network House: An Overview. In: Niklasson, L., Boden, M. (Eds.), Current Trends in Connectionism. Erlbaum, Hillsdale, NJ, USA, pp. 371–380.

Mozer, M. C., Miller, D., 1998. Parsing the Stream of Time: The Value of Event-based Segmentation in a Complex, Real-world Control Problem. In: Giles, C. L., Gori, M. (Eds.), Adaptive Processing of Temporal Sequences and Data Structures. Springer-Verlag, Berlin, Germany, pp. 370–388.

Murphy, K. P., 1998. Switching Kalman Filter. Technical report, DEC/Compaq Cambridge Research Labs.

# BIBLIOGRAPHY

Murphy, K. P., 2002. Dynamic bayesian networks: Representation, inference and learning. Ph.D. thesis, University of California, Berkeley, CA, USA.

Murphy, K. P., Paskin, M. A., December 3–8 2001. Linear Time Inference in Hierarchical HMMs. In: Advances in Neural Information Processing Systems: Proceedings of the 14th Conference on Neural Information Processing Systems: Natural and Synthetic, NIPS. MIT Press, Vancouver, BC, Canada, pp. 833–840.

Musso, C., Oudjane, N., Le Gland, F., 2001. Sequential Monte Carlo Methods in Practice. Springer, Berlin, Germany, Ch. 3 Strategies for Improving Sequential Monte Carlo Methods: Improving Regularized Particle Filters, pp. 247–269.

Neal, R. M., 1996. Bayesian Learning for Neural Networks. No. 118 in Lecture Notes in Statistics. Springer-Verlag, New York, NY, USA.

Neisser, U., 1967. Cognitive Psychology. Appleton-Century-Crofts, New York, NY, USA.

Newcomb, A. F., Bukowski, W. M., Pattee, L., January 1993. Children's Peer Relation. Psychological Bulletin 113 (1), pp. 99–128.

Newell, A., 1990. Unified Theories of Cognition. Harvard University Press, Cambridge, MA, USA.

Newell, A., Simon, H. A., 1972. Human Problem Solving. Prentice-Hall, Englewood Cliffs, NJ, USA.

Nguyen, N. T., Bui, H. H., Venkatesh, S., West, G., June 16–2 2003. Recognising and Monitoring High-Level Behaviours in Complex Spatial Environments. In: Proceedings of the IEEE International Conference on Computer Vision and Pattern Recognition, CVPR. Vol. 2. IEEE Computer Society Press, Madison, WI, USA, pp. 620–625.

Nicholson, A., 1992. Monitoring Discrete Environments Using Dynamic Belief Networks. Ph.D. thesis, Oxford University.

Orr, R. J., Abowd, G. D., April 1–6 2000. The Smart Floor: A Mechanism for Natural User Identification and Tracking. In: Extended Abstracts on Human Factors in Computing Systems, CHI. ACM Press, The Hague, Netherlands, pp. 275–276.

Paternò, F., 1999. Model-Based Design and Evaluation of Interactive Application. Springer-Verlag, London, UK.

Patterson, D. J., Liao, L., Fox, D., Kautz, H. A., October 12–15 2003. Inferring High-Level Behavior from Low-Level Sensors. In: Proceedings of the 5th International Conference on Ubiquitous Computing, Ubicomp. Springer-Verlag, Seattle, WA, USA, pp. 73–89.

Patterson, D. J., Liao, L., Gajos, K., Collier, M., Livic, N., Olson, K., Wang, S., Fox, D., Kautz, H. A., September 7–10 2004. Opportunity Knocks: A System to Provide Cognitive Assistance with Transportation Services. In: Proceedings of the 6th International Conference on Ubiquitous Computing, Ubicomp. Springer-Verlag, Nottingham, UK, pp. 433–450.

Payne, S. J., Green, T. R. G., 1986. Task-Action Grammars: A Model of the Mental Representation of Task Languages. Human-Computer Interaction 2 (2), pp. 93–133.

Pitt, M. K., Shephard, N., 1999. Filtering via Simulation: Auxiliary Particle Filters. Journal of the American Statistical Association 94 (446), 590–630.

PlaceLab, 2008. PlaceLab: A House_n + TIAX Initiative [online], (Accessed: April 26, 2008). URL http://architecture.mit.edu/house_n/documents/PlaceLab.pdf

Ponnekanti, S., Robles, L. A., Fox, A., June 20–21 2002. User Interfaces for Network Services: What, from Where, and How. In: Proceedings of the 4th IEEE Workshop on Mobile Computing Systems and Application, WMCSA. IEEE Computer Society Press, Callicoon, NY, USA, pp. 138–148.

Rabiner, L. R., 1989. A tutorial on hidden markov models and selected applications in speech recognition. Proceedings of the IEEE 77 (2), 257–286.

Reisner, P., March 1981. Formal Grammar and Human Factors Design of an Interactive Graphics System. IEEE Transactions on Software Engineering 7 (2), pp. 229–240.

Rich, E., October 1979. User Modeling via Stereotypes. Cognitive Science 3 (4), 329 – 354.

Rivera-Illingworth, F., Callaghan, V., Hagras, H., June 28–29 2005. A Neural Network Agent Based Approach to Activity Detection in AmI Environments. In: Proceedings of the IEEE International Workshop on Intelligent Environments, IE. IEEE Computer Society Press, Colchester, UK, pp. 92–99.

Rosenblatt, F., November 1958. The Perceptron: A Probabilistic Model for Information Storage and Organization in the Brain. Psychological Review 65 (6), 386–408.

# BIBLIOGRAPHY

Roweis, S., Ghahramani, Z., 1999. A Unifying Review of Linear Gaussian Models. Neural Computation 11 (2), 305–345.

Rumelhart, D. E., Hinton, G. E., Williams, R. J., 1989a. Parallel Distributed Processing: Exploration in the Microstructure of Cognition. In: Rumelhart, D. E., McClelland, J. L., the PDP Research Group (Eds.), Learning Internal Representations by Error Propagation, ninth Edition. Vol. 1: Foundations. MIT Press, Cambridge, MA, USA, Ch. 8, pp. 318–362.

Rumelhart, D. E., McClelland, J. L., the PDP Research Group, 1989b. Parallel Distributed Processing: Exploration in the Microstructure of Cognition, ninth Edition. Vol. 1: Foundations. MIT Press, Cambridge, MA, USA.

Russell, S., Norvig, P., December 2002. Artificial Intelligence: A Modern Approach, 2nd Edition. Prentice Hall, Englewood Cliffs, NJ, USA.

Saboune, J., Charpillet, F., 2005. Using interval particle filtering for marker less 3d human motion capture. In: ICTAI '05: Proceedings of the 17th IEEE International Conference on Tools with Artificial Intelligence. IEEE Computer Society, Washington, DC, USA, pp. 621–627.

Saul, L. K., Jordan, M. I., 1995. Boltzmann Chains and Hidden Markov Models. Advances in Neural Information Processing Systems 7, 435–442.

Savvides, A., Srivastava, M. B., 2005. Advances in Pervasive Computing and Networking. Springer, Ch. 8 A Self-Configuring Location Discovery System for Smart Environments, pp. 167–177.

Schultz, T., Waibel, A., Metze, F., Ries, K., Schaaf, T., Pan, Y., Soltau, H., Westphal, M., Yu, H., Zechner, K., April 9–11 2001. The ISL Meeting Room System. In: Proceedings of the International Workshop on Hands-free Speech Communication, HSC. Kyoto, Japan.

Schulz, D., Fox, D., Hightower, J., August 9–15 2003. People Tracking with Anonymous and ID-Sensors Using Rao-Blackwellised Particle Filters. In: Gottlob, G., Walsh, T. (Eds.), Proceedings of the 18th International Joint Conference on Artificial Intelligence, IJCAI. Morgan Kaufmann, Acapulco, Mexico, pp. 921–928.

Shafer, S., Krumm, J., Brumitt, B., Meyers, B., Czerwinski, M., Robbins, D., July 30–31 1998. The New EasyLiving Project at Microsoft Research. In: Proceedings of the DARPA/NIST Smart Spaces Workshop. DARPA, Gaithersburg, MD, USA, pp. 127–130.

Shaw, M. E., 1978. Communication Networks Fourteen Years Later. In: Berkowitz, L. (Ed.), Group Processes. Academic Press, New York, NY, USA, pp. 351–362.

SmartKG, 2003. Smart Kindergarten: Annual Report 2003 [online], (Accessed: April 26, 2008).
URL http://nesl.ee.ucla.edu/projects/smartkg/docs/AR03.pdf

Srivastava, M. B., Muntz, R., Potkonjak, M., July 16–21 2001. Smart Kindergarten: Sensor-based Wireless Networks for Smart Developmental Problem-solving Environments. In: Proceedings of the ACM SIGMOBILE 7th Annual International Conference on Mobile Computing and Networking, MobiCom. Rome, Italy, pp. 132–138.

Suchman, L., September 1995. Making Work Visible. Communications of the ACM 38 (9), 56 – 64.

Sutton, R., Barto, A., March 1981. Towards a Modern Theory of Adaptive Networks: Expectation and Prediction. Psychological Review 88 (2), 135–170.

TechWeb: TechEncyclopedia, 2008. Definition of *"Zeroconf"* [online], (Accessed: June 12, 2008).
URL http://www.techweb.com/encyclopedia

Tuckman, B. W., 1965. Developmental Sequences in Small Groups. Psychological Bulletin 63 (6), pp. 384–399.

Tuckman, B. W., Jensen, M. A., 1977. Stages of Group Development revisited. Group and Organizational Studies 2, pp. 419–427.

Ubisense, 2008. Claims [online], (Accessed: June 12, 2008).
URL http://www.ubisense.net

van der Merwe, R., de Freitas, N., Doucet, A., Wan, E., November 27–30 2000. The unscented particel filter. In: Proceedings of the Neural Information Processing Systems Conference (NIPS). Denver, CO, USA, pp. 584–590.

Wageman, R., 2001. The Meaning of Interdependence. In: Turner, M. E. (Ed.), Groups at Work: Theory and Research. Lawrence Erlbaum Associates, Mahwah, NJ, USA, pp. 197–217.

# BIBLIOGRAPHY

Waibel, A., Bett, M., Finke, M., February 28–March 3 1998. Meeting Browser: Tracking and Summarizing Meetings. In: Proceedings of the DARPA Broadcast News Workshop. Herndon, VA, USA.

Waibel, A., Schultz, T., Bett, M., Denecke, M., Malkin, R., Rogina, I., Stiefelhagen, R., Yang, J., April 6–10 2003. SMaRT: The Smart Meeting Room Task at ISL. In: Proceeding of the 28th IEEE International Conference on Acoustic, Speech, and Signal Processing, ICASSP. Vol. 4. IEEE Signal Processing Society Press, Hong Kong, China, pp. 752–755.

Wan, E., van der Merwe, R., 2001. The Unscented Kalman Filter. In: Haykin, S. (Ed.), Kalman Filtering and Neural Networks. Wiley Publishing, pp. 221–280.

Want, R., Hopper, A., Falcao, V., Gibbons, J., 1992. The Active Badge Location System. Tech. Rep. 92.1, Olivetti Research Ltd., Cambridge, UK.

Ward, K., Marshall, C. R., Novick, D. G., 1995. Applying Task Classification to Natural Meetings. Tech. Rep. CS/E 95-011, Oregon Graduate Institute, Portland, OR, USA.

Weiser, M., September 1991. The computer for the 21st century. Scientific American 265 (3), 94–104.

Weiser, M., July 1993. Some Computer Science Issues in Ubiquitous Computing. Communications of the ACM 36 (7), pp. 75–84.

Wikipedia, 2008. Definition of *"Trie"* [online], (Accessed: April 22, 2008).
URL http://en.wikipedia.org/wiki/Trie

Wojek, C., Nickel, K., Stiefelhagen, R., September 3–6 2006. Activity Recognition and Room Level Tracking in an Office Environment. In: Proceedings of the IEEE International Conference on Multisensor Fusion and Integration for Intelligent Systems, MFI. Heidelberg, Germany, pp. 25–30.

Yang, J., Zhu, X., Gross, R., Kominek, J., Pan, Y., Waibel, A., April 12–14 2000. Multimodal People ID for a Multimedia Meeting Browser. In: Proceedings of the International Conference onComputer Assisted Information Retrieval, RIAO. Paris, France.

Zhang, D., Gatica-Perez, D., Bengio, S., McCowan, I., Lathoud, G., 2004. Modeling Individual and Group Actions in Meetings: A Two-layer HMM Framework. In: Proceedings of the

Conference on Computer Vision and Pattern Recognition Workshop, CVPRW. Vol. 7. IEEE Computer Society, Washington, DC, USA, p. 117.

Zhang, D., Gatica-Perez, D., Bengio, S., Roy, D., 2006. Learning Influence among Interacting Markov Chains. In: Weiss, Y., Schölkopf, B., Platt, J. (Eds.), Advances in Neural Information Processing Systems 18. MIT Press, Cambridge, MA, USA, pp. 1577–1584.

# Appendix A

# Core Tool Features

This appendix list the features of the three Core Tool components Adapter, Filter, and Learner. Because these components are commandline tools for the representation of their feature sets the usage listing was chosen that will be returned when typing the '-h' option at the prompt.

*Appendix A*

```
[floyd:~] magier% ubi2pfl -h
usage: ubi2pfl [-b] [-f <trimsecs>] [-r] [-t <tstep>] {[-l <nr>=<id>]} [-u] [-q]
        -b          skip data outside bounding box ((0,0),(703,681))
        -c          use CSV-mode (separate fields by ","
        -f <s>      skip first <s> seconds
        -i          skip truth data ('i <time> <state> <action>')
        -l <nr>=<id> set tag <nr> to <id> (MAX_LABEL is maximum nr)
        -n <nl>     set number of labels to process. <nl> must be smaller than MAX_LABEL: 100
        -p <s>      set data unseen from time <s> in seconds on
        -r          use Raw data (default: Filter)
        -t <s>      fill in missing data every <s> seconds
        -u          force line bUffer mode
        -q          quiet mode
    example: ubi2pfl -b -f3 -r -t.25
[floyd:~] magier%
```

Figure A.1: Adapter module's usage listing.

```
[floyd:~] magier% pfilter -h
usage:
    pfilter [-L dir] -M name [-P name] [-X dir] [-a <num>] [-b <num>] [-d path] [-e path] [-f mode]
            [-n np] [-p ps] [-r thr] [-s path] [-u] [-v path]
    pfilter [-L dir] -M name [-P name] [-X dir] -l
        -L <dir>    : use <dir> as plib-directory (default: /usr/local/lib/plib)
        -M <name>   : use model <name>
        -P <name>   : use static model params file <name>
        -X <dir>    : use <dir> for reading model files / writing executables (default: cwd)
        -a <num>    : relative weight of sensor data (0.0 .. 1.0, default 1.0)
        -b <num>    : minimal particle weight (0.0 .. 1.0, default 0.0)
        -d <path>   : dump particle data to file <path>
        -e <path>   : collect #effective particles statistics in file <path>
        -f <mode>   : use filter mode <mode>
                     (<mode> = forward, viterbi, smoothing, default forward)
        -l          : print filter params to stdout (in format usable for -p
                     option) and quit
        -n <np>     : use <np> particles in filter
        -p <ps>     : initialize statistic params from param string <ps>
                     (individual params separated by space, so typically <ps>
                     needs to be included in quotes)
        -r <thr>    : use resampling threshold <thr> (0.0 .. 1.0, default 1.0)
        -s <path>   : save sensor data in file <path>
        -u          : force line bUffer mode
        -v <path>   : collect votes in file <path>
[floyd:~] magier%
```

Figure A.2: Filter module's usage listing.

```
[floyd:~] magier% plearn -h
usage:
    plearn [-L dir] -M name [-P name] [-X dir] [-e path] [-i nr] [-n np] [-p ps] [-r thr] [-s path]
           [-u] path ...
    plearn [-L dir] -M name [-P name] [-X dir] -l
        -L <dir>    : use <dir> as plib-directory (default: /usr/local/lib/plib)
        -M <name>   : use model <name>
        -P <name>   : use static model params file <name>
        -X <dir>    : use <dir> for reading model files / writing executables (default: cwd)
        -e <path>   : collect #effective particles statistics in file <path>
        -i <nr>     : use <nr> learning iterations
        -l          : print filter params to stdout (in format usable for -p
                     option) and quit
        -n <np>     : use <np> particles in filter
        -p <ps>     : initialize statistic params from param string <ps>
                     (individual params separated by space, so typically <ps>
                     needs to be included in quotes)
        -r <thr>    : use resampling threshold <thr> (0.0 .. 1.0)
        -s <path>   : save intermediate statistic params in file <path>
        -u          : force line bUffer mode
[floyd:~] magier%
```

Figure A.3: Learner module's usage listing.

# Appendix B

# Results Experiment #2

This appendix contrasts the results that the different parameter configurations achieved in the three tests of experiment #2. Each of the following double pages shows all results of one aspect of these tests. Starting with initial precision test, the appendix continues with the precision results of the test that used trained parameters for the sensor model. Then the results of the reliability test follow. Finally, three double pages show the results of the robustness test. In the first of these three robustness runs the sensor data of A was lacking. Then B's sensor data was skipped. Finally the sensor data of C was not available.

The abbreviations utilized to label the parameter configurations in the figures stick to the following conventions. The first letter denotes the agenda compliance, where $c$ means compliant, $n$ says non-compliant, and $a$ is all or both respectively. The second letter identifies the sensor model used. Here, $g$ stands for Gaussian and $c$ means Cauchy-distributed. The last letter indicates the configured timer model, where $g$ again means Gaussian-distributed and $e$ denotes the Exponential distribution. Then usually follows a real number or the term *UNI*. The numbers represent the probability $P_{follow}$ that the team will follow its preliminary meeting agenda. *UNI* indicates that this an agenda-free model, where agenda information has not been used.

*Appendix B*

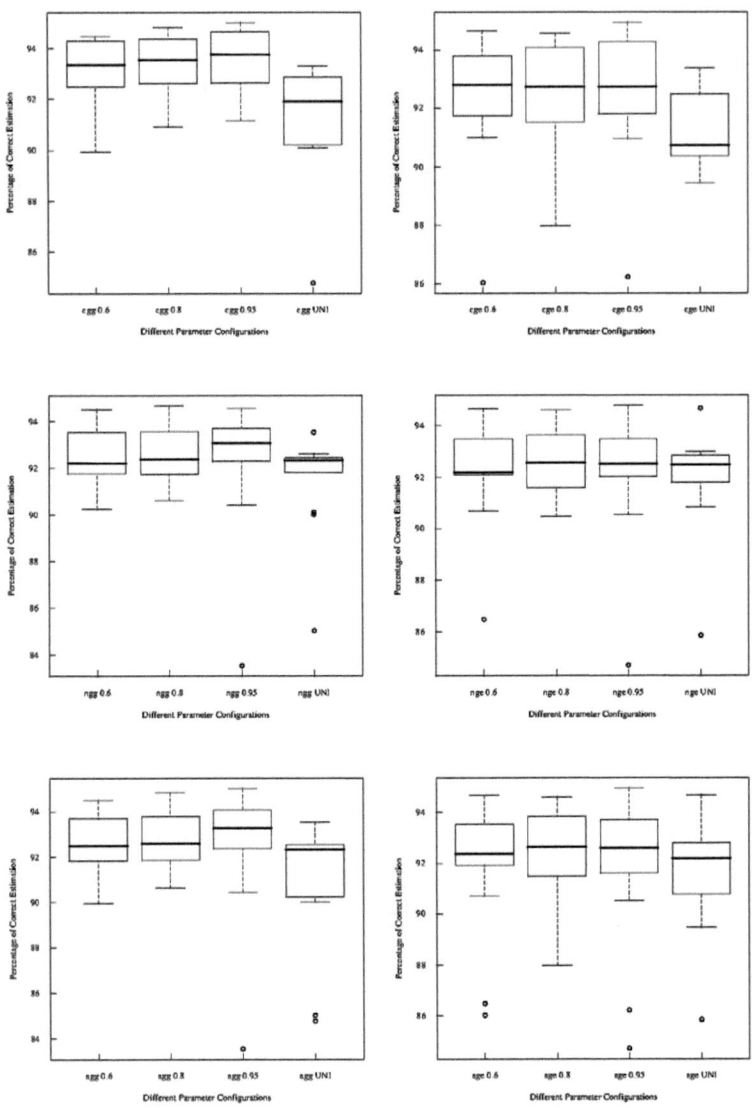

Figure B.1: Precision tests with the Gaussian-distributed sensor model that was configured with an initial parameter setting.

*Results Experiment #2*

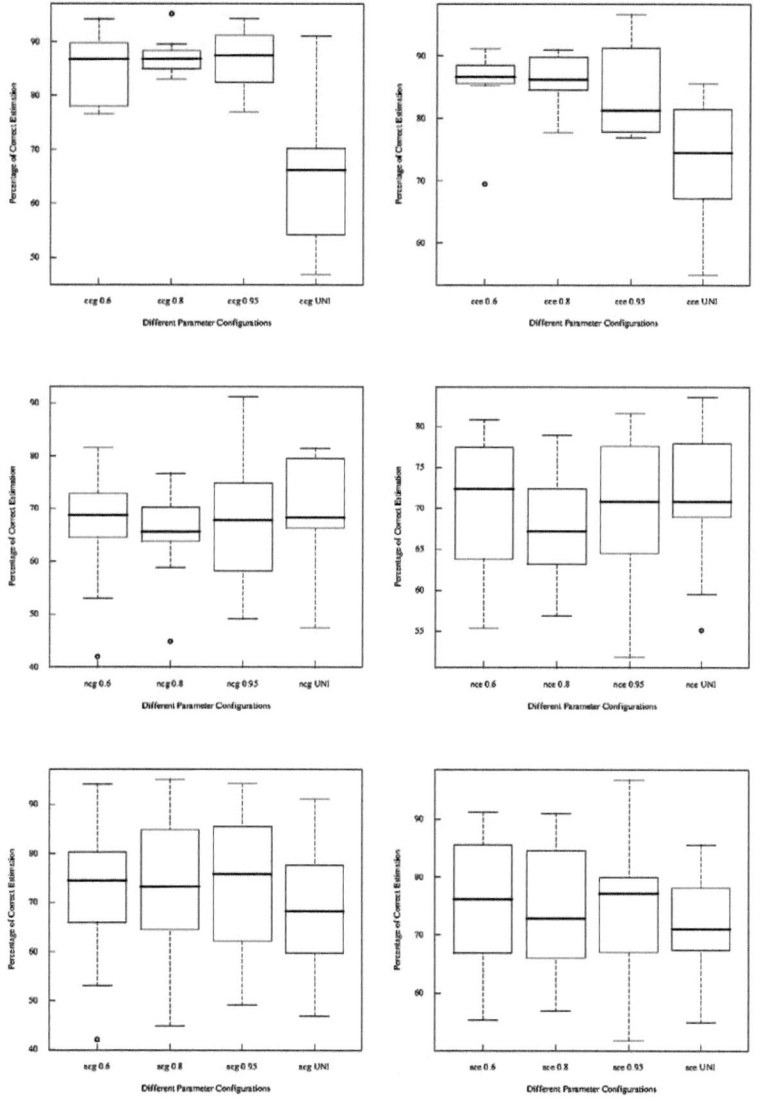

Figure B.2: Precision tests with the Cauchy-distributed sensor model that was configured with an initial parameter setting.

Appendix B

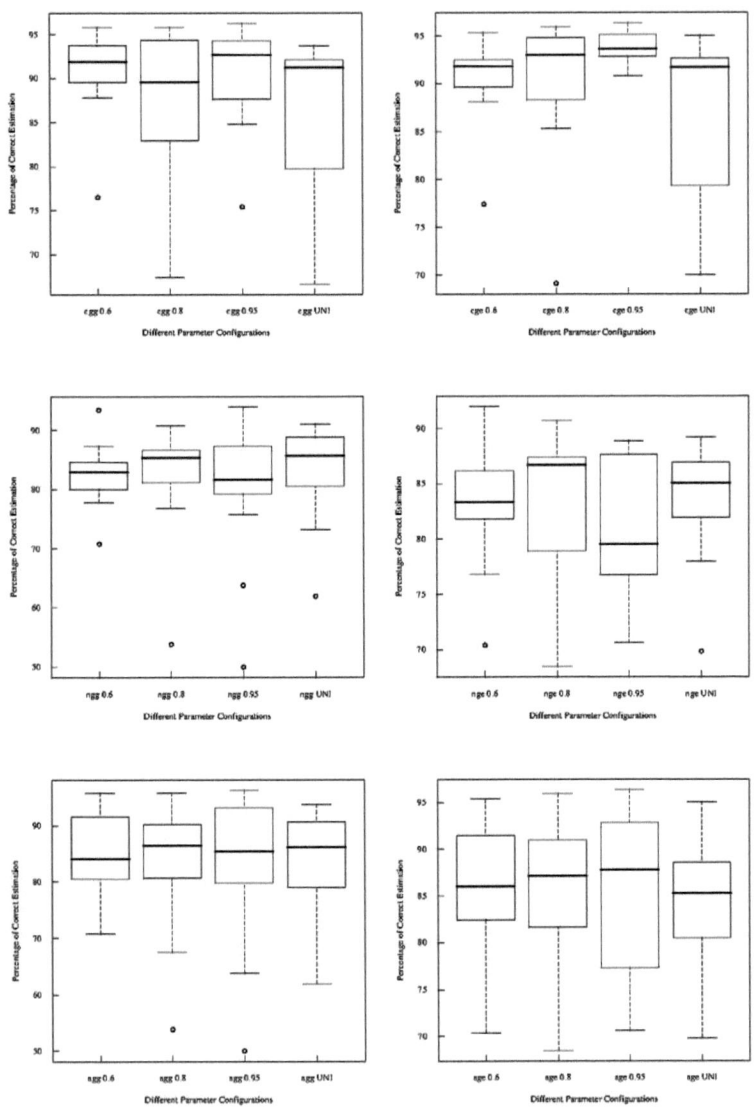

Figure B.3: Precision tests with the Gaussian-distributed sensor model that was configured with a trained parameter setting.

Results Experiment #2

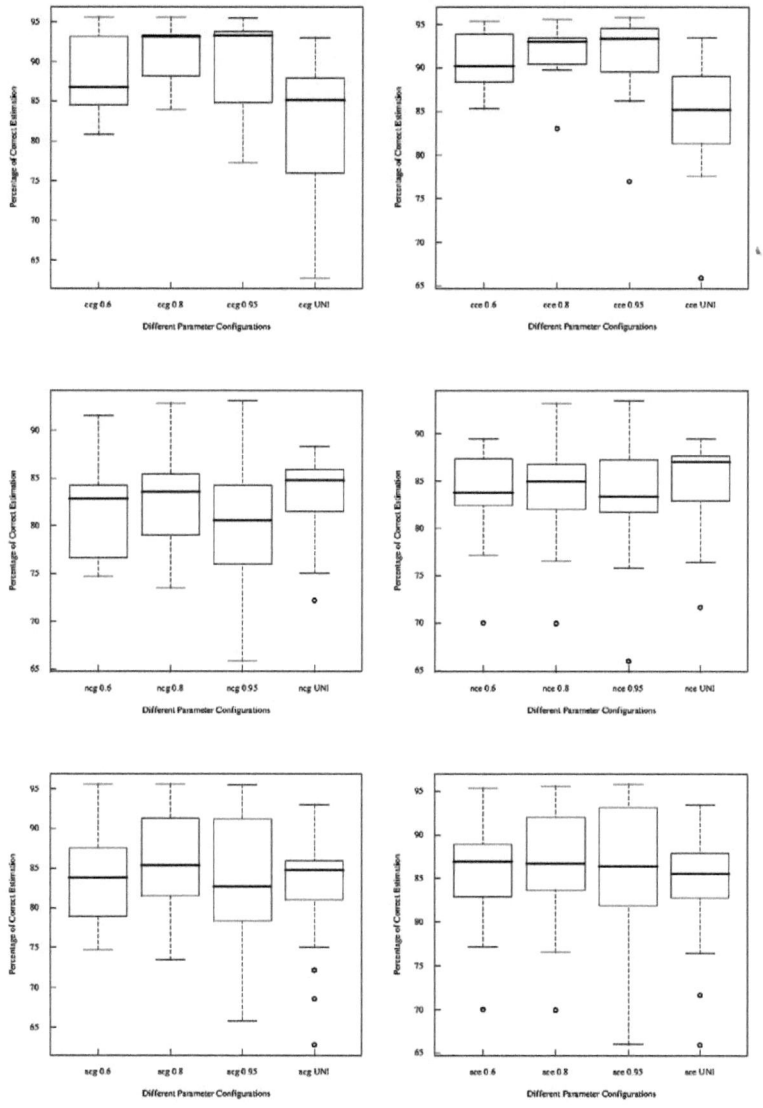

Figure B.4: Precision tests with the Cauchy-distributed sensor model that was configured with a trained parameter setting.

*Appendix B*

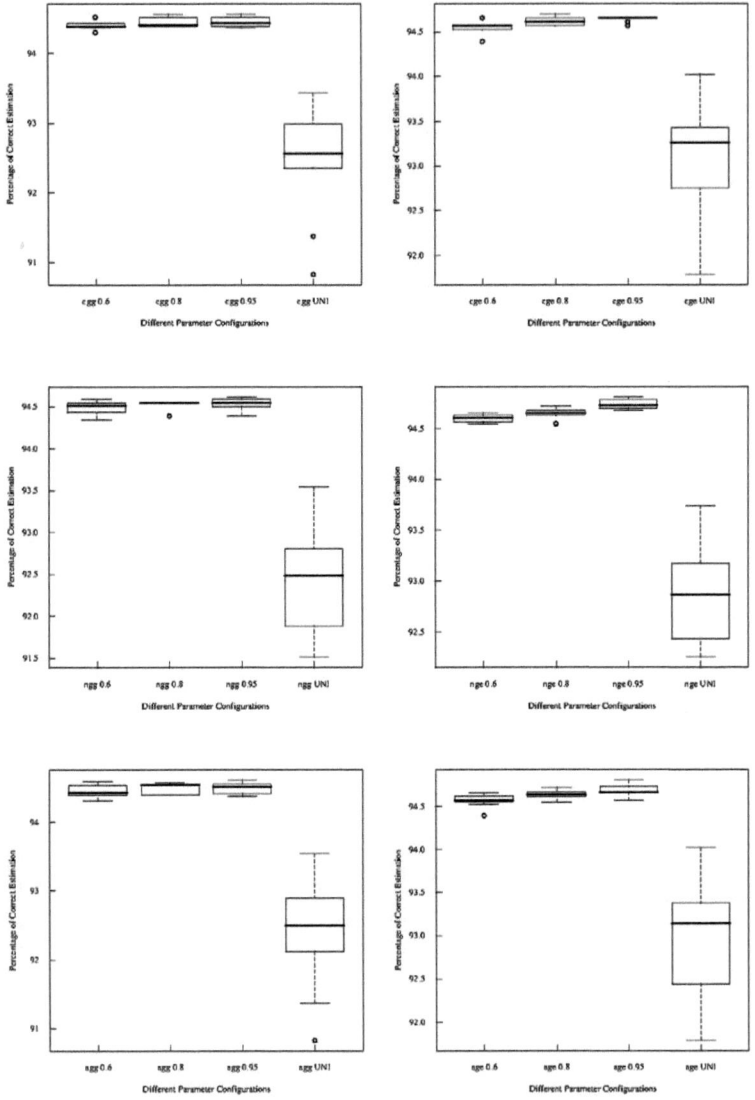

Figure B.5: Reliability tests with the Gaussian-distributed sensor model that was configured with an initial parameter setting.

## Results Experiment #2

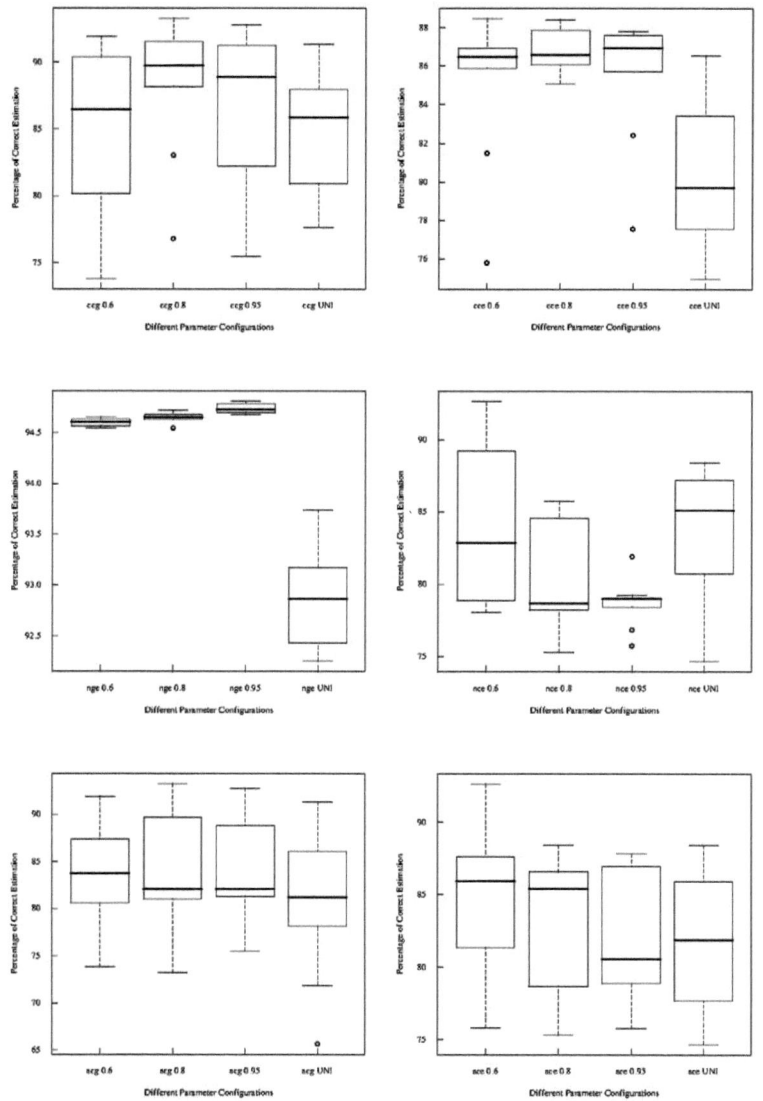

Figure B.6: Reliability tests with the Cauchy-distributed sensor model that was configured with an initial parameter setting.

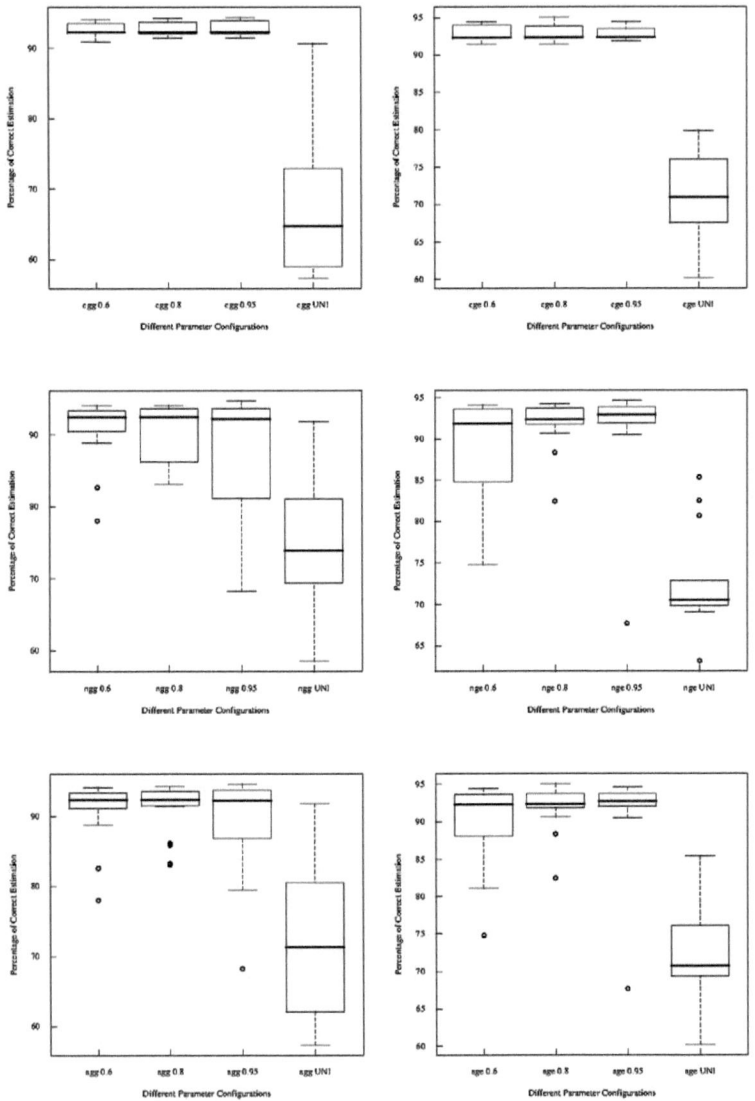

Figure B.7: Robustness !ABC tests with the Gaussian-distributed sensor model that was configured with an initial parameter setting.

# Results Experiment #2

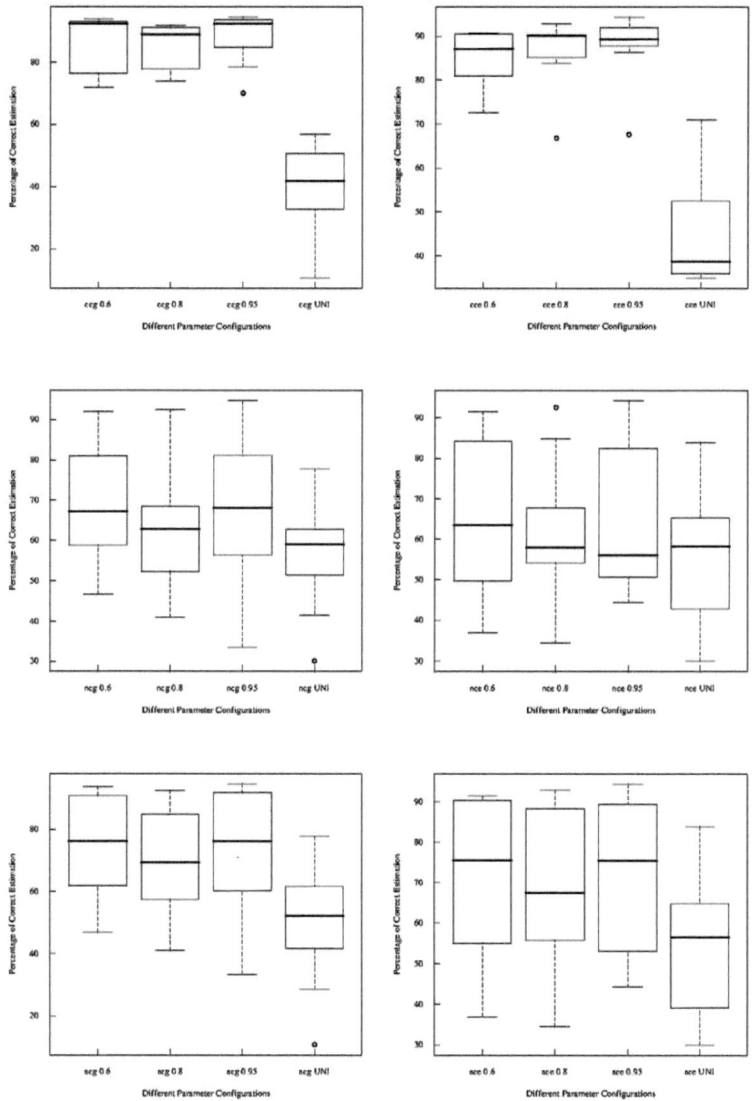

Figure B.8: Robustness !ABC tests with the Cauchy-distributed sensor model that was configured with an initial parameter setting.

Appendix B

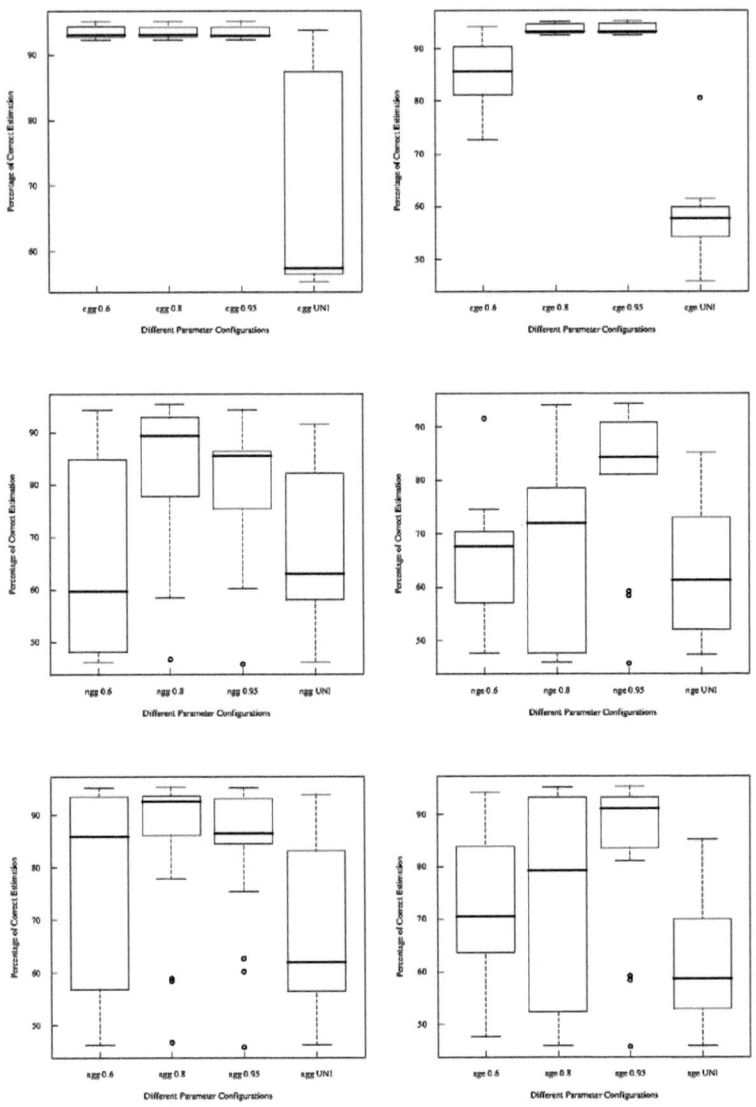

Figure B.9: Robustness A!BC tests with the Gaussian-distributed sensor model that was configured with an initial parameter setting.

Results Experiment #2

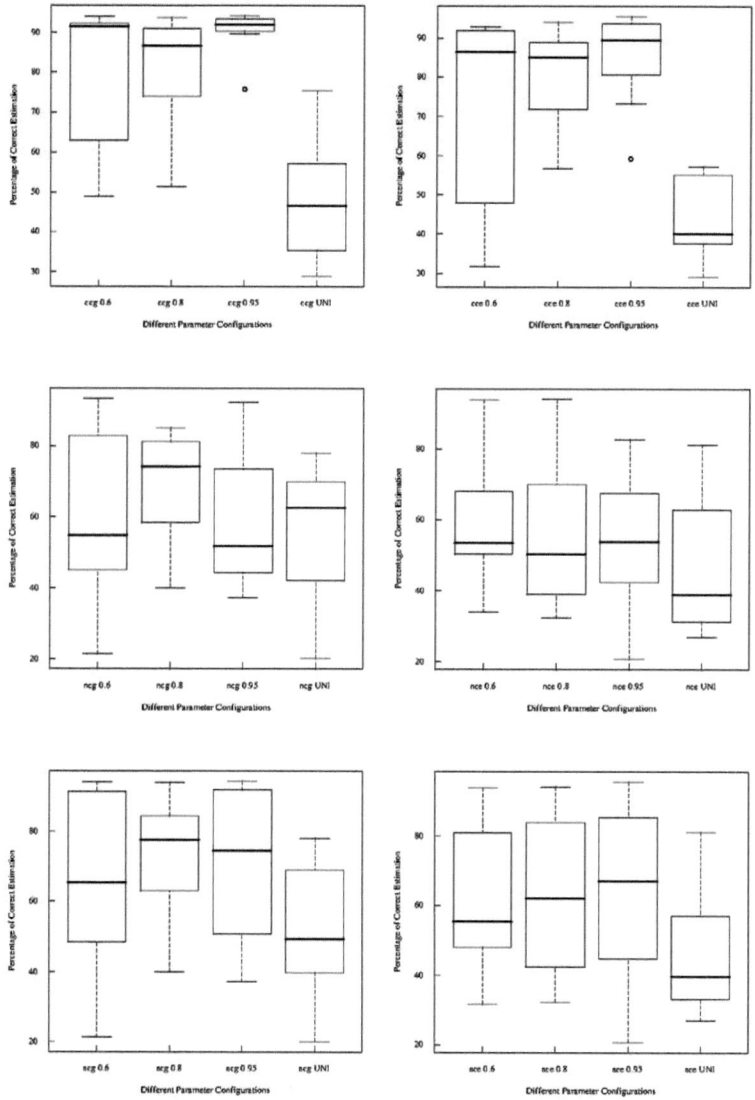

Figure B.10: Robustness A!BC tests with the Cauchy-distributed sensor model that was configured with an initial parameter setting.

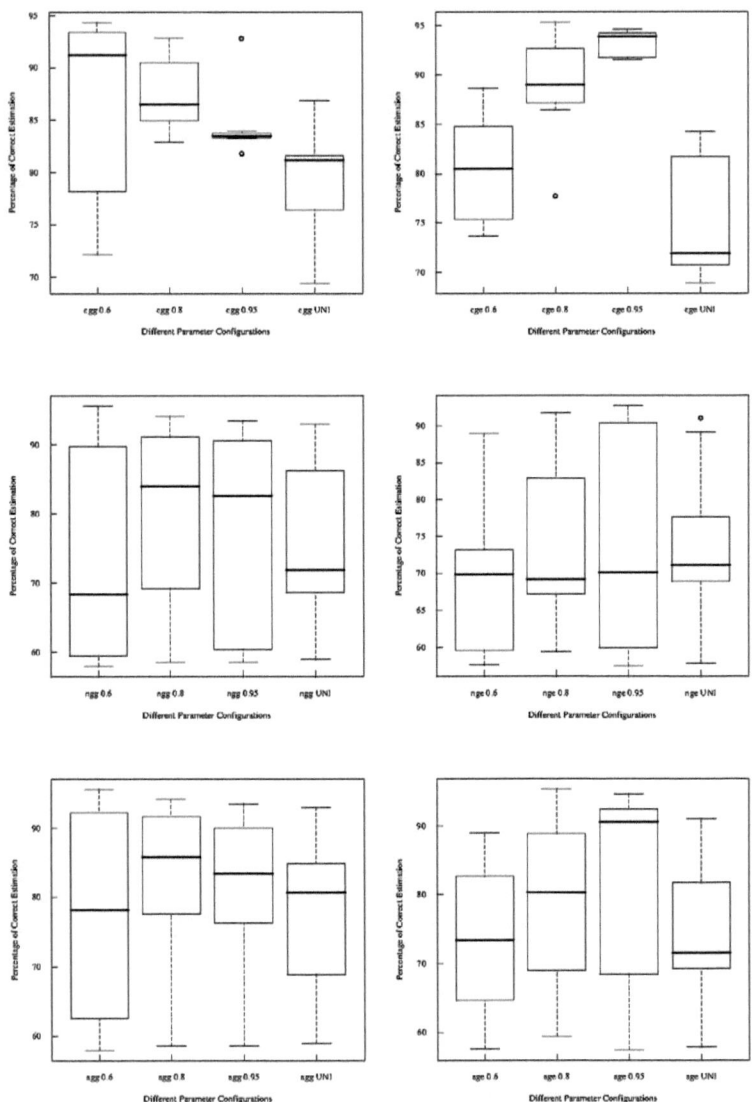

Figure B.11: Robustness AB!C tests with the Gaussian-distributed sensor model that was configured with an initial parameter setting.

## Results Experiment #2

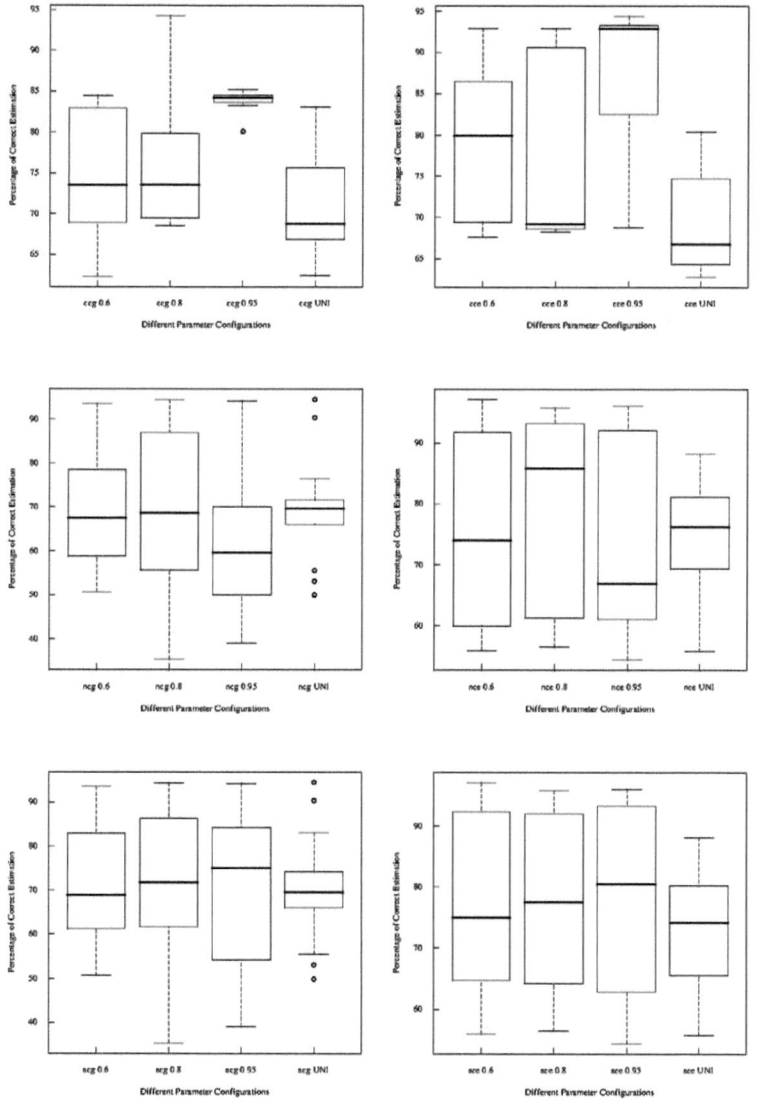

Figure B.12: Robustness AB!C tests with the Cauchy-distributed sensor model that was configured with an initial parameter setting.